A STORY
FORGOTTEN . . .

A STORY
FORGOTTEN...

Karen Geisler

Pleasant Word
A Division of WINEPRESS PUBLISHING

Printed in the United States of America

Packaged by Pleasant Word, a division of WinePress Publishing, PO Box 428, Enumclaw, WA 98022. The views expressed or implied in this work do not necessarily reflect those of Pleasant Word, a division of WinePress Publishing. Ultimate design, content, and editorial accuracy of this work are the responsibilities of the author.

ISBN 1-57921-702-8
Library of Congress Catalog Card Number: 2003107029

Table of Contents

Introduction

The oldest story ever told is forgotten . . .

There is a generation that was taught to be religious out of fear. Fear of hell, fear of church leaders, or fear of breaking strict and rigid rules all contributed to their misconception of who God is and His love for them. This generation chose to live their lives without guilt and took a break from the church.

There is a second generation who didn't even have a chance to learn about God because their parents chose to take a break. They learned to place priority on anything but God.

There is now a third generation that may know there is a God but knows nothing about Him, why He would send a Messiah nor why the Messiah would have to die.

To know God is to love Him, and if you love Him, it becomes easy to do what He commands.

It is for all of these reasons I have written this simple story . . . a story that shouldn't be forgotten.

Chapter 1

LAYING THE FOUNDATION
(Genesis 1:1–5)

*I*n the beginning God created the heavens and the earth. Even though God is Spirit and not flesh and bones, He is able to reveal Himself in whatever form He desires that will provide for us to know Him. He is whatever we need Him to be, when we need Him. He cannot be measured because nothing can be compared to Him. Perfection is the very essence of Him. There is no point in time that can be said was the beginning of God, nor will there ever be an end to God. He has always remained the same and will never change. His Word is His Word and can be trusted for eternity. God's knowledge is infinite, and in the beginning He knew the end. God is all powerful and does what He does because He simply desires to do it. Everything about God is beyond man's ability to scientifically explain.

In the beginning, God was present in three persons: Father, Son, and Holy Spirit. The Son is the Word and He is God. The Holy Spirit is the power of God and it is by the power of the Holy Spirit that people are healed, through which God is revealed, and by whom we are taught.

In God's heavenly kingdom there were also angels and other creatures. One angel who was referred to as the most beautiful angel in His kingdom was named Lucifer. Lucifer, as well as all the other angels and creatures, was created by God for His purpose to accomplish His plan. From the beginning God has had a plan. His plan was to create a people of flesh and bones, breathe His very likeness into these people, and then pour out His love towards them. He would walk with them, talk with them, and give them the desires of their hearts. His plan was to have a people in His image with His attributes; a people that would love Him with all their heart and all their soul and all their mind, and also love one another as they loved themselves. It was His great desire to create a world of peace and love, but would allow His creation the choice to live by His ways or live for ourselves. God would not force Himself or His ways upon His creation.

God's plan included such detail that He knew who the first man and first woman would be, and how they would respond to His desire for them. He knew how their children would respond, and their children's children, and the generations after them. He knew how technically advanced we would become thousands of years later and how we would strive to take control of our own destiny. To this He knew that even His foolishness would be wiser than man's greatest wisdom. Despite all that He knew about the choices we would make, He still loved us enough to create us.

The angel called Lucifer, more commonly known as Satan, was obsessed with the desire to rule God's creation. It was almost as though he had a prideful nature that could not be satisfied as long as God was the one in control of this new kingdom. He was so determined and convinced that he could take the loyalty of this creation away from God, that he proceeded to convince one third of the angels to follow him in his endeavor. His strength was in his cunningness and craftiness. However, instead of totally destroying Satan as well as the angels he had manipulated, God responded by expelling him and his followers from His heavenly kingdom. When Jesus was with His disciples He said, "I saw Satan fall like lightning from heaven." Once expelled, Satan and his angels began immediately to establish his kingdom of darkness on the earth that God had just created.

The earth was a swirling mixture of soil and water that was formless and empty. The darkness of Satan's kingdom filled the earth with death, destruction, ignorance, sorrow, and wickedness. But, the Holy Spirit of God was hovering over the darkness, waiting for God's command to establish His kingdom of light on the earth. God spoke and said, "Let there be light," and there appeared the presence of happiness, clearness and a radiance that separated Satan's dark kingdom from God's kingdom. This marked the beginning of Satan's never ending conniving and plotting to turn the loyalty of this creation away from God and to himself.

Now that God had drawn the boundaries between Satan's kingdom and His, He would begin His creation.

THE CREATOR
(Genesis 1:6–2:25)

In just five days, God would create a place for man to live by virtually speaking what He desired. He spoke what He wanted, and it was. God knew what He wanted to create, how it would look, how every creature would survive, and how the plants would provide for food as well as shelter. God also knew how man would respond to His creation, from the first man to those who will be living at the end of time. Like a puzzle, everything would be in perfect balance with a purpose of fitting somehow or some way into His plan. Some things were created to provide sustenance, and some things were created to provide beauty and give us pleasure. All things were created by God for a purpose.

On the second day God spoke to the waters that there would be a separation between the waters above the earth, and the waters on the earth. The vast space above the earth He called heaven. On the third day God spoke to the waters under heaven and commanded that they be gathered together into one place so dry land would appear. Then God spoke to the dry land and commanded there be grass, herbs, flowers, fruit trees, and all kinds of vegetation. God saw that what He had done so far was good and was pleased with it.

The next day God created two lights to separate the day from the night, and to also provide for months, years, and seasons. God created the sun to give light during the day and the moon to give light at night. He also filled the heavens with stars to give us pleasure at night. As countless as the stars were, God knew every one of them by name. When He saw what He had done on this fourth day, He knew it was also good.

It was now the fifth day and God began creating living things that would dwell on earth. He spoke to the waters and commanded that they be filled with living creatures, and also that birds would fly above the earth across the sky. The waters became filled with fish of every kind big and small, and the sky was filled with every kind of winged bird. God gave these living creatures His blessing and told them to multiply and fill the waters and the earth. The sixth day God spoke to the land and commanded that it produce living creatures such as livestock, creatures that crawl on the ground, and wild animals. Just as He spoke, it was so.

On this same day, God formed man from the dust of the ground and breathed His likeness into him. Man would be a reflection of

God's image. It must have been like birthing a child, the first child of God.

God provided for a mist to come up from the earth to water the ground so that all He had just created would grow and flourish. God also created a garden in the east filled with all kinds of trees that were good for food as well as for beauty. There was a great river that ran through the garden, and then split into four rivers. This garden was gorgeous and God called it Eden, then placed the man there to live.

God graciously gave all that He had created as a gift to man. He gave him all the creatures and the birds, as well as the authority to rule over them. Then He told man that every seed-bearing plant and tree would be his for food, and all the other plants and shrubs would be food for the animals. He then began to bring all the living creatures to this man, one by one, and let this man give each of them their names. How wonderful it must have been for God to have this relationship with man. Even though He was Spirit, He was able to make Himself known to man, to walk with him and talk with him. He poured His love out to man in everything He created or accomplished.

After God had brought all the animals to man for him to name, He knew that none of the animals would provide the companionship that man needed. So, with great love and a desire to meet the needs of this man, He caused him to fall into a deep sleep. He took a rib from the man's side and created a companion for him from that rib. When the man saw the companion God had created for him, he gave her the name woman because she had been taken out of man. They were both naked as they walked about the garden but felt no shame because where there was no sin, there was no guilt.

God told the man they were free to eat of any tree in the garden except from the one tree that would give them knowledge of good and evil. God cautioned them that if they were to eat from this tree they would die. God wanted to have an endless relationship with His creation so He also gave them a tree that would give them eternal life, and placed no restrictions on it. God loved them so much that He gave them the right to choose. The choice was to live in God's kingdom of light, or to accept compromised values presented by the kingdom of darkness. Leaving the choice to them, God blessed them and told them to increase in number and fill the earth.

The next day was the seventh day and God's creation was finished. It was a beautiful place that could resemble heaven as we might imagine it, where man would live with a love for God and a love for his neighbor. It was a place where God offered man the choice of living forever, a place where no one would ever get sick.

There wouldn't be any contention among the animals because they would feed on the vegetation, just as man would. There would also be no contention among people because they would treat each other as they themselves desired to be treated. There would be no distinctions among races nor greed for personal gain because man's attention would be focused on God and each other, not on himself.

God's plan for man was beyond anything that could be imagined. He took great pleasure in spending time with His creation and was often heard walking in the garden. God rested on the seventh day and blessed it, then declared it a holy day.

MAKING A CHOICE
(Genesis 3:1–24)

Throughout the seven days of God's creation, Satan appeared to be inactive. Yet, he was roaming back and forth around the earth looking for who or what he might use to move the focus of this creation away from God. He found a willing messenger through the serpent. His plan was to convince man to eat from the one tree God told them not to eat from. If he could get them to even taste the fruit, it would mark their willingness to be disobedient to God and then they would be destined to die.

The serpent tried to confuse the woman regarding what God had said about eating from the tree that would give them knowledge of good and evil, asking "Did God really say that?" The woman was sure God had gone so far as to say they couldn't even touch the forbidden tree or they would die. Satan challenged them by saying 'certainly God would not allow you to die.' In theory, why would He? He went through so much to create a wonderful place for them and if they died, who would take care of God's creation? Not only that but God clearly loved them with such an unconditional love. Surely God wouldn't do such a cruel thing to them.

The serpent continued by suggesting they would actually become more like God by eating the fruit, because it would make them more knowledgeable about good and evil. The woman took a piece of the fruit from the serpent and tasted it, then handed it to her husband. She obviously didn't die, so he tasted it too. The ability to feel guilt was instantaneous with the sin of being disobedient to God. It was as if their eyes were suddenly opened and they realized they were both naked. Feeling a need to cover their bodies, they sewed fig leaves together and covered themselves as best they could.

God knew from the beginning of creation that this man and woman would be convinced through Satan's cunningness to sin against Him, and a personal relationship with man would become impossible. Because of God's absolute holiness, man could not survive His presence if there was any blemish of sin. God had such an unrelenting love for man that in the hour of confronting them for their sin, God still had a loving and merciful heart.

It was the cool part of the day when they heard God walking in the garden. They instinctively felt a need to hide from God because of the guilt they were feeling, and hid among the trees. How grievous it must have been for God to know they were trying to hide from Him, and called out to them asking, "Where are you?" The man answered, "I heard you in the garden and I was afraid because I was naked, so I hid." The effects of Satan's kingdom was penetrating fast, as fear is a characteristic of his darkness.

God asked him, "Who told you that you were naked? Have you eaten from the tree that I commanded you not to eat from?" This was not a question of God not knowing, but rather God's gracious way of calling them to account for what they had done. Instead of the man repenting of his sin, he blamed the woman and said, "The woman you put here with me gave me some fruit from the tree, and I ate it." With this God said to the woman, "What have you done?" She too refused to repent of her sin, and blamed the serpent saying, "The serpent confused me and I ate the fruit."

God responded by judging them not out of anger or disappointment, but from righteousness. God cursed the serpent above all livestock and wild animals, and said he would crawl on his belly all his life. In addition to this, the woman's offspring would hate him and strive to kill him. The serpent's only recourse would be to strike at man's heel. God told the woman she would bear children with great pain. Also, her relationship with her husband would be one where she would have a deep need and desire for him, while he would rule and have dominion over her.

Lastly, God looked to the man and explained that because he listened to his wife and was convinced by her to do what God had told him not to do, the ground would be cursed. Life would be different because of what he had done. Life was going to be hard, all the days of his life would be painful, and he would struggle to survive. His life would come to an end and when it did, he would return to the ground and become dust because that was what he was created from.

Not only did their sin bring death, it would also expose them to all the other horrible attributes of Satan's dark kingdom. They would now live a life much different than what God would have desired for them. All of man's offspring would be blemished and vulnerable to the darkness of Satan's kingdom as well.

God banished them from the Garden to prevent them from eating from the tree of life, because this was no longer an option for them. Before God left them, He knew they had a need to be clothed and wanted to help them with this need, so He made garments from animal skins and clothed them. This marked the end of a truly unique relationship with God they could never again fully enjoy.

LEARNING TO LIVE
(Genesis 4:1–5:31)

The man called himself Adam and named his wife Eve, who gave birth to a son they named Cain. She gave birth to a second son and named him Abel. Adam and Eve had other children as well, and their children had children. They were increasing in number, but daily living was a challenge just as God said it would be. Yet, even though they would never have a relationship with God that equaled their memories of the garden, God was always there, guiding them and helping them.

God wanted them to live by the standards of His kingdom so that there would be justice and fairness among the people, and a sincere love for one another. One of the principles He taught them was to give joyfully, which was demonstrated by them offering their first fruits to God as a willing sacrifice. Abel was a shepherd over a flock of sheep, and he brought the first fat and healthy lambs that were born to his flocks to God with a heart to honor Him. God received Abel's offering with compassion and respect for him, and was pleased with Abel.

Cain was a farmer and took his time bringing his offering to God because his heart just wasn't in it. God knew Cain's heart and did not receive his offering like He did Abel's, so Cain became aggravated and angry. God asked Cain, "Why are you angry? Why is your face downcast? If you do what is right, will you not be accepted?" God tried to explain to Cain that if he allowed himself to feel offended and didn't get control of it, it would swallow him up. God wanted so much to help him understand that sin was crouching at his door and was eager to have him. Yet just as He did for Adam and Eve, God would allow Cain to make the choice of embracing His kingdom or Satan's.

Cain made his choice and invited Abel to go out to the field with him, then killed him. Abel's life was over before he even had a chance to live it. Yet, God was gracious and gave Cain an opportunity to be accountable for his sin and asked him "Where is your brother Abel?" Instead of confessing his sin, Cain said with almost a sarcastic response, "I don't know, am I my brother's keeper?" With that God said, "What have you done? Listen! Your brother's blood cries out to Me from the ground. Now you are under a curse and driven from the ground which opened its mouth to receive your brother's blood from your hand. When you work the ground, it will no longer yield its crops for you. You will be a restless wanderer on the earth."

Cain, as did his parents, had come to understand the hard way that God cannot turn His back to sin. His righteous nature could not let sin go unpunished. Cain was tormented with the realization of the consequences of his sin and said to God, "My punishment is more than I can bear. You're driving me from the land, and I'll be hidden from your presence; I'll be a restless wanderer on the earth, and whoever finds me will kill me." Still feeling compassion for him, God made provisions for him and said, "Not so; if anyone kills Cain, he will suffer vengeance seven times over." God put a mark on Cain that would prohibit anyone from killing him, then Cain left God and went to live in a land called Nod, which was east of the Garden of Eden.

Cain's wife went with him and gave birth to a son named Enoch. They had other sons and daughters also. Cain was fairly isolated so he built a city where he lived and named it after Enoch. Enoch had a son named Irad, who had a son named Mehujael, who had a son named Methushael, who had a son named Lamech.

Lamech had progressive sons who invented things that would improve their way of life. While some of his sons were content to live in tents and raise livestock, one was noted to be a musician and invented musical instruments. Another son was known for developing the art of making tools from bronze and iron.

There was progress and growth among Cain's families, but there was also an increase of sin. The sin of Cain perpetuated itself down through the generations even to Lamech. Out of anger, Lamech killed a man for injuring him, and a young man for hurting him.

After Cain left home as a fugitive, God saw the pain Adam and Eve felt from losing their two sons. He extended His love to them by giving them yet another son they called Seth. Adam was 130 years old when Seth was born, and it seemed like an eternity since Adam walked with God in the Garden of Eden. The demands and struggles of life seemed to separate them from God more and more. It wasn't until Seth was 105 years old and had a son named Enosh that people realized their separation from God and began to seek Him. Even though God had never left them for a second, it must have caused quite a celebration in heaven when even a few of the people turned their hearts back to Him.

Enosh had a son named Kenan, who had a son named Mahalalel, who had a son named Jared, who had a son named Enoch. Enoch discovered the joy of walking with God and knowing His great unconditional love. It was a walk in which Enoch was consumed with devotion to God in every detail of life. Perhaps Adam, who was still living in Enoch's day, shared with him the memories from the Garden. Enoch pleased God so much that He provided for Enoch to never have to experience death. God just took him away to be with Him where He was. Enoch had a son named Methuselah, who had a son named Lamech, who had a son named Noah.

The life span was so long that Noah would hear nearly first hand about the creation of heaven and earth (see Illustration 1). He heard how God brought the animals to Adam one by one to name, of how wonderful it was to know God when there was no blemish of sin. Noah would hear all about the memories of the garden from his father who heard it from Adam first hand.

It would be through Seth's generations that life would flourish. When God created man His intention for man was to live, not die. Adam lived to be nine hundred thirty years old, but twenty-one generations later the life expectancy would decrease to an average of one hundred fifty years. As sin increased from generation to generation, man's life span became shorter and shorter. By the time God's creation was one thousand five hundred thirty-six years old, the people had become entirely wicked. Their motives were wrong all the time, their hearts had only evil intents and they lived every day for themselves doing whatever pleased them. The darkness of Satan's kingdom was thriving among the people, but God allowed them a choice and sin was their choice.

God was grieved in His heart that man would choose to live in wickedness, and was truly sorry that He had made man. God considered destroying His creation, not out of anger, but because of the grief He felt for the choices they had made. Yet because there was one single man that was righteous, a remnant of the people would be spared. While Enoch's son was counted as one among the wicked, his great grandson Noah had the same passion for God that Enoch had. God graciously warned them one hundred and twenty years in advance that He was going to destroy them if they continued to live their lives of wickedness. Yet, they would still die because when given the choice, they would choose sin.

Chapter 1

A New Start
(Genesis 5:32–9:19)

The earth had become fairly populated by now. There were communities of people from both Cain and Seth's descendants, as well as the descendants of Adam and Eve's many other children. The days of Noah were dark days because of the wickedness that consumed the people. Noah was the tenth generation on earth since the creation, and he was the only one left who knew God or walked with God. God's heart was filled with pain and He was grieved for the people. The people were not strong at all when it came to making a good or right decision. Their motives and intentions were wrong all the time and they no longer had any knowledge of God. The earth was filled with violence.

Noah had remained faithful and was a delight to God. Because of this, God chose to spare him and his family from the destruction He had warned that He would bring to His creation. Noah's family included him and his wife, their three sons Shem, Ham and Japheth, and their wives. God instructed Noah to build a large ark four hundred and fifty feet long, seventy-five feet wide and forty-five feet high. It would have many rooms on three levels, with a door and window built on the side. A roof would cover the ark with a space of thirteen inches above the top floor to allow for air ventilation.

With only himself and his three sons working on it, it could very well have taken them all of the one hundred and twenty years of the warning period God had given the people, for them to build it. Noah's father may have also helped with the building of the ark, as he died only five years before it was completed.

The people of Noah's time had never seen rain because the vegetation was still being watered by a mist that came up from the ground. God told Noah the earth was going to be flooded with water but it was probably a concept too difficult to comprehend.

23

Building such a large vessel in preparation for a flood must have appeared to be eccentric, but God told Noah to build the ark and he did what God told him to do.

When the ark was finished, Noah stored away enough food to feed all the animals that would share the ark with him and his family. God told Noah the rain would begin to fall in seven days, so Noah and his sons quickly began rounding up animals and birds. They brought two of every kind of animal, creature and bird into the ark, but seven of any animal or bird used as offerings to God. Noah was six hundred years old when he finished doing everything God had told him to do, and on the seventh day they entered the ark. Once they were in, God shut the door.

It must have been a solemn moment when that door closed, as it closed on relatives, friends, neighbors, and even on Noah's grandfather. On the seventeenth day of the second month the earth opened up and water burst forth. It was too late for all those people outside the ark, but this was the result of the choice they made to sin. The gates of heaven opened and floods of water poured out onto the earth, and the ark began to float. Noah watched out the window as the mountains slowly disappeared, and were covered by more than twenty feet of water. Everything that was left on the land died. Only Noah and those with him in the ark remained alive. After forty days of heavy rain, it stopped, and the waters began to slowly recede (see Illustration 2).

It was exactly five months from the time the rain started that the waters had receded enough for the bottom of the ark to rest on the top of a mountain. In took another two and a half months before the tops of the mountains became visible. Forty days later, after they had been in the ark for nearly nine months, Noah opened the window he had built into the side of the ark and began sending out first a raven and then a dove to see if they could find dry land. The raven kept flying back and forth above the water, but the dove returned because it found no place to land.

Noah waited another week and sent the dove out again. This time the dove returned with a freshly picked olive leaf in its mouth. After one more week, Noah sent the dove out again but it did not return. Five and a half months after the ark had come to rest on top of the mountain, Noah took the top covering off but stayed in the ark another two months. They had been in the ark a total of one year and ten days when God told Noah to come out. It was an amazing moment as Noah and his family watched all the animals, birds, and creatures step out on dry ground; then God commanded them to multiply and fill the earth once more.

Noah built an altar to God and honored Him with a sacrifice which pleased God. God said to Noah He would never again curse the ground or destroy all the living creatures because of man, no matter how bad man became. He told Noah that as long as the earth endures, the time of planting and the time of harvest, the cold and the heat, the summers and the winters, and the day and night would never cease. God also gave them the right to eat of anything that lives or moves in addition to the green plants, but warned them not to take the life of any man because man was made in God's image. God told them He would demand an accounting of anyone who takes the life of a man, whether it was taken by man or beast.

God made a covenant, a promise to Noah and all His creation that He would never again cut off life by a flood that would destroy the earth. Then God gave them a rainbow in the sky and said, "Whenever I bring clouds over the earth and the rainbow appears in the clouds, I will remember My covenant between Me and you and all living creatures of every kind. Never again will the waters become a flood to destroy all life. Whenever the rainbow appears in the clouds, I will see it and remember the everlasting covenant between Myself and all living creatures of every kind on the earth." And so, life began again.

NATIONS BIRTHED
(Genesis 9:18–11:9)

After the flood, Noah went back to farming and one of his joys was his vineyard. One night he enjoyed the fruit of his grapes a bit too much and his youngest son Ham found him passed out in his tent naked. Instead of showing compassion and honoring his father by covering him, he went out and told his brothers about it. They had heard the story about Adam and Eve many times and how they realized their nakedness after they sinned, so Shem and Japheth were compelled to discretely cover their father's nude body. The next day when Noah learned what had happened he cursed Ham for what he had done, but blessed Shem and Japheth. Noah told Ham his descendants were cursed and someday they would become servants to Shem's descendants. Noah lived three hundred and fifty years after the flood then died at the age of nine hundred and fifty.

Japheth had seven sons; some notable nations that emerged from his descendants were Russia, Mede, Celtic, Greece, and Spain. Ham had four sons named Cush, Mizraim, Put, and Canaan; two notable nations that emerged from their descendants were the Philistines and Canaanites who lived primarily in the areas of what is known today as Israel and Egypt. Shem had five sons and his descendants would became known as the Persians, Assyrians, Arabians, Syrians, Lydians, and Israelites. They lived in areas known today as Syria, Iraq, Iran, Saudi Arabia, and Jordan.

As they grew in numbers and spread throughout the land, they became more and more focused on satisfying their own needs and wants. The more they focused on themselves, the more they drifted away from God. While Adam and Eve tried to hide from God because of their sin, the descendants of Noah went beyond hiding and created their own imaginative gods to fit their lifestyles. They built high pyramid like towers to offer sacrifices to these fabricated gods.

They couldn't approach the true God of Adam because of how wicked they had become, but they weren't willing to give up their sinful lifestyles. Instead, they became determined to build a tower that would reach heaven, a tower tall enough that would enable them to approach God their own way. They were so consumed with their self ambitions that they couldn't see or realize how foolish they were.

God did not react with anger but instead, out of mercy and compassion, tried to humble them. He confused them by causing each family to speak a different language. When they couldn't understand one another enough to communicate, they abandoned the tower project and the unfinished tower became known as the Tower of Babel. The foreign languages became a point of separation among the descendants of Noah, which ultimately gave way to the birth of nations, nations that did not remember God.

Chapter 2

CHOOSING A PEOPLE
(Genesis 11:10–13:18)

*E*ven though the descendants of Noah were becoming more and more separated as individual nations, some still remembered their beginnings. The story about creation was still being told just as they heard it from Noah, who heard it from his father, who heard it from Adam. Even though this story was told with a freshness, for many of them their understanding of God had grown stale. They had heard how Adam's grandson Enosh had called on God but it wasn't something many of them did anymore. Satan had been quite successful in drawing them away from God, but God longed for His creation to know Him, and to know who He was.

God had a plan to select a people in which He would reveal Himself through. A plan that would ultimately include sending His only Son to be born through this chosen people. His Son would sacrifice His life to pay the price for God's creation to be free from

Satan's grip. God would accomplish His plan through a descendant of Shem named Abram, and in time he would become known as Abraham.

Arphaxad was born to Shem two years after the flood. It was with this generation that men began having children in their thirties rather than in their hundreds as many of their forefathers did. Sin was taking a toll on the people, which was evidenced by their shortened life span. Arphaxad lived less than half as long as his grandfather Noah, and the average life span decreased significantly with each generation after Arphaxad (see Illustration 3).

Arphaxad had a son named Salah, who had a son named Eber, who had a son named Peleg, who had a son named Reu, who had a son named Serug, who had a son named Nahor, who had a son named Terah. Terah lived east in the land of Ur, and had three sons named Abram, Nahor, and Haran. His sons were the twentieth generation since God created man.

Terah's son Haran died, so he moved west taking Abram, Abram's wife Sarai, and Haran's son Lot with him, and settled in a place they called Haran. His son Nahor remained in the land of Ur in the town of Nahor.

It had been about three hundred and seventy years since the flood, and while people weren't known to have had a personal relationship with God, God specifically called out to Abram. Abram was seventy-five years old when God asked him to leave his father and move to a land that would be completely strange and unknown to him. If he was willing to do this, God would bless those who blessed him and curse those who cursed him. God also promised that He would bless all the families of the earth through him. Abram left Haran without hesitation and took with him his wife Sarai, his nephew Lot and all the people and possessions he had acquired while in Haran. God was going to take Abram through varying circumstances to teach him that he could always trust Him.

Abram traveled to the land of Canaan, a land inhabited by the descendants of Ham. God met Abram there and assured him that his descendants would someday own this land. Abram built an altar there to honor the place where God had appeared to him and then moved on further into the land. He pitched his tents on a mountain between Bethel and Ai, built an altar and called out to God.

There was a famine in the land of Canaan, so Abram headed south in search of food and traveled all the way to Egypt. When they arrived in Egypt, Abram became concerned for his life. Even though his wife Sarai was in her sixties, she was so beautiful that Abram was sure Pharaoh would kill him to have Sarai in his harem. Abram introduced Sarai as his sister. It wasn't a total fabrication because they both had the same father, but not the same mothers.

Pharaoh did take Sarai into his harem but shortly after, Pharaoh's people were hit with a plague. When Pharaoh realized it was Abram's God who sent the plague, he tried to appease God by sending Abram, Sarai, and Lot away with a great deal of wealth. Abram was beginning to understand just how powerful his God was. He also realized how little he had trusted God to help him through the famine and protect him from Pharaoh. He returned to the altar he had built between Bethel and Ai and humbly called on God once again.

Because of the wealth of goods Abram and Lot had accumulated in Egypt, in addition to what they had from Haran, it wasn't long before their herdsmen began to quarrel because of the lack of grazing space for their animals. As much as Abram had come to love Lot as the son he never had, he knew they had to move apart and offered Lot first choice of the land. Lot chose to take the best of the land and settled in the area of Sodom. With Lot gone, the reality of having no children was setting in.

God spoke to Abram and told him to lift up his eyes. God didn't want Abram to focus on his situation but rather focus on what God had promised him. It became a lesson in trusting God. God knew Abram's heart and told him that he would have descendants. His descendants would not only own this land but they would be like the dust of the earth, so many that no one would be able to count them. Abram was encouraged, moved to a new place and built another altar to honor God.

THE PROMISE
(Genesis 14:1–17:27)

A man from Sodom came to Abram pleading for help. The kings of Sodom and Gomorrah had joined with three other kings to gain their freedom from the king of Elam. They were defeated when the king of Elam came against them with the help of three other kings. His nephew Lot had become a victim of this massive war and was taken captive. All of Lot's family, his servants, and all he owned had been carried away by the conquering kings.

With God's help, Abram and three hundred and eighteen of his servants not only rescued all that had been taken, but drove the four kings out of the land. Lot was able to return with all of his possessions. The king of Sodom offered Abram all the wealth he had recovered as a reward, but Abram refused it. Abram knew it was God that had provided the victory and refused to take the credit by accepting his extravagant offer. Abram had set his heart to trust God, and was determined that his life would be committed to trusting and honoring Him.

It pleased God that among the many that chose to abandon Him, there was one that would still choose to trust Him. God spoke to Abram and reassured him that He would be his protector and his reward. For the first time Abram had an exchange of conversation with God and asked what was all his wealth good for if he didn't have a son to inherit it. God brought Abram outside and showed him the stars in the sky, then promised he would have a son, and that his descendants would be as numerous as the stars in the sky.

Abram believed God but couldn't comprehend how he could possibly come to own the land of Canaan. God told him to offer a sacrifice, after which he fell into a deep sleep. When a great horrible darkness fell on Abram, God told him his descendants would go to another land and be afflicted and treated as slaves. After four hundred years, the fourth generation would leave that land with great wealth and return to Canaan. It would be then that God would take Canaan from Ham's descendants, and give it to them. God said it, so Abram believed it.

As time passed, the promise seemed to be more and more out of reach. It had been ten years since Abram and Sarai moved to Canaan and they still had no children. Sarai was seventy-five years old and Abram eighty-five. Sarai was certain she was beyond her child bearing years and decided that her Egyptian maidservant Hagar should be a surrogate mother for her. Abram agreed and Hagar became pregnant with Abram's child.

After Hagar became pregnant she despised Sarai, so Sarai treated her harshly. Hagar reacted by running away into the desert where an angel of the Lord met her. He told her she would have a son and was to name him Ishmael. Ishmael would be like a wild man, always struggling and fighting against everyone, and everyone would be at war against him. On the advice of the angel, Hagar returned and gave birth to Abram's first son and they named him Ishmael. Abram was eighty-six years old when Ishmael was born, and the modern world would come to know Ishmael's descendants as the Arab nations.

It had been thirteen years since Ishmael was born, and God spoke to Abram again, reminding him that he must trust Him and not live like the other people in the world. If he was faithful in this, God would certainly keep His promise to make him the father of many nations. God changed Abram's name, which means *father*, to Abraham, which means *father of multitudes*. God told Abraham His promise was a covenant not only with him, but between God and Abraham's descendants. He would give them this land as a permanent possession. God instructed Abraham to indicate his commitment to this covenant by circumcising not only himself but every male in his house.

God also changed Sarai's name to Sarah which means *queen*, because she would be the mother of many nations. God promised Sarah she would bear a son and they were to name him Isaac. Abraham was really struggling in his heart with the idea of having a child with Sarah, because he was now one hundred years old and Sarah was ninety. In desperation he asked God to bless Ishmael, the only son he knew. God said no, Ishmael's descendants would become a great nation but His covenant would be with the descendants of Isaac. That day, Abraham ordered every male in his house be circumcised, no matter how old or young they were.

SODOM AND GOMORRAH DESTROYED
(Genesis 18:1–21:7)

Abraham was sitting under some trees by his house trying to stay cool from the early afternoon sun when the Lord and two angels came by. Abraham brought water to wash the hot dust from their feet and prepared food for the three strangers. While they ate, they encouraged Abraham by reminding him that he and Sarah would have a child. When Sarah laughed to herself at the thought of this, the Lord confronted her disbelief and asked if there was anything too difficult for the Lord to do. It scared Sarah that this man would know her thoughts, so she denied that she had laughed. Yet the Lord was still firm about what He knew.

By now Abraham had realized who they were. They told Abraham about their plans to destroy Sodom and Gomorrah because their sin was grievous, and the outcry against them was just too much. The two angels left for Sodom, but Abraham was concerned for Lot and pleaded with the Lord not to destroy the righteous with the wicked. After a great deal of pleading and bargaining, the Lord agreed to spare Sodom if ten righteous men could be found in the city. Then the Lord went on His way.

Lot was sitting at Sodom's gate when the two angels arrived. Knowing how dangerous it would be to stay at the gate after dark, he invited them into his home to eat and rest for the night. When darkness fell "all" the men of the city, both young and old, came to Lot's door and demanded the two visitors come out so they could have sex with them. Lot stepped outside and pleaded with them to go away, even offering them his two daughters rather than defiling the two angels. After they nearly broke down the door, the angels pulled Lot inside the house and struck all the men outside the door with blindness.

They instructed Lot to gather his family and prepare to leave because God was going to destroy the city. When Lot could not convince his future son-in-laws to go with them, his wife and two daughters left with him in haste. The angels warned them to head for the hills and not look back. After they left, the Lord rained down brimstone and fire on Sodom and Gomorrah, devastating the cities and all their inhabitants, as well as all the surrounding plains. Lot's wife chose to disregard the warning of the angels and looked back toward Sodom. When she looked back she turned into a pillar of salt. Lot was so full of fear that he took his two daughters and hid in a cave.

His daughters were sure that all the people on earth were destroyed in the fire and were afraid they would never have the experience of bearing children. They plotted with one another to get their father drunk, and then laid with their father in order to get pregnant. The oldest daughter was the first to lay with him and the second daughter laid with him the next night. Lot had gotten so drunk that he had no idea what his daughters had done to him. Lot's oldest daughter had a son who would become the father of the Moabites, and the youngest daughter had a son who would become the father of the Ammonites. These two nations would survive for five centuries and become enemies to Abraham's descendants.

Abraham got up in the morning only to see the smoke rising from the land toward Sodom and Gomorrah. It was a painful sight because for only ten righteous men, God would have spared these cities. Abraham had no idea what might have happened to his nephew Lot, and decided to move south from there to a place called Gerar. Just as he did in Egypt, he failed to trust God when he arrived at Gerar and called Sarah his sister. Because the king of Gerar thought she had no husband, he took Sarah to be a maidservant.

God protected Sarah and got the king's attention by preventing any of his wives or maidservants from becoming pregnant. Before the king even had opportunity to violate Sarah, God came to him in a dream. God told the king he was a dead man for making Sarah his maidservant. The king immediately returned Sarah to Abraham, compensating him with sheep, oxen, servants, and silver, then begged him for his help. After Abraham interceded to God for the king, his wives and maidservants began to have children again.

The Lord also opened Sarah's womb and at the age of ninety she gave birth to Abraham's second son. It was a happy occasion and they named him Isaac, which means "laughter."

TRUST TESTED

(Genesis 21:8–22:24)

Ishmael was about fifteen years old when Isaac became weaned, and Abraham threw a great feast to commemorate the event. When Sarah found Ishmael bantering and laughing at Isaac, she insisted Abraham send him and his mother Hagar away. Abraham was distraught over the suggestion of sending his son Ishmael away and turned to God for guidance. God told Abraham not to be grieved at sending them away because He would protect Ishmael, and just as He had promised, Ishmael would become a great nation. God comforted Abraham and reassured him that it would be through Isaac that He would bless the world.

Abraham gave Hagar and Ishmael provisions of water and food then sent them away. When they found themselves in the wilderness with no more food or water, they sat down and prepared to die. But the angel of God spoke to Hagar and reminded her that God would provide for Ishmael to become a great nation. Then God opened her eyes to see a well in the middle of the wilderness. Ishmael survived and married an Egyptian girl, and the wilderness became his home.

Ishmael had been gone for some time now, but Isaac had more than made up for this loss to Abraham. Abraham had come to hear God's voice clearly and to trust His Word. He loved his son Isaac and it was no doubt that he was a most precious gift from God. God had a plan for Isaac and Abraham's descendants. He would call Abraham's descendants His own people, and He would be known as their God. He would demonstrate to the world His mighty power and His endless love through them. He was looking for a people that would stand the test of time, to remain faithful to Him, and trust Him for all things so He could bless the world through them.

Abraham's trust for God had grown strong and had withstood many situations, but he was about to face the test of his life. God knew Abraham loved Isaac dearly, but spoke to him and asked him to do the unexpected. God told Abraham to bring Isaac to the land of Moriah and offer him as a burnt offering. Abraham had to fall back on God's Word that He had spoken and promised so many times. He knew God's Word could be trusted.

God had said his descendants would be as numerous as the stars of the sky, like the dust of the earth. God said it would be through Isaac that He would bless the earth. He didn't know what God's plan was but He just knew that if God asked him to give his son as a sacrifice, God would make a way to still make His Word remain true and faithful. He put his trust in God, and early the next morning he saddled his donkey and left with Isaac and two servants, bringing with him wood for the fire.

When they reached the mountain, Abraham left the two servants behind as he and Isaac made their way up the mountain carrying the fire, the knife, and the wood. When Isaac questioned his father about a lamb for the sacrifice, Abraham assured him that God would provide. When they reached the top of the mountain, Abraham built an altar, arranged the wood on it and then bound Isaac and laid him on the wood. Just as Abraham stretched out his hand to slay his son with the knife, an angel of God called out to him to stop. God was pleased that Abraham would fear Him more than anything, even to the point of sacrificing his only son. Abraham took Isaac off the altar and when he looked up he saw a ram caught in the bushes, a ram provided by God for the sacrifice.

God told Abraham, "By Myself I have sworn, because you have done this thing, and have not withheld your son, your only son, in blessing I will bless you, and in multiplying I will multiply your descendants as the stars of the heaven and as the sand which is on the seashore, and your descendants shall possess the gate of their enemies. In your seed all the nations of the earth shall be blessed, because you have obeyed My voice."

In the span of eternity, this truly was a marked day. This was a day that God clearly declared that the descendants of Abraham would be His people. This would be the nation in which He would reveal Himself to the world. This would be the people through whom He would send His Son to pay the price for sin, and offer freedom from the hold of Satan.

A Bride for Isaac
(Genesis 23–24)

God had blessed Sarah and Abraham abundantly, but even they could not escape death, and at the age of one hundred twenty-seven, Sarah died. Abraham had become extremely wealthy with sheep, cattle, silver, gold, servants, camels, and donkeys, but had no land to bury his beloved wife. Abraham went to the city gate in Hebron to bargain with the elders for a piece of land. He proposed to purchase the cave at Machpelah, which was near Hebron so he could bury Sarah. The owner sold him the cave and the field in front of it for ten pounds of silver then deeded it to him. Abraham was now able to lay Sarah to rest, in the cave at Machpelah.

Isaac was thirty-seven years old when his mother died, and shortly after traveled south to live in the Negev. Abraham was concerned that he might marry one of the daughters of the Canaanites, so he sent his chief servant on a mission to find Isaac a wife from one of his own relatives. Abraham had learned to trust God and knew with absolute certainty that God would provide a wife for Isaac from his own family line, perhaps from the family of his brother Nahor. His servant wasn't as confident but gave his word to Abraham that he would do his best. He loaded ten camels with fine cloths, silver, gold, and gifts, then he and a few other servants headed northeast into Mesopotamia to the city of Nahor.

When they arrived, they stopped at a public well just outside the city of Nahor. The chief servant wasn't sure how to find Abraham's relatives, and even if he found them, how would he know what girl to select for Isaac. He knelt down near the well and prayed to the God of Abraham asking that God would bring the girl to him. He asked God to not only bring her to the well, but that she would give him water to drink and also draw enough water for his camels. If she did all this, then he would know it was the girl God had chosen for Isaac.

Before the servant had finished praying, a beautiful young girl came to the well to draw water. The servant asked her for a small drink and she quickly lowered her jar and gave him a drink. After he drank from her jar she offered to draw water for his camels too, and emptied her jar into the trough. After she had drawn enough water for the ten camels, the servant was sure this was the bride God intended for Isaac. Believing God had answered his prayer, he gave her a gold nose ring and two gold bracelets, then asked, "Whose daughter are you, and is there room in your father's house for us to spend the night?" She told him her name was Rebekah and her father was Bethuel who was the son of Nahor, then welcomed them to come to their home. Before he went with her, he felt compelled to bow down and worship God, for He had brought the grand-daughter of Abraham's brother Nahor to meet him at the well.

Rebekah went home to her mother's house and reported to them what had happened. Her brother Laban saw the gold gifts and immediately went out to the well to find the man his sister was talking about. Laban found him at the well with the camels and brought him back. The camels were given straw and fodder, and they gave the men water to wash their feet. When food was brought for them to eat the chief servant refused to eat until he could bring closure to the mission his master Abraham had sent him on. He proceeded to explain who Abraham and Sarah were, how God had blessed them abundantly, and how Abraham wanted a wife for his son Isaac from among his own relatives. He told them how Abraham was unwavering in his faith, but confessed his own doubts and how he had prayed at the well. He described how Rebekah came to the well and gave him and his camels water, just as he had prayed to Abraham's God.

Rebekah's father Bethuel and her brother Laban were absolutely taken back at the servant's story. The servant finished his story and asked them to please give him an answer regarding Rebekah: will they or will they not allow her to return with him to become Isaac's wife. Bethuel was so overwhelmed by how God had intervened that he agreed Rebekah would become the wife of Abraham's son. With that, the servant gave Rebekah gold and silver jewelry as well as fine clothing, and gave costly gifts to Rebekah's mother. They ate and celebrated but spent only one night. In the morning the caravan returned to the land of Canaan with Rebekah, her nurse, and maids. They were returning home with Isaac's bride.

Isaac had just returned home from the Negev and was still grieving for his mother. He went out into the field to be alone and meditate. As the sun was setting he looked out on the horizon and saw camels coming, so he walked towards their direction. Rebekah took her veil and covered herself as soon as she saw Isaac walking towards them. Isaac met them in the field and the chief servant explained to him every detail of what had happened. Isaac took Rebekah into his mother's tent and married her. He loved Rebekah and was comforted by her after his mother's death.

A New Generation
(Genesis 25–27:41)

After Sarah's death, Abraham remarried and had six sons. In addition to this, he had concubines who became pregnant giving birth to even more sons. Yet, he sent all of these sons away with gifts to live in the east, and left his fortune to his son Isaac. His son Ishmael also prospered by having twelve sons that became twelve large tribes known today as the Arab nations. Ishmael's descendants settled near the borders of Egypt and hostility became a way of life among them.

While Abraham and Ishmael were having sons, Isaac remained childless. After being married for nearly twenty years and still no children, Isaac didn't know what else to do except seek help from God. God answered Isaac's prayer and Rebekah became pregnant with twins. It was a difficult pregnancy because the babies were extremely active, so Rebekah turned to God to try and understand what this meant. God told her the babies in her womb represented two nations, and the nation of the older child will serve the nation of the younger. When the babies were born the first twin had a lot of hair so they named him Esau which means "hairy." The second twin was born holding onto Esau's heel so they named him Jacob which means "deceives."

Isaac favored Esau because he loved to hunt and do "man" things. On the contrary, Rebekah favored Jacob because he loved to stay indoors and do "feminine" things. They had developed two distinctively opposite personalities. One day Esau came in from hunting when Jacob had been cooking a pot of red stew. It smelled wonderful and Esau was absolutely starved. Jacob lived up to his name by convincing Esau to trade his birthright for a meal of stew and some bread. The birthright provided for the first son to inherit a double portion, but Isaac seemed rich enough to make him a wealthy man even with a single portion. His decision labeled him with the nickname Edom which means "red" because of the red stew he bought with his birthright. Esau came to regret what he had done and his nickname was a nagging reminder of it.

Esau and Jacob were about fifteen years old when their grandfather Abraham died. He lived to be one hundred seventy-five years old. Ishmael and Isaac came together to bury their father beside

Sarah in the cave of Machpelah. It had been nearly thirty-eight years since Isaac said goodbye to his mother, and felt blessed to have had Rebekah help him through that loss. Now he had her and his sons to help him get beyond the loss of his father.

Rebekah would not become pregnant again, and it was culturally difficult to live with the idea of having no more than two sons. Isaac also struggled with the people in the land, and to make matters worse, there was a famine in Canaan. Isaac was tempted to go to Egypt to survive the famine but God encouraged him to remain in the land of Canaan, promising him He would make his descendants as numerous as the stars in the sky. God also told Isaac He would not only give his descendants the land of Canaan but all nations would be blessed through his offspring.

Even though Isaac still had only two sons, he trusted God's Word and moved to the southwestern-most corner of Canaan and planted his crops. God blessed Isaac with huge crops that produced a hundred times more than what he had hoped for. He became so wealthy with flocks, herds, and servants that the Philistines in the area envied him. They harassed him by plugging up the wells he used, the very wells his father Abraham had dug. In the end, Abimelech, the leader of the Philistines asked him to leave the area.

Isaac was a humble man and never aggressively pursued the Philistines for the wrongs done to him over the wells. Instead he moved north until he found a well with fresh clean water. It wasn't long before the Philistines moved in and refused him access to this well also, claiming it was theirs. So Isaac dug a new well but they quarreled over that one too. Once again Isaac moved farther north and dug another well in a part of the country that appeared to be peaceful towards him, and was quick to give credit to God. He continued on to a higher elevation where God appeared to him and consoled him. God assured Isaac that He was with him and would bless him, so Isaac built an altar there to honor God and also dug another well. It wasn't long after this that Abimelech realized

God was blessing Isaac and came to him seeking a peace treaty. Isaac, being the humble man he was, graciously agreed and swore an oath to live in peace with the Philistines.

Isaac was now a hundred years old, and even though he was living peacefully with his neighbors, trouble was brewing in his home. Esau had turned forty and decided to get married. He not only married once, but took a second wife, both of whom were Hittite women. They were descendants of the people that Abraham had purchased the cave from to bury Sarah. This was hard for both Isaac and Rebekah because of the importance Abraham had placed on Isaac marrying someone from within their father's people. On the other hand, Jacob had made no indications he was ready to get married.

Isaac was getting old and blind, and spent his days in bed. He wanted to pass God's blessings on to the next generation before he died, so he called for his oldest son Esau. He asked Esau to go hunting and bring the fresh wild game he loved to eat, then he would give him his blessings. Esau took his bow and went out.

Rebekah overheard what Isaac said to Esau, and plotted with Jacob to steal Esau's blessing. First they prepared food just the way Isaac liked it. Then Jacob dressed in Esau's clothes and with goat skin covering his smooth hands and neck, he brought the food into Isaac posing as Esau. Isaac suspected he was Jacob, but Jacob swore to him he was Esau. After smelling Esau on his clothes and feeling his hairy hands, Isaac took Jacob's food and ate it. Then thinking he was Esau, blessed Jacob instead.

Jacob had barely left Isaac when Esau came in to receive his blessings. Isaac was stunned when he realized it was not Esau he had blessed. Esau pleaded with his father to give him blessings also, but Isaac could not. It would be Jacob that would now have the blessings, and there was no way for Isaac to undo that. Esau was devastated and swore he would get even with Jacob. Jacob had deceitfully stolen not only his birthright from him but now had even stolen his blessings from him. He was determined, that after his father died, he would kill Jacob.

JACOB'S LIFE TAKES A TURN
(Genesis 27:42–31)

After learning of Esau's intent to kill Jacob, Rebekah plotted one more time to ensure Jacob's safety. Her plan was to send him off to find a wife in her brother's house, away from Esau's harmful reach. She complained to Isaac about the Hittite women Esau had married, and that her life would not be worth living if Jacob also married women from the land of Canaan. Isaac gave Jacob instructions to go to his mother's homeland, specifically to the house of his Uncle Laban to find a wife. Isaac then reaffirmed the blessings already given to Jacob and sent him on his way. Rebekah promised Jacob she would secretly send word for him to return as soon as Esau's fury had subsided.

Jacob was seventy-six years old when he left for his mother's homeland. Yet, even at this age it had to be an enormous step for Jacob to leave his mother's protection and go out on his own. The first night he laid his head on a rock under the stars and fell asleep. In his dreams he saw a stairway to heaven with angels coming and going on it, then he heard God speaking to him. God reassured him he would be safe, that He would watch over him wherever he went and He would bring him back home. Then God addressed the bigger picture by promising Jacob He would cause his descendants to be as numerous as the dust of the earth, and they would not only own the land he was lying on, but all the people of the earth would be blessed through his offspring.

Jacob woke up in the morning encouraged by everything he heard. He placed the stone he had used as a pillow on a pillar, then poured oil on it and called that place "Bethel" which means house of God. Jacob vowed that if God would be with him, protect and provide for him, and bring him back, he would always give God a tenth of everything he earned. Jacob then continued on his journey.

Jacob arrived at a well just outside of Haran where shepherds were gathering to water their flocks. He asked them if they knew his Uncle Laban. Just as he was asking, a young girl came to the well with a flock of sheep. They introduced her as Rachel, Laban's daughter. Jacob was so taken by her beauty that he kissed her, and then began to weep as he poured out his heart to her and how he came to be there. For Jacob it was instant love. Laban opened his home to Jacob and offered him a job tending his flocks. Jacob wanted nothing more than to have Rachel as his wife and proposed he work for Laban seven years in exchange for her. Laban agreed to his proposal.

The seven years seemed like only days to Jacob because his love for Rachel was so intense. At the end of the seven years Laban threw a great party but deceived Jacob by sending his oldest daughter Leah to him in the night instead of Rachel. The next morning Jacob was stunned and enraged when he realized he had been tricked, and it was Leah not Rachel he had made love to. He confronted Laban but Laban argued that no matter what their agreement had been, their customs would not allow the younger daughter to marry before the older daughter. If Jacob wanted to have Rachel as his second wife, he would have to work another seven years. Jacob agreed to work another seven years but Laban also agreed he could marry Rachel right away. After one week Jacob married Rachel and even though he remained married to Leah, he gave all his love to Rachel.

God had compassion on Leah because she was not loved by Jacob, and while Rachel could not get pregnant, Leah gave Jacob four sons. They were Reuben, Simeon, Levi, and Judah. Rachel was determined to give Jacob children one way or another, and convinced him to let her maid Bilhah be a surrogate mother for her. Bilhah gave Jacob two sons, Dan and Naphtali. Leah decided she could do the same and her maid Zilpah also became a surrogate mother and gave Jacob another two sons, Gad and Asher. The battle for Jacob's attention became quite the competition.

One day Leah's oldest son Reuben discovered some aphrodisiac plants. Thinking it would please his mother and help her in gaining his father's love, he brought them to her. Rachel heard about the plants and was convinced they would help her get pregnant, so she bartered with Leah, promising her a night with Jacob in exchange for the plants. Leah agreed but it was not Rachel that got pregnant, it was Leah. Leah gave Jacob two more sons and a daughter, named Issachar, Zebulun, and Dinah.

Rachel was getting old and distressed at the thought that she may never give Jacob a child. In desperation she called out to God and God blessed her. Jacob was ninety years old when Rachel gave birth to his eleventh son, and she named him Joseph (see Illustration 4).

Jacob worked for Laban twenty years and God blessed Jacob in everything he did. Laban recognized this and out of greed, tried many times to manipulate Jacob's wages. Yet despite Laban's attempts of manipulation, Jacob's wealth increased tremendously because of God's blessings. Laban's sons became extremely jealous of Jacob, and Laban too had developed an indifferent attitude toward Jacob. They all viewed Jacob's wealth as wealth that should belong to themselves.

God intervened and told Jacob to return to the land of Canaan. So, at the age of ninety-seven, Jacob secretly called his wives and children to the field and without telling Laban, fled with his family and all the goods he had accumulated. They had been gone for three days before Laban discovered they had fled, and it took Laban a week to catch up with them in the hills of Gilead. However, before Laban caught up with Jacob, God spoke to Laban and warned him not to say anything to Jacob, good or bad.

Because Laban feared the God of Abraham, he could only question Jacob why he left like a thief in the night. Laban was also looking for small idols someone had taken from his home. While it was Rachel who had stolen them, no one knew it was her nor did they discover them in her tent. After much searching and discussion, Jacob challenged Laban which resulted in a pact between them. Jacob agreed to treat his wives and children well, and Laban promised he would never pursue Jacob for harm.

The next morning Laban returned to Haran and Jacob continued his journey to the land of Canaan.

Chapter 3

THE ISRAELITE NATION EMERGES

(Genesis 32–35)

*I*n the twenty years Jacob had been gone, his mother never once sent word that Esau's anger had subsided against him. Jacob was convinced that Esau was still angry with him for deceiving him out of his birthright and deceitfully taking his blessings. He was so worried about what Esau would do to him that God sent angels to meet him and encourage him. Jacob was encouraged, but eventually his overwhelming fear got the best of him and he became determined to fix the problem himself.

Jacob figured that if Esau knew how well he had done over the last twenty years, he would realize there was no need to share their father's inheritance with him. This would not only give Esau his birthright back, he could have it all. Figuring this news might temper Esau's anger, Jacob sent messengers ahead to tell Esau about all his possessions. He wanted Esau to know that he was on his way back and he hoped to find him a peaceful man.

Jacob became terrified when his messengers returned with word that Esau was on his way to meet him with four hundred men. He was sure Esau intended to destroy him and his family. At first he divided all his possessions and people into two groups so that if Esau attacked the first group, perhaps the second group would be spared. But, convinced Esau would still kill all his children and their mothers, Jacob franticly cried out to God in fear.

He wanted so badly to believe God's promise about making his descendants like the sand of the sea shore, yet it was just too hard to do nothing and stand on faith in the face of crisis, so he decided to appease Esau by sending gifts to him. First he sent two hundred and twenty goats, then two hundred and twenty rams, then thirty camels with their young ones, then fifty cows and bulls, and finally thirty donkeys. Each group was instructed to tell Esau they were gifts from his brother Jacob.

When darkness fell he led his children, their mothers, and all his remaining possessions across the river and returned to the other side to be alone. This was a pivotal point in Jacob's life. He couldn't go back to live with Laban because God had called him to return home. He was afraid to go home because he was sure his brother would kill him and all his children. Throughout the night Jacob struggled with God, not wanting to settle for anything less than to absolutely know he had God's blessings. God did bless Jacob that night, and he knew it because God had touched him on his hip socket, causing him to limp. God also blessed him by changing his name from Jacob "the deceiver" to Israel because he "struggled with God" and prevailed.

God was taking Jacob through some difficult moments so Jacob could learn to trust Him, just as his grandfather Abraham did. Jacob didn't totally get it that God was with him and the nagging fear lingered. As he limped forward to encounter his brother, he separated his family into three groups with Bilhah, Zilpah and their sons going first, then Leah and her children in a second group, followed by Rachel and Joseph in the rear. The reunion of the two brothers was not the embittered massacre Jacob had feared, but instead a reunion of embracing, weeping, and kissing.

Esau was overwhelmed by the gifts Jacob had given him but told Jacob he was quite wealthy and didn't need his gifts. Jacob, not ready yet to let God be in full control, insisted Esau keep his gifts. Esau wanted so badly to escort them home but Jacob again insisted Esau and all his men go ahead while he took his time traveling with the young children. He told his brother all he wanted from him was his favor. Esau agreed and headed home, south of the Dead Sea to Seir. Jacob, on the other hand, changed his direction and headed north of the Dead Sea to Succoth. From Succoth Jacob moved directly west to Shechem where he purchased a plot of ground from Hamor, the leader of Shechem. Jacob set up an altar and declared that the God of Israel was a mighty God.

While Jacob declared this with his mouth, God wanted him to know it in his heart. Jacob was about to go through another difficult situation that would again give him a greater understanding of God. Hamor's son Shechem was attracted to Leah's daughter Dinah and seduced her. Hamor was more interested in Jacob's wealth, and proposed their two families become one through intermarriage, starting with the marriage of Shechem and Dinah. Hamor was willing to pay whatever they required for Dinah, but her brothers refused to accept a dowry and insisted all the men in their town would have to be circumcised. The people in Shechem considered circumcision a small price to pay for the wealth they would inherit, so they agreed.

Three days after all the men had been circumcised and still in pain, Dinah's brothers Simeon and Levi attacked and killed every male in town. They ransacked their homes taking all their valuables, seized their flocks and took the women and children captive. When Jacob saw what they had done he was overwhelmed with fear again because he was a nobody in the land of Canaan and when word got out, he was sure the neighboring people would destroy them. God was quick to speak to Jacob, telling him to return to the place where God had met him when he was running from Esau twenty years ago. Somehow Jacob knew God wasn't just asking him to physically return to that place, but to return to God with his whole heart.

Jacob ordered all his children, their mothers, and his servants to get rid of any foreign gods and idols. They were to change their clothes, take off the jewelry and humble themselves before God. Jacob took anything that would distract them from God and buried it all beneath an oak tree at Shechem. Now Jacob felt he was ready to lead them to Bethel, the place where he had met God twenty years ago. When they arrived at Bethel, Jacob built an altar to honor God. God spoke to him and reminded Jacob that his name is Israel, "the one who struggles with God." God also reminded him of what he had learned in Shechem, that He is an almighty God. He assured Jacob that his descendants would become nations and kings, and they would own the land of Canaan.

Jacob moved on from there but life would still be difficult. His beloved wife Rachel became pregnant but died giving birth to Jacob's twelfth son. Jacob named him Benjamin which means "son of my right hand." Jacob was devastated over her death and buried her near a town known today as Bethlehem. Jacob's oldest son Reuben, perhaps out of anger for his mother Leah always taking second place to Rachel, seduced Rachel's maid Bilhah who was the surrogate mother for two of Jacobs sons. Jacob's grief and problems were too much, so he returned home to his father Isaac at Hebron. Isaac died peacefully at the age of one hundred eighty, and his sons Esau and Jacob buried him.

This brought to a close one generation, and marked the beginning of a new generation that would be a nation chosen by God. This nation would be the twelve sons of Israel who would eventually become known to the world as the nation of Israel.

Chapter 3

Joseph Goes to Egypt

(Genesis 36–41)

Esau's descendants lived in the hill country of Seir, south of the Dead Sea. They became known as the Edomites, which came from Esau's nickname he inherited when he gave up his birthright for a bowl of red stew. It had been about ten years since Jacob left Laban and was now settled in Canaan where his father Isaac had lived. With Rachel gone, Jacob focused his love towards their son Joseph who was now seventeen. Jacob treated Joseph special and loved him more than any of his other sons. He even gave Joseph a gorgeous colorful coat. Joseph, of course, took advantage of his father's doting and when opportunity presented itself, would snitch on his brothers. Joseph's brothers hated him and never had one good thing to say about him.

One day Joseph told his brothers about a dream he had and how their piles of grain gathered around his pile and bowed down to it. They were insulted and angry that Joseph would insinuate that they would, or ever could, bow down to him. He told them about a second dream he had and how the sun, moon, and eleven stars bowed down to him. Jacob was surprised that Joseph would suggest even he would bow down to him, but dismissed it for the dream that it was. The hate Joseph's ten brothers had for him intensified out of pure jealousy, and their hatred and jealousy would soon change the course of the Israelite family.

Joseph's ten brothers went north towards Shechem so the flocks could graze in the fields there. Jacob was still concerned about retaliation for what they did to the people in Shechem, so he sent Joseph to find his brothers and report back on how they were doing. Joseph traveled north to the grazing fields only to discover they had gone even farther north to Dothan. He continued on, determined to find them, but when they saw him coming, their anger got the best of them and they plotted to kill him.

Reuben, thinking he needed to save him for their father's sake, convinced his brothers to throw him into a deep hole. After they stripped him of his colorful robe and threw him in the hole, Reuben returned to the sheep thinking he would rescue him later. While he was gone, a caravan of Ishmaelites came by on their way to Egypt. Judah knew it would be wrong to let him die in that hole, so he convinced his brothers to sell Joseph to the Ishmaelites who were willing to pay them eight ounces of silver. By the time Reuben came back and discovered what they'd done, it was too late. So they dipped his colorful coat in some goat's blood and returned to convince their father a wild animal must have devoured Joseph. First it was Rachel and now he had lost Joseph. Jacob could not be consoled.

Joseph was taken to Egypt and sold to one of Pharaoh's officials, the captain of the guards. His name was Potiphar. God gave Joseph success in everything Potiphar gave him to do. Potiphar was pleased with Joseph and trusted him to be in charge of everything he owned. God blessed Potiphar solely because of Joseph.

Potiphar's wife secretly tried several times to seduce Joseph but he refused her temptations. Joseph's refusals turned her desire into anger and she accused him of trying to take advantage of her. Potiphar was furious and placed him in prison, in the section where the king's prisoners were held. Again, God gave Joseph success in everything he did, so the prison guard put Joseph in charge of all the prison affairs for his section.

Eleven years passed since Joseph was sold by his brothers when two of Pharaoh's chief servants were sent to prison. Pharaoh's cupbearer and his bread maker had offended him and were now in prison, assigned to Joseph. After being in custody for some time, they each had a dream and God enabled Joseph to interpret their dreams for them. He told the cupbearer that Pharaoh would restore him to his position in three days on Pharaoh's birthday, but the bread maker would be executed. Joseph pleaded with the cupbearer to help him get free after he was restored to his position, but after he was released he forgot about Joseph.

Two years later Pharaoh had a dream that seven ugly, skinny cows rose up and devoured seven healthy, fat cows. It was so troublesome it woke him up. He fell asleep and had a second dream that seven thin, scorched heads of grain rose up and devoured seven healthy, good heads of grain. In the morning he called all his magicians and wise men of Egypt but no one could interpret his dreams for him.

The cupbearer remembered how Joseph was able to interpret his dream, and promptly told Pharaoh. As soon as they could get Joseph shaved and cleaned up, they brought him before Pharaoh to interpret his dreams. Joseph made it clear to Pharaoh that it was not his ability to interpret dreams but God's. With that, Joseph listened to Pharaoh's dreams and informed him that God had revealed to him through his dreams, His plans for Egypt. God would give Egypt seven years of bountiful harvests but at the end of the seven good years, would come seven bad years of famine and drought. He suggested Pharaoh put a wise man in charge of the land to preserve enough of the harvest in the seven good years to last through the seven years of famine.

Pharaoh recognized that the very spirit of God was in Joseph, so at the age of thirty Joseph was given charge of the whole land of Egypt. There was no one greater than Joseph in the land other than Pharaoh. Pharaoh changed Joseph's name to Zaphenath-Paneah and gave him the priest's daughter to be his wife. During his first seven years of governing Egypt, Joseph had two sons named Manasseh and Ephraim.

Joseph was thirty-seven years old when the famine began, and it reached far beyond just Egypt. The whole world was hit by the famine, but only Egypt had food. People came to Egypt from every corner of the world to buy grain, and they came to Joseph—*the lost son of Israel*—who had been sold by his brothers for a mere eight ounces of silver.

A Family Reunited
(Genesis 42–45)

Most of Jacob's sons were married and had families of their own. Of Leah's children, Reuben had four sons, Simeon six, Levi three, Judah five (two were dead) and two grandsons, Issachar four sons, Zebulun three and her daughter Dinah had none. As for Leah's maid Zilpah, her son Gad had seven sons, and Asher had four sons, one daughter and also two grandsons. Rachel's son Benjamin had ten sons, and Bilhah's son Dan had one son and Naphtali had four. Jacob lived among his sixty-six children, grandchildren and great grandchildren, but life just wasn't good for him anymore like it was when Joseph was living. He never fully recovered from the loss of Joseph.

They were about two years into the famine and even in his depressed state, Jacob knew they had to seek food if they were going to survive. He had heard that Egypt was selling food so he sent all his sons except Benjamin to Egypt to purchase grain.

The ten brothers arrived in Egypt and it was Joseph they had to go to, to buy grain. It had been more than twenty-two years since they had seen him, and that, combined with the fact that they weren't expecting to see Joseph, added to their inability to realize it was him. But Joseph recognized them. When they bowed down to him he couldn't help but remember the dreams he had when he was seventeen. His brothers had hated him for those dreams and now here they were years later bowing to him and they didn't even know it.

Chapter 3

So much had happened since then and the reality of it was all just too overwhelming. In anger he accused them of being spies, but spoke to them through an interpreter so they wouldn't know he knew their language. They insisted they were not, that they were just a plain ordinary family of twelve brothers; one was dead and the youngest was at home with their father in the land of Canaan. He continued to insist they were spies and demanded they bring him proof of their story. He would allow one of them to go home and return with their younger brother while the other nine brothers remained in prison until they could prove their innocence. With that he threw them all in prison to think about it.

On the third day Joseph told them he had decided to let nine go home with grain for their families, but one would have to remain in prison until they returned with their younger brother to validate their story. Thinking he could not understand their language, they discussed freely how sure they were this was happening because of the horrible things they had done to Joseph more than twenty years ago. Listening to them talk about it and their regrets was too much for Joseph, and he turned away and wept. Joseph returned to them and had Simeon bound and taken off to prison. Then he gave orders to the Egyptian workers to fill their sacks with grain but return their silver by hiding it in their sacks.

The brothers returned home with plenty of grain to feed their families but it was not a pleasant trip. Simeon was left behind, and on the way home they discovered their payment for the grain was in their sacks. But worse than anything, the Egyptian official had insisted they could only return if Benjamin returned with them. They arrived home but wanted to return immediately to rescue Simeon. Reuben even offered his father the lives of two of his sons if he didn't return safely with Benjamin. Jacob wouldn't consider it, not for Simeon, not for Reuben's sons, not for anybody. He had lost Joseph and he wasn't taking any chances on losing Benjamin. Yet, in a few short months they ran out of grain and they would have to return to Egypt for more if they wanted to survive.

Jacob insisted they go back for more grain, but they refused to go unless Benjamin went with them. After a lot of wasted time and arguments, Judah told Jacob he would take personal responsibility for Benjamin's safety. Jacob knew he had to let Benjamin go for the family to survive the famine, so he agreed and sent double payment as well as several gifts for the Egyptian officer. The brothers returned to Egypt as quickly as they could. When Joseph saw them with his brother Benjamin waiting in line for food, he ordered they be brought to his home and a feast prepared for them. They didn't expect to be brought to the officer's home and were sure this meant something bad. They tried to explain to the guard what had happened on the previous trip, the money in their sacks, and how they brought back the silver from their sacks plus enough to buy more grain. While they were trying to explain, Simeon was reunited with them at Joseph's house.

They still didn't know what to think, and when Joseph came in they bowed down to him and presented all the gifts in hopes to appease him. Through all his questions about their father and accepting their gifts, Joseph couldn't take his eyes off his brother. Benjamin was only three years old when Joseph was taken prisoner to Egypt and now he had to be about twenty-six years old. It was all too much for Joseph and he had to leave the room so they wouldn't see him weeping for the joy of the moment. After he regained his composure, he returned to them to share in a feast fit for a king, with Benjamin getting five times more food than anyone. It turned into a wonderful time for them all.

When it was all over, Joseph gave orders to his servants to fill their sacks with grain and to also put their silver back in their sacks. In addition, he told them to hide his personal silver cup in Benjamin's sack. The next day after they had left, Joseph sent his servants after them to accuse them of stealing his personal cup.

Chapter 3

The brothers knew they hadn't stolen anything and reacting with confidence, vowed that if any one of them was found with the cup, he should be killed and the rest would become Joseph's slaves. The brothers were horrified when the cup was found in Benjamin's sack and returned to face the consequences. They told Joseph they knew they couldn't prove their innocence and accepted the fact that they would become his slaves. Joseph said no, they were to return to their father but Benjamin would have to remain in Egypt.

Judah pleaded with Joseph, telling him how their father had loved Benjamin's older brother more than anyone, but he died. Their father refused to let Benjamin go to Egypt but was eventually forced to in order for the family to survive. Judah had vowed to give his own life for the safety of Benjamin and pleaded with Joseph to let him stay in Benjamin's place. Judah was certain that because his father was old; it would kill him if Benjamin didn't return. Judah had no desire to go home and watch his father die.

Joseph couldn't control himself any longer. He demanded all his servants leave at once then told his brothers who he really was. They were terrified when they realized it really was their brother Joseph, and how angry he must be for what they did to him. But Joseph convinced them it was all events that had to happen so God could provide for them to survive the famine that wouldn't end for another five years. This was all part of God's wonderful plan to save them because of the promises He had made to their fathers Abraham, Isaac, and Jacob. They were His chosen people and God would bless the world through them and their descendants.

It was a wonderful reunion of embracing, weeping, and forgiving. The news of Joseph's family spread fast and everyone was really happy for Joseph. Even Pharaoh was pleased to hear the news and offered Joseph the best of the land for his family and encouraged them to move to Egypt. Pharaoh ordered carts to be sent to Canaan to carry back all the wives and children of Joseph's brothers, as well as his father. The brothers returned home with gifts of clothing, food, bread, grain, and silver, and couldn't wait to tell their father they had found Joseph alive.

It was too much for Jacob to believe that Joseph was alive, but when he saw the gifts from Pharaoh it was as though his own life had been revived. He believed and became determined to travel to Egypt to see Joseph before he died.

JACOB GETS THE BIG PICTURE
(Genesis 46–50)

When Jacob was one hundred thirty years old he moved his entire family to Egypt, to the area called Goshen. Joseph traveled into Goshen to meet them and it was an emotional reunion for Jacob and Joseph as they hugged and wept for a long time. Joseph brought his brothers and father in to meet Pharaoh who was delighted to have them in Egypt. Pharaoh offered them land in the best part of Egypt which was Goshen, sometimes called Rameses. He also suggested to Joseph that if his brothers had skills, he should hire them and place them in positions of leadership. Jacob prayed a blessing over Pharaoh then returned to Goshen with his family. Jacob appreciated being treated so well and being given the best of the land in Egypt, but he made Joseph promise to bring him back to the land of Canaan when he died. He wanted to rest in the cave at Machpelah with Abraham and his father Isaac. Joseph gave him his word.

The famine lasted for another five years but Jacob and all his family were extremely well taken care of, including their flocks and herds. With the exception of Joseph's family and Pharaoh's priests, all the people of the land were required to find a type of payment for their food. At first Joseph accepted their money in payment for the grain. When their money ran out he accepted their livestock in exchange for grain. When all their livestock was turned over to Pharaoh, Joseph accepted their land as payment. For the remainder of the famine the people agreed to continue working the land and producing what little they could, and for this Joseph allowed them to keep four-fifths of the harvest. Even after the famine was over Pharaoh maintained ownership of the livestock and the land, and the people continued to be taxed one-fifth of their harvests. Pharaoh's wealth increased far more than he could have hoped for and his delight was reflected in the favor he showed to Joseph's family.

Jacob had lived in Goshen for seventeen years, and his family had definitely been blessed by God. They were no longer the sixty-seven that had come down from the land of Canaan, but a large community. Their wealth also increased because of how God had blessed them through Pharaoh's good will.

Joseph could see Jacob was close to dying so he brought his two sons to him so he could bless them. Jacob rallied all the strength he could and sat up in bed to greet them. He reminded Joseph of God's promise to give his descendants the land of Canaan and he really believed God would still do this. When this happened, more than anything he wanted Joseph to have the birthright portion. This would give him double what any of his brothers got, but Joseph was his eleventh son, not the first. So Jacob, being the clever person he always had been, declared Joseph's sons Manasseh and Ephraim "his sons", and any other children born to Joseph would be treated as Jacob's grandchildren.

Now just as Jacob's mother had predicted he would be greater than his older brother Esau, Jacob also predicted Ephraim would be greater than his older brother Manasseh. This troubled Joseph so Jacob reassured him Manasseh would be great also, but Ephraim would be greater. Then Jacob put his hands on their heads and blessed them. He prayed that the God of Abraham and Isaac, the God who had been his shepherd, the God who had been with him all his life even to this day, the God who had kept him from harm, that *this God* would bless these boys as though they were his own, and that their descendants would be many.

Jacob didn't like getting old because it was a humbling experience. He had always been so independent and strong willed, and for most of his life he was very much in control. He was a twin, and just because he was born second didn't mean he didn't deserve to have everything a first son would normally have. He did what he had to do to get Esau's birthright as well as the blessings his father intended to give his brother. When he met Rachel, it was love at first sight and he did what he had to do to have her as his wife. When his father-in-law deceived him and gave him Rachel's older sister instead, he just worked harder to have Rachel. He wanted to be wealthy, and while he knew God was blessing him, he did what he had to do to give himself the full advantage. When it was time to leave his father-in-law and go back to his father, nothing was going to stop him and nothing did. Jacob was self reliant but it was always fear that God used to get his attention.

When he returned to the land of Canaan it was the fear of meeting Esau that made him turn to God for help. He fought with God in prayer all night and by morning Jacob literally walked away limping in the battle of wills of doing it God's way versus Jacob's way. God changed his name to Israel as a reminder of his struggle with God. Yet Jacob still didn't quite get it, and manipulated the meeting with Esau to give himself every advantage. It was just his nature to do that.

It wouldn't be long and he found himself out of control with fear again as a result of his daughter being raped. Again he turned to God, but this time God said come back to Me but come back with your whole heart. Jacob's idea of this was to get rid of all the idols, earrings and stuff that kept them from looking like godly people. Then he returned to the place where he had heard God speaking to him more than twenty years ago. Soon life went back to normal. Normal until his son Joseph turned up missing, and then he gave up on life completely.

Jacob was never able to grasp what God had been trying to accomplish through him. God's plan was to save the whole world through his descendants and God needed him to teach his sons, the nation of Israel, to be grounded in an understanding of who God was. They had to learn to trust God. God needed these people He had chosen to stand the test of time, to survive all of Satan's attempts to destroy His creation by destroying them. Now that Jacob was old and able to reflect on how God had worked through his life, he was finally beginning to understand that God had a plan. Somehow, in his heart he began to discern the roles his sons would play in God's plan.

He knew he didn't have much time left and he needed to tell them before he died. Jacob called his sons to his bedside to explain how each would play out in God's great plan for mankind. They would return to the land of Canaan and God would give them that land. Jacob addressed each one of them, but it was Judah's descendants that would have the greatest role of them all. The brothers heard their father explain how Judah's descendants would become great and rule nations with the strength of a lion. Judah would rule forever. It is doubtful they could, even in the smallest sense, understand the enormity and depth of what Jacob was telling them. It was impossible for them to grasp the idea that the Son of God would be born through Judah's descendants to save the world from Satan, then rule for eternity.

Jacob may not have grasped the clarity of God's plan as we know it today, but he was able to understand that God had a plan and his descendants held a pivotal role in that plan. Jacob finally got beyond the need to control his life; he accepted the name God had given him, lay back down in his bed and died. Just as he requested of Joseph seventeen years ago, his sons carried his body back to the land of Canaan and he was laid to rest in the cave at Machpelah with Abraham and his father Isaac.

With probably the same level of fear that always brought Jacob back to God, his sons developed a tremendous fear that Joseph would now take revenge on them for what they had done to him when he was young. But Joseph reassured them he felt no animosity whatsoever towards them and there would be no revenge. The one most valuable thing he learned from his father through it all was that God had a plan.

Chapter 4

FROM RICHES TO BONDAGE

(Exodus 1–2:15, Reference Books)

The pharaohs that reigned during the period when Israel moved his family to Egypt were of the Twelfth dynasty, and ruled from 1991 to 1786 B.C. This was one of the greater dynasties to rule in Egypt. It was probably Senusert II who was the Pharaoh that Joseph interpreted dreams for, and who appointed Joseph to his position of authority. However, his reign lasted only a few short years and his successor Senusert III reigned during the seven years of famine. Joseph and his family continued to hold the favor of each succeeding Pharaoh for several years.

Joseph died at the age of one hundred and ten during the reign of Amenemhet III. In fact, all of his brothers had passed away but their children had become like a nation within Egypt. By now, they were so wealthy and self sufficient they no longer needed Pharaoh's favors. They became known as the community of Hebrews because they had moved to Egypt from Hebron. Life had become quite good for these Hebrews in Egypt and they were in no hurry to go back to the land of Canaan.

All the Pharaohs of this dynasty were natives of Egypt. However, within seventy-five years of Joseph's death, outsiders were able to overthrow the Egyptian government and begin a new dynasty of authority over Egypt. This new dynasty, called the Hyksos, was few in number, and felt vulnerable to the huge community of people called Hebrews. There was a lot of concern that the native Egyptians would conspire with this community to overthrow them. Almost overnight the tables were turned for the children of Israel. The new Pharaoh made them his slaves and forced them to build the cities of his new capital, Pithom and Rameses. He was ruthless in forcing them into every kind of hard labor, making life bitter for them.

The Hebrews suffered under the bondage of this dynasty for almost one hundred fifty years, but hoped life would change for them when an Egyptian and his followers overthrew the Hyksos dynasty. Finally, an Egyptian called Ahmose became the new Pharaoh of Egypt and ruled for twenty-four years. He and his successor, Amenhotep I, who ruled for another twenty-one years, not only chose to continue the Hebrew's bondage but ordered the midwives to kill all the boys born to their women.

They weren't going to take any chances of being vulnerable to outsiders again, including the foreigners living within their boundaries. Despite the attempts to minimize the size of this foreign community of people called Hebrews, God continued to bless them and they increased in numbers much faster than normal. At the end of the reign of Amenhotep I, a fourth generation of Israel's descendants were being born and the midwives were ignoring the orders to kill the baby boys.

Thutmose I was now the third Pharaoh since the Hyksos dynasty, and he was even more ruthless than his two predecessors. When he realized the midwives had ignored their orders, he commanded that all baby boys born to the Hebrews be thrown into the Nile River.

One Hebrew family who were descendants of Levi had two children, a three-year-old son named Aaron and a seven-year-old daughter named Miriam. They had just given birth to another son when Pharaoh gave this horrible order. For three months she hid her baby to protect him from this order, but knew she had to do something drastic to spare his life. She coated a basket with tar so it wouldn't leak water, placed her baby in the basket, then let the basket drift down the Nile River. Her young daughter followed the basket so she would know what became of her son, whether it was good or bad. All she could do was pray that someone down river would rescue her son.

Miriam couldn't believe it when Pharaoh's own daughter found him while taking a bath in the river. She was Hatshepsut, the queen's daughter who was born to Thutmose I as well as three other children. Hatshepsut's siblings died, leaving her the only child of Pharaoh's queen. Hatshepsut wanted the title of Pharaoh more than anything but women weren't allowed to hold this prestigious title. She was aggressive, a bit mannish and it was not uncommon for her to dress like a man. On occasion she was even known to wear a fake beard, perhaps to somehow convince her father she deserved the title of Pharaoh.

When Hatshepsut saw the baby boy, she thought adopting him as her own might be to her advantage in getting the title of Pharaoh. She called him Moses because she had pulled him out of the water. When Miriam realized Hatshepsut intended to keep the baby, she came out of the reeds and told her she could find a Hebrew mother to nurse the baby for her. Hatshepsut agreed and paid Miriam's mother to care for him until he was weaned. Hatshepsut gave Moses every advantage a pharaoh's son could have.

When Hatshepsut's father died, the closest she could get to the title of Pharaoh was to marry the next pharaoh, which was her half brother. He was born to a lesser wife and called himself Thutmose II. As queen she was obliged to give him children to inherit the title Pharaoh, but was only able to give him one daughter who died at a young age. His reign lasted only ten years before he died, and a son from a lesser wife was appointed the title Pharaoh. He called himself Thutmose III.

Hatshepsut could not tolerate her lack of power so she aggressively assumed joint control with him which lasted for twenty-two years until she died. Thutmose III regained his sole authority after her death and ruled for another thirty-two years, but his experience with Hatshepsut made him bitter and angry.

Four years before Hatshepsut died, Moses was forty years old and found himself drawn to the Hebrew people. He often went out to watch them in their hard labor. It's not clear who or how many people knew Moses was a Hebrew, but Moses did. On one visit to observe the Hebrews, he found himself intervening for one who was being beaten by an Egyptian. He killed the Egyptian to save the Hebrew and carefully buried the body, hoping no one would find out. He knew how much Pharaoh hated Hatshepsut, and there was nothing that would please Thutmose III more than to kill Moses just to hurt her. The next day he discovered the word was out about the killing. As Moses expected, Pharaoh was determined to kill him so he immediately fled for his life into the desert. It would be another forty years before he would see Egypt again.

Life continued to be almost unbearable for the children of Israel who remained in Egypt, and often deadly for the weak. In the little more than four hundred years they had been in Egypt, life had gone from one extreme to the other. Of course they had heard all the stories about the God of their fathers but where was this God now? Why didn't He hear their prayers?

They prayed earnestly to this God to deliver them from their enemies and to save them from this torture. Their situation seemed impossible and the best they could do to survive was to pray, to wait, and to hope for someone to deliver them out of their bond-age.

They needed a deliverer, a deliverer that only God could pro-vide.

THE DELIVERER
(Exodus 2:16–4)

Overnight, Moses went from riches to rags, from a queen's son to a homeless nobody. He was able to make it through the desert and came to the region of Midian. It seemed to be his nature lately to come to the rescue of those in need, and he rescued seven women from some bullish shepherds when they tried to water their sheep at a well. These were the daughters of Jethro, who welcomed Moses into his house and family by giving him his oldest daughter Zipporah as a wife. She gave birth to a boy and Moses named his son Gershom, which means alien in a foreign land.

Moses remained in this foreign land and took care of his father-in-law's sheep. He had all the advantages of being raised in Pharaoh's house but he didn't have the advantage of being told all the stories of his ancestors. He didn't realize he was following in his great great grandfather's footsteps by meeting his wife at the well and tending his father-in-law's sheep. Like Jacob, Moses would have the enor-mous privilege to be used by God to accomplish His great plan of salvation.

It had been many years since Moses left Egypt and he was soon to have one of many encounters with God, unlike anyone else since the days of Adam in the Garden of Eden. He led his father-in-law's sheep to the western side of the desert to graze by the great moun-tains of Sinai. Mount Sinai was only a three-day journey from Egypt, almost too close for his comfort, but he was curious because he had heard this was the mountain of God.

Moses was raised in a house that believed in many gods, most made of wood or metals. But he had heard the God of his fathers was like no other God; He was a God above all gods. He climbed the great mountain and saw a bush on fire, but it didn't burn up. As he walked closer to the bush to try and figure it out, he heard a voice from the bush calling his name. He answered and the voice told him not to come any closer, but to take his shoes off because the ground he was standing on was holy. The voice said, "I am the God of your father, the God of Abraham, the God of Isaac, and the God of Jacob."

Moses turned and hid his face out of fear. But the voice continued by declaring He had heard and seen the misery and suffering of His children in Egypt, and that He wanted to rescue them. He wanted to bring them to the land He promised to give to their fathers, a rich land flowing with milk and honey, the land of Canaan. He told Moses to go to Pharaoh and inform him he was taking the Israelites out of Egypt, and bringing them into the desert to this mountain to worship God.

Moses was stunned and asked, "What if they want to know Your name?" God said His name is *Yahweh* meaning He is and will be what He will be. God knew Moses was afraid and would have a tendency to doubt, so God made it clear to him that Pharaoh would refuse his request, but God would stretch out His hand and change his heart by performing miracles. God told Moses they would also plunder the Egyptians before they left by merely asking for their silver, gold, and clothing.

This was all so overwhelming to Moses and he knew the people wouldn't believe him. How could they believe that slaves could so easily walk off, and with Egypt's wealth? How could they believe that he had been sent by the God of their fathers? God told him to throw his staff on the ground, and when he did it turned into a snake. When he picked up the snake it turned back into a staff. God told him to put his hand inside his coat, and when he did it turned white with leprosy. When he put his hand inside his coat again, the leprosy disappeared. If these two signs weren't enough to convince them, God told Moses to pour water from the Nile on the dry ground and it would turn into blood.

Moses always had a problem with stuttering and questioned why God would choose him to go speak to Pharaoh. God told Moses it was "Him" who gave him his mouth, and "He" would help him speak and teach him what to say. Moses was such a timid, humble man and so afraid to go back. With as much reverence as Moses could muster, he asked God to please send someone else, not him. God was angry with Moses for his lack of willingness to be obedient but was gracious by offering to send his brother Aaron with him to speak to the people on Moses' behalf. God told Moses his brother would speak for him but it would be clear to everyone it was Moses who had been given the authority by God, and it would be Moses who would perform all the miracles.

Moses traveled back through the desert to his father-in-law and asked permission to go back to Egypt to see if any of his people were still alive. If Moses was looking for Jethro to give him reason not to go back, he didn't get it. Jethro told him to go and wished him well. Moses was still afraid to go back but God spoke to him in Midian and reassured him that the Pharaoh who wanted to kill him was dead. God also reminded him that the new Pharaoh would refuse to let the people go even after all the miraculous signs Moses would perform for him. God told Moses that in the end, He would kill Pharaoh's first born son because of Pharaoh's refusal to let them go.

Moses left for Egypt with his wife and son. Before arriving in Egypt, God wanted to break Moses completely away from his learned Egyptian culture and in doing so, brought him to the point of death. His wife instinctively knew what had to be done and she circumcised their son. When she touched Moses' feet with the foreskin, God spared him and he revived. Moses had fled Egypt forty years ago as an Egyptian but was now returning as a child of Israel who had spoken with their God. God had also spoken to Aaron instructing him to go into the desert to meet Moses, and they met at the mountain of God.

Moses told Aaron all the things God had instructed him to say including all the miracles God commanded him to perform. As soon as they reached Egypt, they met with all the elders of the Israelites and Aaron told them everything Moses had told him. It was the miracle they had prayed for, finally God was going to deliver them out of the hand of their enemy. They bowed down and worshipped God.

THE EXODUS
(Exodus 5–13:16)

In the forty years Moses was in the region of Midian, his adoptive mother Hatshepsut died, as well as his step brother Thutmose III, the one determined to kill him. His son Amenhotep II was now Pharaoh and by now, Egypt had come to depend on the hard labor of the Hebrew community. While they didn't enforce laws to kill the children anymore, they were still just as ruthless towards them and didn't value the life of a Hebrew slave other than for the work they could do.

Word was getting out and spreading fast that Moses had returned at the command of the God of their fathers to lead them out of Egypt. There was hope and excitement among the children of Israel. Moses was also encouraged because Pharaoh did not try to kill him as his father did. It was around this time that Zipporah gave birth to their second son and Moses named him Eliezer, which means God is my help. Moses wanted to honor God for saving him from Pharaoh's sword. Moses sent her and his two sons back to Midian to stay in the safety of Jethro's house while he remained in Egypt to do what God instructed him to do.

Amenhotep II had become Pharaoh when he was sixteen, and now six years later was agreeing to meet with Moses. While he had never met his great Aunt Hatshepsut, he certainly had to know his father's hatred for her. It would be entertaining to meet her adopted son, the one who had fled so cowardly from his father. Moses was direct and commanded Pharaoh to allow the Hebrews to make a three-day journey into the desert so they could worship their God. He informed Pharaoh he stood before him on behalf of the God of the Israelites and if he refused, Egypt could be stricken with plagues or by the sword.

Pharaoh of course refused, and out of arrogance he commanded no more straw be provided to the Hebrews, that they find their own straw for making bricks. The Hebrew foremen immediately went to Pharaoh in hopes they could convince him to change his mind and give them straw. Instead Pharaoh called them lazy for wanting to go into the desert to worship and not only insisted they find their own straw but their quotas for bricks would remain the same.

The people became angry with Moses and accused him of putting a sword in Pharaoh's hand to kill them. This certainly wasn't the outcome Moses had expected, and out of desperation went to God for help. God told Moses He made a promise to Abraham, Isaac, and Jacob to give them the land of Canaan and He would do what He had promised. He told Moses that up to now, no one really knew Him and He would reveal Himself and His mighty power to the children of Israel through His dealings with Pharaoh. Moses relayed this to the children of Israel but they didn't want to hear it because of the added hardships Moses had caused them.

Moses didn't know what to do and told God, if they won't listen to me how can I expect Pharaoh to listen to me. God assured Moses that Pharaoh would listen and respect him as though he were a god himself. So Moses returned to Pharaoh and again demanded he let the people go. This time Moses threw his staff on the floor and it turned into a snake. Pharaoh had his magicians do the same, and even though Moses' snake swallowed up their snakes, Pharaoh refused to consider Moses' demands, just as God said he would.

God instructed Moses to go to Pharaoh in the morning at the Nile River, repeat the demands and then turn the water into blood when he refused. Moses did what God commanded but Pharaoh's magicians were able to turn water into blood also, so Pharaoh ignored Moses once more. A week later God told Moses to go back to Pharaoh and warn him that if he refused to let His people go, God would plague Egypt with frogs. When Pharaoh refused, all of Egypt was crawling with frogs. They were in their beds, their kitchens, in their bread, everywhere. The Egyptians complained to Pharaoh. Even though Pharaoh's magicians were able to magically produce frogs also, it was Moses he called on to end the plague by promising he would let the people go. But when the plague stopped, Pharaoh changed his mind and refused to let them go. When Pharaoh went back on his word, Moses struck the ground with his staff and the dust turned into gnats.

For the first time, Pharaoh's magicians could not duplicate Moses' miracle but Pharaoh still wouldn't let the people go. Moses returned to Pharaoh and told him if he didn't let the people go, God would cover the land with flies but not the land of Goshen. Pharaoh refused and the land became full of ugly, disgusting black flies. Pharaoh called Moses back and promised the people could go worship if he got rid of the flies. So Moses prayed and God caused the flies to go away, but again Pharaoh changed his mind and refused to let the people go.

Moses threatened Pharaoh with a plague on their livestock but he still refused to let the people go. By the next day nearly all the horses, donkeys, camels, cattle, sheep, and goats in Egypt were dead, but not in Goshen. Still Pharaoh would not let the people go. So Moses took handfuls of soot and, throwing it into the air, told

Pharaoh it would cause festering boils to break out on their skin. Everyone in the whole land except the Hebrews broke out with boils on their skin, even the magicians who couldn't come to Pharaoh anymore because of the boils on their feet.

Early the next morning Moses returned to Pharaoh and told him his very existence was allowed by God in order to reveal His power and strength, and that God's name would be proclaimed throughout all the world. Moses also told Pharaoh that God was going to send a hailstorm worse than Egypt has ever seen. He advised Pharaoh that if there were any livestock or people in the fields that had survived the previous plagues, they be given shelter because they would not survive this one.

Pharaoh ignored Moses and then the hail fell. The storm was intense with severe thunder and lightning and it destroyed all the flax and barley that was ready for harvest, as well as any livestock that had been left in the field. Yet the storm did not pass over Goshen. Pharaoh called for Moses and admitted he had sinned and promised they could go if he would only stop the storm. As soon as the storm stopped however, he changed his mind and refused to let the people go.

Moses returned to Pharaoh and told him if he didn't let the people go, tomorrow God would send a plague of locusts like Egypt has never seen. He warned him that even though their wheat crops survived the hailstorm, they would not survive the locusts. After Moses and Aaron left, Pharaoh's officials told him that Egypt was in ruins because of these plagues. They told Pharaoh that enough was enough and begged him to let the people go, so Pharaoh called Moses back.

When Moses returned, Pharaoh told him they could go but he was only willing to let the men go. He didn't trust them to return if the women and children went also. Pharaoh refused to completely comply with Moses' demands and sent him away. That day and for the rest of that night an east wind blew, bringing with it locusts that covered the ground until it was black. Nothing green was left in all of Egypt except in Goshen. Pharaoh called Moses once again confessing he was wrong, but when Moses prayed for the land and the locusts left, Pharaoh again refused to let them go.

God caused a darkness to cover the land for three days. It was so dark you could feel it, and only those who lived in Goshen were able to leave their homes. Pharaoh called Moses and told him the people could go, women and children too, except they had to leave their livestock behind. Moses said that was impossible because they needed to make sacrifices to God. Pharaoh got so angry he told Moses to get out of his sight and if he ever saw him again it would cost him his life.

God told Moses there would be just one more plague and then Pharaoh would let the people go. He told Moses to instruct the people to prepare for their journey by plundering the Egyptians. They would only have to simply ask them for their silver, gold, and fine cloths and the Egyptians would willingly give it all to them. While the Hebrews went door to door plundering the Egyptians, Moses went to Pharaoh one last time to inform him of the final plague.

Moses was not afraid of Pharaoh anymore but angry instead. He told Pharaoh that at midnight God would go throughout the land and every first born son would die. From the first born son of Pharaoh to the first born son of a slave girl, including the first born of their cattle. There would be a wailing in Egypt like never before or ever will be again. He went on to tell Pharaoh that even his officials would come to him in Goshen begging him to lead the people out of Egypt, *then we will leave.*

The children of Israel were instructed to slaughter a year old male lamb at midnight and wipe its blood on their door posts. When God passed through Egypt in the night to kill the first born sons, He would pass over those households that had the blood of a lamb on their door. They were to cook the lamb in fire and eat it in its entirety. If one lamb was too much for any given household they were to combine households so that none of the lamb was left un-eaten. They were to eat it quickly because the hour was coming soon for them to leave Egypt.

They did exactly as they were instructed and throughout the night, they heard their Egyptian neighbors crying out. There wasn't a home in all the land that didn't have someone dead, except for those homes where the lamb's blood had been applied to the door posts. During the night Pharaoh sent word demanding Moses lead the people out of Egypt immediately. They didn't even want them to wait until morning because they were afraid by then they would all be dead. So before they could even add the yeast to the bread they were making, they were forced to leave their homes and head out into the desert in the night. With their bread dough still on the kneading boards and with all of Egypt's valuables, they left.

It was the fourteenth day of the month Abib, also known as the month of Nisan, and it was an event that would be celebrated for years to come. Moses told the people that God viewed them as His firstborn son. He redeemed them from the harsh hand of Egypt and they were to give back to God the first born of every womb, including their livestock. They would sacrifice a lamb unto God for each of their firstborn sons and when their children ask why, they will tell them it is because God killed every firstborn in Egypt when Pharaoh refused to let them go. It would be a perpetual re-minder to never forget that they came out of their bondage only by God's mighty hand.

They would celebrate their departure from Egypt every year with seven days of eating bread without yeast. The only work they would do during those seven days would be to prepare food, but the prepared lamb could only be eaten by those who were circum-cised. For the children of Israel, this day would be remembered, not only as the day they left Egypt, but the day death passed over their door because of the blood of the lamb.

They called it the "Feast of Unleavened Bread," but now know it as the day of Passover.

GOD PARTS THE RED SEA
(Exodus 13:17–18)

This community of Hebrews had grown to more than two million men, women, and children when they left Egypt. It was a tremendous undertaking to lead them out. God knew their faith in Him was not strong enough to overcome the enemies in the Promised Land and would return to Egypt at the first sign of a battle. So instead of allowing them to go directly into the Promised Land, He took them into the desert towards the Red Sea.

God was always with them, and encouraged them by providing a visible sign that He was making the way before them. He appeared as a pillar of cloud during the day and a pillar of fire at night. When they reached the Red Sea they set up camp, but God warned Moses that Pharaoh would hear where they were, change his mind about letting them go and pursue them with his whole army. However, God assured Moses that all this would happen so the people of Israel as well as the Egyptians would know once and for all, that He was a mighty God.

When the Israelites saw their backs were to the sea and Pharaoh's huge army headed straight for them, they became terrified. The people lashed out at Moses in anger and fear, accusing him of dragging them out to the desert to be killed by Pharaoh's sword. They complained that they had told Moses to leave them alone when they were back in Egypt. Moses assured them that God would fight for them, to just be still and trust God.

Moses held his staff over the water and a tremendous wind parted the Red Sea, making an escape route for them. Then the pillar of cloud and fire went behind them forming a wall of darkness for Pharaoh's army, but a light for the Israelites. All night they traveled as quickly as they could to the other side of the sea, with walls of water raging on both sides.

By morning they were on the other side when the pillar lifted, allowing Pharaoh's army to pursue them through the walls of water. God confused the Egyptians and caused the wheels of their chariots to come off. They began to realize they were up against a God too big for them and tried to retreat out of the sea. But God told Moses to stretch his staff over the sea once more, and when he did the sea closed in on Pharaoh's army. Not one soldier survived.

They had grown up in a land that believed in many gods, but as they watched in quietness as the bodies of the soldiers washed up on shore, a reverent fear for Jehovah came over them. It was an awesome moment for the Israelites to realize the tremendous power their God had to deliver them. They had heard the promises God made to Abraham, Isaac, and Jacob many times, but it just never seemed as real to them as it did this moment.

From that day forward they knew in a way they had never understood before that their God was more powerful than any god. They also realized they needed to show more respect to Moses because he was a servant of that God. It was an awesome deliverance from their enemy so they celebrated with singing, dancing, and worship. When the celebration was over, Moses led them into the desert.

They had traveled into the desert for three days without water, and when they finally found water, it was so bitter they couldn't drink it. They complained, so God instructed Moses to throw a piece of wood into the water, and when he did the water turned sweet. There wasn't anything magical about the wood, it was just a visible way for God to show them He changed the water because He wanted to. God had chosen them to be His people and He wanted them to know that it was His desire to provide for them. They were part of His plan to bring salvation to the world, and He would not let them die of thirst.

God spoke to the people through Moses, who tried to explain that if they would just trust God and follow His instructions, God would take care of them. They would never experience any of the diseases the people in Egypt had, but instead they would come to know God as their healer. This was one of many attributes they would discover about their God if they would just trust Him. Then God led them to a place in the desert where there were twelve springs of water. They camped there for a while, then traveled on towards Mount Sinai.

It was now one month since they left Egypt, and traveling through the desert wasn't wonderful. They were often thirsty but now they were hungry, and even though they hated the bondage and hard labor of Egypt, they missed the wonderful meats and fruits. Moses tried to warn them that their grumbling and complaining is really against God, not him. But God was gracious and sent them quail that evening to satisfy their hunger for meat. In the morning He covered the ground with a dew that looked like a flaky frost after it dried, and the people called it manna.

The manna had the texture of white coriander seed and it tasted like wafers made with honey. Moses instructed them to collect only what they would eat for the day because each morning God would provide fresh manna. The only exception would be the sixth day in which they would collect a double portion so they would have enough for the Sabbath. Every day except the Sabbath, they would collect and prepare the manna by boiling it or baking it.

There were some who didn't listen to Moses and tried God's patience once more. They collected more than what they needed for the day, and by the next day the leftover manna stunk and was crawling with maggots. God was gracious over their grumbling, but when they chose to be disobedient in such a small thing He became angry. Every day they realized God's faithfulness through the manna He provided, and they would always have the manna until they reached the Promised Land.

As the pillar of cloud and fire moved on, the Israelite community followed it. They reached a place where they were able to spread their camp out and called it Rephidim. There was no water there so they complained to Moses again. They were so angry and out of control that they were on the verge of stoning Moses. God told Moses to bring the elders with him outside the camp where he would find a large rock. Moses was to strike the rock, and water would come out from the rock for the people to drink. The people got their water but Moses named that fountain Massah and Meribah, which means testing God and quarreling. Moses didn't want the people to forget the ugly attitudes they showed towards God.

While camped at this place, a band of fighters from a community of people called the Amalekites came out and attacked them. Moses told his aide Joshua to organize an army to fight the Amalekites. When they went out to fight, Moses would assure their victory by standing on the hill and holding out his staff.

The next day they went into battle with the Amalekites and as long as Moses held the staff up they were winning, but when his arms got tired and he lowered the staff, they would start to lose. Aaron and another official named Hur gave Moses a rock to sit on and held his arms up for him. This gave absolute victory to Joshua's army and taught them a new attribute of God. He is Jehovah Nissi which means, He is their banner.

It was while they were here that Moses' father-in-law Jethro came to visit Moses, bringing with him Zipporah and her two sons. Moses told Jethro everything from his first visit with Pharaoh, to their exodus and everything that had happened since they left including their most recent experience of going to battle against the Amalekites. The next day however Moses couldn't visit with them because he was busy from morning until evening, listening to issues the people had with one another and making judgments for them according to God's laws.

Jethro observed this process, and told Moses he was doing a noble thing but it would ultimately be too much for him and he would break under the stress of it all. He suggested Moses teach the people God's laws, then select trustworthy men of integrity and establish a court system where issues could be decided with only the most difficult issues escalating to him.

Moses took his father-in-law's advice and established a system of officials in a pyramid fashion. The easy issues would be settled in the lower courts and as the issues became more difficult, they would be escalated to the higher courts for judging. After Moses finished putting this system in place, his father-in-law returned home to Midian.

The pillar of cloud and fire lifted, leading them into the desert of Sinai where they camped by the mountain of God. It was the mountain where Moses first met God.

THE COVENANT
(Genesis 19–24)

The Israelites arrived at the mountain of God in Sinai exactly two months to the day after they left Egypt. So far it had been somewhat of a difficult journey with the lack of water and food, then the attack of the Amalekites. But God was always faithful to provide whatever they needed including victory on the battlefield.

Moses went up the mountain to meet with God, and returned to tell the people that if they would obey God, He would treat them like a treasured possession. The people were enthusiastic and united in their response, and agreed to obey God. Because of their willingness, Moses told them God would descend on the mountain and the people could stand around the mountain and observe His presence. They had three days to clean the desert dust off themselves, put on clean clothes and become ceremonially clean. Moses headed back up the mountain to meet God, but first he reminded the people they were to observe only, and warned them not to even touch the mountain.

Three days passed and just as Moses said, God descended on the mountain. God came in the form of fire that was so powerful, the mountain shook violently. There was a sound like a trumpet that got louder and louder, and the entire top portion of the mountain was engulfed with smoke that billowed upwards like smoke from a furnace. The people absolutely shuddered in terror at this awesome but curious sight. God gave Moses only ten commandments then instructed him to return to the people before they tried to climb the mountain to see more.

If the people even touched the mountain they would die, because their lack of holiness could not withstand the absolute holiness of God. Moses went back down the mountain to the people with the ten commandments and found them overwhelmed with fear. They were so afraid they would die if they heard God's voice that they told Moses they preferred to have God speak to him on their behalf. Moses tried to calm the people and told them not to be afraid, but when he returned to meet with God they kept their distance from the mountain.

God gave Moses ten commandments for the people to follow. Jehovah will be their only God, they are not to make any kind of an idol nor worship any idols, they are not to misuse the name of God, they must keep the Sabbath day holy by resting, they must honor their parents, they must not murder, they must not commit adultery, they must not steal, they must not give false testimony against anyone, and they must not envy their neighbor for anything.

God also gave Moses laws about how to treat their servants fairly, how to respond when someone is injured or killed intentionally or accidentally either by man or by man's livestock, how to respond when personal property is damaged, how to help and respect one another and the consequences of personal abuse. In all their judgments, they are expected to treat everyone with justice and mercy no matter what the person's social standing is. As for the land, they are to harvest their crops for six years but let the land rest in the seventh year.

Three festivals are to be observed each year, the Feast of Unleavened Bread to celebrate when they came out of Egypt, the Feast of Weeks to celebrate the first fruits from their crops, and the Feast of Tabernacles to celebrate the end of the harvest. When they enter the Promised Land, they are to come together to celebrate these festivals, to a place that God will designate.

All the commandments and laws God gave them to live by were good and would result in a caring and healthy community. It would be a community that would stand out as being uniquely and distinctively different from any other people on earth. The commandments and laws would provide an environment that resembled God's kingdom, and God emphasized to Moses that "*all*" the commandments and laws were important. If the people are careful to follow them, He would be an enemy to anyone that opposed them. He would also send His terror ahead of them and make their enemies turn and run.

God would not drive out all the enemies in the Promised Land in a single year because the land would become desolate and the wild animals would get over populated. Instead, little by little He would drive out the enemy until the Israelites increased enough to take the whole land. In the end, they would own the land from the Red Sea to the Mediterranean Sea, and from the desert to the Euphrates River. God warned Moses that the Israelites were not to make any agreements with the people in the land, nor to allow them to live among them. If they did, the temptation for the Israelites to worship their false gods would always be there.

Moses returned to the people and read all the commandments and laws God had given him, and the people agreed to live their lives God's way. Moses built an altar at the foot of the mountain with twelve pillars to represent the twelve tribes of Israel. Then he offered burnt offerings on this altar to God.

Moses took the book with the commandments and laws and read it one more time to the people to make sure they understood it completely. They reaffirmed their commitment to obey everything God had asked. With this, Moses sprinkled the blood from the sacrifice on the book making it a covenant, an agreement between God and His people. God would give them the Promised Land and be an enemy to their enemies, and the people in turn would follow His commandments and laws.

They entered into a covenant that sealed their role in God's divine plan to bring salvation to the world. God was pleased and called Moses, Aaron, and his two sons, as well as the seventy elders of Israel to the top of the mountain to see the God of Israel. They were bowed down in a reverent fear when they saw God's feet on a pavement of sapphire as clear as the sky itself. Seeing God and entering into a covenant with God were both historic events, and they returned to the people in the camp to celebrate with eating and drinking.

Moses left the celebration and returned to the mountain with Joshua who faithfully took his place at some point half way up the mountain. Moses continued to the top, to meet with God again.

THE MEETING PLACE
(Exodus 25–31)

On their two-month journey to Mount Sinai, Moses would meet with God in a tent set up outside the camp which he called the tent of meeting. Moses' aide Joshua not only went with Moses but he rarely left the tent of meeting. When God spoke to Moses, the pillar of cloud would descend to cover the entrance and the people would stand at their tent doors and worship. When Moses returned to the camp, the pillar of cloud would lift and the people would go about their business.

But now they were at Mount Sinai and Moses and Joshua headed up the mountain to meet with God. Joshua stopped half way up the mountain while Moses continued to the top and entered the thick cloud. The people watched from the camp as God's glory blazed like a consuming fire that almost seemed to swallow Moses up. Moses and Joshua were both gone for forty days and forty nights and had nothing to eat or drink. It was during this long visit God described in vivid detail the tabernacle they were to build that would replace the tent of meeting. The tabernacle would be mantled and dismantled many times as they traveled through the desert on their way to the Promised Land. The tabernacle would be where Moses would meet with God, and it would be a most holy place.

The most sacred article in the tabernacle would be the ark. God's presence would rest above the ark and this would be the place where He would speak with them. The ark would be made of wood overlaid with pure gold inside and out, measuring 45" long, 27" wide and 27" tall. It would have four gold rings attached to the feet with poles made of wood and gold to carry it. The cover for the ark would be pure gold and have two angels on each end with their wings spread upward. When the ark was finished and anointed, no one could touch it and live because the holiness of God's presence would be on it.

They were to make a table made of wood overlaid with pure gold measuring 36" long, 18" wide and 27" tall. The plates and dishes used in the temple would be placed on this table as well as twelve loaves of bread. This bread represented the twelve tribes of Israel and would always be present on the table before God. The table would have four gold rings attached to the legs with poles made of wood and gold to carry it.

They were to make a lamp stand using seventy-five pounds of pure gold. It would have three branches extending out from both sides, each having three cup-shaped almond flowers placed intermittently down each branch. Each branch would also have a fourth flower where it was joined to the lamp stand, and a cup-shaped flower for the center light. They were to also make seven lamps, wick trimmers and trays of pure gold for the lamp stand. The lamps were to burn from evening to morning using only clear olive oil.

They were to make an altar of incense out of wood overlaid with pure gold, measuring 18" long, 18" wide and 3' tall. It would have a gold horn on each corner as well as gold rings, and transport it using poles made of wood and gold. Only sweet incense could be burned on this altar in the morning and in the evening, to provide a sweet fragrance to God.

They were to build a hollow altar made of wood overlaid with bronze measuring 90" square and 54" tall. It would have a bronze grate, a horn on each corner as well as bronze rings. Poles to carry the altar would be wood overlaid with bronze, but all the pots for removing ashes, the shovels, sprinkling bowls, meat forks, and fire pans used at the altar would be solid bronze. This would be used for the sacrifices made to God by fire. Sacrifices for the atonement of sins required the shedding of blood, a necessary extreme to come into the presence of a most holy God.

They were to build a portable tabernacle which would consist of forty-eight wood frames overlaid with gold and placed in silver bases. The frame would be covered with five layers of curtains made from fine blue, purple and scarlet linen with angels woven into them using pure gold thread. These delicate linen curtains would be protected with a layer of curtains woven from goat hair, a second covering of protective curtains made from ram skins dyed red, then a third covering made of goat skins. The final measurements of the tabernacle would be 45' long by 15' wide, but a curtain would hang inside to divide it into two rooms. The first room, called the holy place, would be 30' by 15'. The second room, called the most holy place, would be 15' square and entered through the inside curtain. The table, lamp stand, and altar of incense would be placed in the larger room, but the ark would go in the most holy place.

They were to build a courtyard 150' long by 75' wide made of twenty posts on the long sides and ten posts on the ends. Each post would be set in a bronze base with silver hooks and hold white linen curtains 7½' high. Curtains for the entrance of the courtyard would be made of blue, purple, and scarlet linen, with the entrance always facing east. The tabernacle would be positioned in the courtyard on the west end with that entrance facing east also. The bronze altar would be placed inside the courtyard entrance, with the bronze basin between the altar and the tabernacle entrance. The basin was to be filled with water and used by Aaron and his sons for washing their hands and feet.

Moses' and Aaron's grandfather was Kohath, the son of Levi who was Israel's third son. Levi had two other sons, Gershon and Merari whose descendants, like Moses and Aaron were also chosen by God to serve in the tabernacle. The descendants of Gershon would be responsible for transporting all the curtains and coverings associated with the tabernacle and courtyard, and Merari's descendants would be responsible for transporting all the poles, bases, tent pegs, and ropes. Kohath's descendants would be responsible for transporting all the furniture and articles used in the tabernacle and courtyard.

The only role Aaron and his sons would have in the transporting of the tabernacle would be to cover all the articles prior to any disassembling. Their main role was to serve the people in the tabernacle as priests. God wanted them to wear garments that would give them dignity and honor. The one serving as priest would put on linen undergarments, then a robe made of blue cloth, having blue, purple, and scarlet pomegranates woven into the hem with gold bells sewn between them. Over the robe he would wear a one-piece apron called an ephod made of gold woven with finely twisted blue, purple, and scarlet linen. It would be fastened at the shoulders with two onyx stones engraved with the names of the twelve tribes of Israel.

The priest would also wear a breast piece for making decisions. The breast piece would be a nine-inch square made of gold woven with finely twisted blue, purple, and scarlet linen, then folded in half. It would have four rows of precious stones, also engraved with the names of the twelve tribes of Israel. Braided gold chains and rings would be used to secure the breast piece to the ephod to keep it from swinging away from the ephod. The priest would also place items called the Urim and Thummim in the fold of the breast piece, which were used as a means of casting lots to make decisions. A final piece of clothing would be an embroidered sash.

The priest would wear a turban on his head made of fine linen. A gold plate would hang from the turban across his forehead, engraved with the words "Holy to the Lord."

God promised the priesthood would belong to Aaron and his sons but they needed to be consecrated and ordained. Moses would prepare them for this by shedding the blood of a young bull and two rams, then placing them on the altar with bread, cakes, and wafers made without yeast. Aaron and his sons were to wear their priestly garments throughout this process which continued for seven days. At the end of the seven days, they and their garments would be consecrated.

To consecrate the altar they had to shed the blood of a lamb and sacrifice it on the altar along with bread and wine. They were to do this once in the morning and once in the evening for seven days. All the offerings made by fire would be a pleasing aroma to God.

Finally, God instructed Moses to blend spices, liquid myrrh, and oils to make a sacred anointing oil. Moses was to use this special oil to anoint the tabernacle and all the articles and utensils after everything was completed. He was also to anoint Aaron and his sons to serve as priests.

It had been more than twenty-five hundred years since Adam sinned against God in the Garden of Eden. But now God was making a way to once again dwell among His creation, and would dwell among them at this meeting place called the tabernacle.

MAKING BAD CHOICES
(Exodus 32–40)

Moses had been on the mountain for forty days and received not only specific instructions from God, but stone tablets containing the covenant, carved by God's own hand. But God became angry and told Moses to return quickly because the people had already broken their covenant with Him. God told Moses He was going to destroy the Israelites because of their continued stubbornness and disobedience. God also assured Moses He would raise up another people through Moses' descendants.

If Moses hadn't been such a humble man he might have jumped at the chance to have his descendants become the chosen people of God, but he truly had a heart for God's people. Moses had no idea what the people had done to break their covenant with God or to make God so angry. He interceded for them because he didn't want God dishonored by the Egyptians. For sure they would accuse God of bringing the Israelites out of bondage only to slay them by His own hand in the desert. He pleaded with God to remember His promise to their fathers, Abraham, Isaac, and Israel. God yielded to the plea of Moses and did not destroy them.

Moses took the stone tablets and headed down the mountain. He met Joshua on his way down who was concerned about the noise he had been hearing from the camp. Joshua thought they might be at war but Moses assured him it was not war he was hearing. As Moses and Joshua made their way to the camp they found the Israelites partying and carousing. In the middle of the partying was a golden calf and an altar. They had sacrificed offerings on the altar to honor the golden idol, giving it credit for bringing them out of Egypt.

Moses became so sickened and enraged that he threw the stone tablets on the ground, smashing them into pieces. In unbelief he cried out demanding Aaron tell him what the people did to make him lead them into committing such great sin against God. Aaron asked him to understand what it was like for them with him being gone for so long. They were sure something must have happened to him and they got scared. Aaron told Moses the people gave him all the gold earrings they had taken from the Egyptians, he threw them into the fire and like magic, this golden calf came out.

With absolutely no pity for them, Moses burned the idol in the fire, ground it into a powder, mixed it with water then forced the people to drink it. Even though the people patronized Moses by drinking the water, few felt any shame for what they did and were still out of control with their carousing. Moses went to the entrance of the camp and called out, demanding anyone that was for Jehovah to come out of the camp and stand by him. To his great disappointment, only the descendants of his great grandfather Levi came out of the camp.

God commanded Moses to instruct the Levites to go through the camp among their relatives and kill them with a sword. It was a difficult thing to do, but they were obedient to God and about three thousand men were killed. Because of their willingness to obey God, the Levites would always serve Him in the work of the tabernacle.

The next day Moses told them he was going back to the mountain to seek God's mercy for them.

Moses pleaded with God to forgive them and if He wouldn't, allow him to carry the guilt for the people. God refused to let Moses carry their guilt and caused a plague to inflict them for their sin. God also told Moses He would send His angel to go ahead of them. God would not go with them because they were stubborn people and He might destroy them out of anger during their voyage. Moses told the people what God had said and they became genuinely sorry for what they had done.

Moses returned to God and reasoned with Him. He argued that if God didn't go with them, the world would not be able to distinguish them from anyone else. Moses told God that if He didn't go with them, they would stay where they were. Again God yielded to Moses' plea but not for the people, but because of how pleased He was with Moses.

Moses had come to know God in such a wonderful way, and the more he came to know God, the more he learned to love God. Moses' heart longed for God and he longed to see God's glory. God wanted to show Himself to Moses, but no one can see God's face and live. God hid Moses in a rock ledge and allowed Moses to see His back as He passed by. Then God told Moses to come back with two stones and He would again engrave the words of the covenant He had made with the children of Israel.

Moses returned to the mountain with the stones and God engraved them one more time. God assured Moses of His commitment to live among the children of Israel, and as long as they lived by the covenant, He would drive out all their enemies from the Promised Land. Again, God warned Moses that they must not intermarry or make any treaties with people in the land, because it would mean their downfall. They were to be aggressive about breaking down the idols and altars in the land, to avoid being lured into pagan worship. They absolutely were not to put anything or any-one above Jehovah because He is a jealous God.

Moses spent another forty days on the mountain, and when he came down about five months had gone by since they left Egypt. The people were a bit afraid of Moses because his face was radiant from being in the presence of God. Because they were so afraid, he wore a veil over his face but would remove it when he went to be with God. Moses reviewed the covenant they had made with God, and reassured them of God's desire to be their God. He explained in detail how they were to build the tabernacle, the articles to be used in the tabernacle, the courtyard, the altar, the garments for the priests, and the anointing oils.

Moses identified two men that God had chosen and enabled to do the unique crafting required to complete the work. These two were from the tribes of Judah and Dan, as well as others God blessed with the necessary skills. Moses invited the people to bring an of-fering for Jehovah to finance this massive undertaking, and the people were moved in their hearts to contribute. Men, women, and children alike brought gold jewelry, yarns, fine linens, goat hair, ram skins, silver, bronze, wood, precious stones, and more. Much of what they brought was the riches they had taken from the Egyp-tians just before they left Egypt.

Day after day people came with offerings of all sorts for the work on the tabernacle. They gave so much that Moses had to or-der them not to bring any more. The total metals used to complete what God instructed them to build was more than a ton of gold, three and three quarter tons of silver and two and a half tons of bronze. Completing this work became their sole focus while camped at the foot of Mount Sinai.

Two weeks away from their one-year anniversary of leaving Egypt, they finished all that Moses instructed them to make. Moses inspected everything from tent pegs to curtains, even including the priestly garments. When he was absolutely certain that everything was made just as God instructed, Moses gave the command to set up the tabernacle and courtyard. Before anything was anointed, Moses placed the stone tablets in the ark, the tablets God had carved with His own hand.

With Aaron dressed in the priestly robes and his sons in their tunics, they consecrated and anointed everything including Aaron and his sons. When it was finished, the glory of God filled the tabernacle so much that even Moses couldn't enter it. In all their travels the pillar of cloud and fire remained over the tabernacle, and when the pillar moved, they moved with it.

Chapter 5

THE SYSTEM OF SACRIFICES

(Leviticus 1–27)

Adam's decision to sin at the beginning of creation resulted in that sin being carried by every person born after him. Because Yahweh is holy, perfect, and pure in every sense, Adam's sin distanced us from God and required atonement. While at Mount Sinai, God helped Moses understand that this atonement could only be achieved through the shedding of blood. A young bull, lamb, goat, dove, or pigeon could be sacrificed but could not have any defects. There were absolutely no exceptions to this rule, the sacrifice had to be the blood of a *perfect* offering.

The system of sacrifices included different types of offerings depending on the occasion. If someone wanted to express adoration or devotion or commitment to Jehovah, a male bull, lamb, goat, dove, or pigeon was sacrificed with a grain offering, and entirely consumed by fire. This was called a burnt offering and was generally initiated by the priests rather than the people. The smoke from this sacrifice would billow upward toward heaven, and become a sweet and pleasing aroma to God.

Another sacrifice was the sin offering which would provide atonement for someone when they unintentionally broke one of God's commands. A young and perfect bull, lamb, goat, dove, or pigeon was acceptable and offered with a grain offering. Unlike the burnt offering, the blood of this offering had to be sprinkled in the tabernacle in front of the curtain leading into the most holy place as well as on the horns of the altar of incense. The remaining blood was poured out at the base of the altar in the courtyard. The head, legs, and hide of this offering were burned outside the camp but the rest of it was burned on the altar in the courtyard. The priest and his sons were allowed to eat from portions of this offering.

Another sacrifice was the guilt offering which would provide atonement for any injustice committed against one another that had monetary value. Examples of injustice done could include things like doing wrong to a neighbor, swearing falsely, not honoring a commitment, or robbing someone. A ram would be offered, but the accused would also be required to provide restitution for the injustice done, plus an additional one fifth of the damage value.

A peace offering was brought to the altar when a person was in good standing with God. It could be a bull, lamb, or goat and was considered a contribution to the Lord. It was an expression of gratitude and joy to Jehovah. An offering called the wave offering generally was a portion of the peace offering, either a breast or thigh, and was given to Aaron and his sons as the portion belonging to them. This had to be eaten in its entirety the day it was offered with only a few exceptions.

The grain offering was made of flour, oil, and incense, and often accompanied the other offerings. Generally, the priest would place a handful in the fire on the altar, and the rest of the grain offering would belong to him and his sons as their portion.

Chapter 5

God gave Moses detailed and specific instructions, and he was careful to teach them to Aaron and his four sons. Aaron's two oldest sons lacked reverence for God and instead of burning incense on the altar in the tabernacle, tried burning some in the firepots. The two were instantly consumed by fire from God and died.

Aaron and his two younger sons were in the process of being anointed and could not leave the tabernacle to bury them, nor could they stop to mourn them. The two were taken out of the courtyard and buried by cousins. Aaron and his two remaining sons, Eleazar and Ithamar, pursued their priestly duties with an absolute reverent respect for the work God had commissioned them to do. It was a hard lesson, but a lesson that was necessary for them to survive the road ahead.

God provided a lot of instructions to Moses for the people during his visits to the mountain. They were instructions that would contribute to a life of quality in the community and ensure individual integrity. The instructions included details regarding what they could or couldn't eat, how to provide for purification after giving birth to a firstborn child, how to protect the community from people having infections or skin diseases, how to protect and purify themselves from mildew problems. The instructions also included rules about sexual relations that were not allowed, rules for priests, rules about honoring the Sabbath, rules and penalties for people who blasphemed, and many more.

God gave instructions to make sure the Promised Land would always be enjoyed equally among the Israelites, by declaring a Year of Jubilee every fiftieth year. The Year of Jubilee provided for all land properties to revert back to its original owner among the Israelites at the end of every fifty years. When selling land, its value would be determined by the number of years remaining before the Year of Jubilee. They were also to offer their workers freedom in the Year of Jubilee and if the workers declined their freedom, they would become their property for life.

Of everything anyone earned, whether it was a harvested crop, earned income, or properties gained, one tenth of it must be given to God as tithe. God knew they would struggle with this, so He challenged them to just try it. God promised to repay them by opening the storehouses of heaven and pouring out so much blessing they wouldn't be able to contain it all.

After the tabernacle was finished and God's presence rested above it, God repeated His promises for their faithfulness. If they stayed true to their covenant with Him, He would bless them in every way. He would provide rain for their crops, they would have tremendous harvests, they would live in peace and their enemies would fear them. He would be their God and they would be His people.

God also reminded them of the consequences of choosing not to live by the covenant they agreed to. They would live with terror and diseases, their crops would not produce a harvest and they would be defeated by their enemies. God lovingly promised He would try over and over to bring them back to Himself by allowing these things to take place. If in the end they still refused to come back to Him, God warned that He would become hostile and scatter them among the nations.

However, in the end He would not destroy them completely because He would keep the promise He made to Abraham, Isaac, and Israel. It was a promise that someday the world would be blessed through them.

A FORTY YEAR JOURNEY
(Numbers 1–21)

It was the fourteenth day of the first month, one year after they had left Egypt. They celebrated the first anniversary of Passover, one of many they would celebrate for centuries to come. A week after their celebration, God began to prepare them for their journey by instructing Moses to take a census of all the men who were able to serve in the army. Starting with age twenty, Reuben's tribe had 46,500 men, Simeon had 59,300, Gad had 45,650, Judah had 74,600, Issachar had 54,400, Zebulon had 57,400, Ephraim had 40,500, Manasseh had 32,200, Benjamin had 35,400, Dan had 62,700, Asher had 41,500 and Naphtali had 53,400. There was a total of 603,550 available men to fight in Israel's army.

God also instructed them to organize their tribal camps around the tabernacle with each having their own banner to identify themselves with the tribe they belonged to. The tribe of Judah would be camped on the east end of the tabernacle, with the tribes of Issachar and Zebulon camped on either side of Judah. The tribe of Reuben would camp to the south of the tabernacle, along with the tribes of Simeon and Gad. The tribe of Ephraim would camp on the west side, with the tribes of Manasseh and Benjamin, and the tribe of Dan on the north with the tribes of Asher and Naphtali.

The Levites would be nestled between the twelve tribes and the courtyard, with Moses, Aaron, and his sons camped on the east side next to the tribe of Judah. The tabernacle workers belonging to the Kohathites camped on the south side, the Gershonites on the west side, and the Merarites on the north.

They organized themselves according to these instructions, displayed their banners, and then assigned unique trumpet blasts to notify each tribe when to move out. When the pillar of cloud and fire lifted indicating it was time to move on, Aaron and his sons covered all the articles in the tabernacle and prepared them for transporting. They blew the trumpets to call out the tribe of Judah, then blew the trumpets again to call out the tribe of Issachar, then Zebulon. These three leading tribes had an army of 186,400 men among them.

In the time it took these three tribes to move out, the Gershonites and Merarites disassembled the tabernacle and courtyard, and packed it all onto six carts pulled by twelve oxen. As the last of the three tribes moved out, they joined in behind them. The trumpets blew again to call out the tribes of Reuben, Simeon, and Gad from the south side of the camp, and they followed the six carts with their army of 151,450 men.

Half of Israel had moved out of the camp, and the Kohathites would follow in the middle of the caravan carefully carrying the holy articles by their poles. By the time they would reach the new site with the holy articles, the Gershonites and Merarites would have the tabernacle and courtyard already set up and waiting for them to arrive. The trumpets sounded again calling out the tribes of Ephraim, Manasseh, and Benjamin from the west side of the camp, and they followed the holy articles with their army of 108,100 men.

The last three tribes to move out were the tribes of Dan, Asher, and Naphtali from the north side of the camp; they traveled with their army of 157,600 men. The Israelite camp traveled out beginning with those on the east side facing the entrance of the tabernacle, and continued in a clockwise direction tucking the tabernacle and its articles among them. But it was always the ark and God's presence above it that led the entire caravan.

The people didn't like having to travel through the desert and began complaining about how hard their lives were. When the edges of the camp were consumed by fire because of God's anger, they frantically cried out for Moses' help. He prayed to God for them and the fire stopped. Not long after this they began to wish they had the food they ate in Egypt. They always had as much fish as they wanted and it was free. They began to despise the manna God provided and craved fresh vegetables, fruit, onions, and garlic.

Moses knew they were complaining all over the camp and felt the weight of them heavy on his shoulders. He was so frustrated that he pleaded with God to take his life if this was the way it was always going to be with these people. God told Moses He would provide meat for them, but first, Moses was to bring seventy leaders to Him. He would fill them with His Spirit and enable them to help Moses in carrying the burden for these people. God filled them with His Spirit and all seventy began to prophesy.

After this God brought quail in a windstorm and dropped them on the ground until they were heaped three feet deep all around them. There was so much quail that everyone gathered at least sixty bushels each. They feasted on the meat and it was just like they remembered back in Egypt, but before they had even finished their first meal, God's anger broke out against them. They suffered a plague because they were too quick to complain and easily lured by the things of Egypt. God moved them out of that place and brought them to Hazeroth.

Again God was tested when Moses' own sister and brother complained to him about his dark-skinned wife. Moses' wife really wasn't the issue. Aaron and Miriam felt they also heard from God and were jealous of the authority Moses had. God called all three of them to the tabernacle and the pillar of cloud descended on them. God spoke harshly to Aaron and Miriam because Moses was a humble man and special to God like no one else. When the cloud lifted, Miriam was white with leprosy and they pleaded with Moses to intercede to God for them. Moses did intercede and God healed Miriam, but by law she was required to remain outside the camp for a week. At the end of the week, God moved the people into the Desert of Paran.

They were camped in the Desert of Paran when God told Moses to send some men to explore the Promised Land. If they saw for themselves the land of milk and honey He had promised to give Abraham, Isaac, and Israel, it would encourage them and make their journey easier to bear. One man from each tribe was selected and the twelve explored the land for forty days. They were amazed at how rich it was, and even a branch of grapes had to be carried by two men.

They returned with a wonderful report on the richness of the land and even brought samples of the fruit to show them. But they also reported that the people were like giants with fortified cities, and convinced the Israelites they were not strong enough to take the land. Two of the spies, Joshua and Caleb disagreed with them and argued that they shouldn't be afraid because anything was possible with God. But the ten went on personal campaigns, spreading bad reports all over the camp. The whole Israelite community lost hope and they cursed Moses for taking them out of Egypt. They would have preferred bondage to dying in the desert. They despised Moses and made plans to stone him. With that, God's glory appeared at the tabernacle.

Moses went to meet with God and again found himself interceding for the Israelites, pleading for God's mercy and compassion. Moses reminded God that He was a God slow to anger and abounding in love and forgiveness. God did forgive the people, but the ten who discouraged the people with their bad report died from a plague because God was angry with them. Also, because the people refused to believe He was able to defeat the giants in the land or break down their fortified cities, that generation would die in the desert and never enter the Promised Land. Their children would enter the Promised Land but would wander in the desert for another forty years, one year for every day the land was explored. However, Joshua and Caleb would enter the Promised Land with the next generation because their faith never wavered.

The people couldn't bear the idea of wandering through the desert another forty years, and if God said they would die in the desert there was a good chance they would. So, they decided to take the gamble and try their luck at going up into the Promised Land the next morning. Anything would be better than doing nothing.

Moses warned them that they would be disobeying God by going in, and they would be going in without God or His protection. They ignored Moses and went anyway, only to be attacked and pushed back by the Amalekites and Canaanites living in the hill country. They had often experienced the impossible when God was with them, but now they knew firsthand just how helpless they were without God.

Twenty years had gone by and they were still wandering from place to place in the desert as the pillar of cloud and fire directed. A man named Korah from the Kohathites was tired of his job transporting the tabernacle furniture, so he conspired with two leaders from the tribe of Reuben named Dathan and Abiram, against Moses and Aaron. They also convinced two hundred and fifty leaders that Moses and Aaron were no better than anyone else in the camp, and that they had assumed too much of a leadership role.

They confronted Moses and Aaron with accusations of appointing themselves to their lofty positions, and that the people didn't necessarily want them to stand between them and God. This devastated Moses because it was God who chose Aaron and his sons to be priests. Moses asked them to come to the tabernacle in the morning with censors filled with burning incense; God would distinguish for them who He wanted to serve the people as priests. Moses was hoping the burning incense would cover the stench of their rebellion and protect them from God's anger.

Dathan and Abiram were belligerent and after accusing Moses of being egotistical, refused to come. Moses became angry because he had never taken advantage of them in his position, but instead had given up everything to serve them. In the morning Dathan and Abiram stood at the doors of their tents while Korah and the two hundred and fifty leaders went to the tabernacle with their censors. God warned Moses and Aaron to move away from them so He could destroy them. While Moses and Aaron pleaded for mercy, the earth opened and swallowed up Dathan and Abiram, their tents and all that belonged to them. Then fire came out from the Lord and consumed Korah and the two hundred and fifty leaders.

By the next day, the people had united with the twisted idea that somehow this was Moses' fault and angrily accused him and Aaron of killing good people, God's people. Moses instinctively knew God would pour out His anger on them for this so he and Aaron went directly to the tabernacle to intercede for them. When they realized God was going to punish the people, Moses ordered Aaron to quickly fill a censer with incense, light it with fire from the altar, then run through the camp. Aaron and his censer literally became a dividing line between the living and the dead; 14,700 died from a plague before it stopped.

Nothing they saw seemed to change their hearts, not even when the earth swallowed up Dathan and Abiram, not when fire consumed Korah and the leaders, and not even when Aaron's censer stopped the plague. God wanted them to believe without a doubt that He had chosen Aaron and his sons to serve as priests. God instructed Moses to have each tribe bring a staff to be placed in the tabernacle in front of the ark. By morning Aaron's staff had blossomed and grown almonds. When the people saw it they were afraid to come near the tabernacle for fear of dying. Moses placed Aaron's staff next to the ark as a reminder to the Israelites that their grumbling is against God, and if they continued they were destined to die.

They moved on to the Desert of Zin and stayed at Kadesh where Moses' sister Miriam died. While Moses was grieving for her, the people began to complain again because they had no water. They would have preferred to have died with the two hundred and fifty leaders that were consumed by fire rather than die of thirst in the desert. Once more they reminded Moses they would have been better off if they had stayed in Egypt. God told Moses to go out and speak to a rock and water will gush out, enough for them and their livestock. God wanted Moses to do this in front of all the people so they would see God's continued desire to provide for them.

Moses wasn't feeling as gracious as God, and was getting real tired of hearing their regrets about leaving Egypt. He led the people to the rock and instead of speaking to the rock and letting them see God's grace, Moses scolded them and hit the rock quite hard with his staff. God still graciously poured water out of the rock. However, because Moses was disobedient and failed to honor God, he would lead the people to the Promised Land but would not enter it himself.

While they were camped by this rock, Moses sent messengers to the Edomites who were the descendants of Esau, the twin brother of Moses' great great grandfather Israel. Moses informed the king they were in Kadesh at the edge of their territory, and requested they be allowed to pass through their land along the king's highway. Moses assured him they only wanted to pass through, nothing else. The king of Edom refused to give them approval to pass through and even sent their large and powerful army out to scare them into taking another route.

They left Kadesh and traveled to Mount Hor which was near the border of Edom. They had been on their journey now for thirty-nine years when Aaron died at the age of one hundred and twenty-three. He was buried at Mount Hor and his son Eleazar assumed his priestly duties. Aaron belonged to the generation that God would not allow to enter the Promised Land.

ALMOST THERE
(Numbers 21–Deuteronomy 34)

They were now in an area called the Negev and the Canaanite king who ruled this area sent his army out and attacked them, taking some of them as prisoners. The Israelites made a vow to God that if

He would deliver this enemy into their hands, they would completely destroy their cities. God provided for the Israelites to destroy them and their cities, and they named the place Hormah which means destruction (see Illustration 5).

They left Hormah and traveled south to go around the land of Edom. It was a journey that took them in the opposite direction of the Promised Land and back into the desert they had traveled through for nearly forty years. The people turned on Moses and complained about their lack of good food and water, that they were tired of eating that miserable manna. God heard their complaining and sent deadly snakes which bit them and caused many to die. When the people repented to Moses for their complaining, he put up a pole with a bronze snake mounted on the top. God provided for those who were bitten to live, by simply looking at the bronze snake on the pole.

The Israelites moved on and set up camp at another eight places. When they came north to a valley in Moab which was east of the Dead Sea, Moses sent messengers to Sihon, king of the Amorites, requesting they be allowed to pass through their territory. Rather than responding by denying them passage, King Sihon sent his entire army out to destroy the Israelites. However, God was with them and the Israelites conquered King Sihon's army and continued their pursuit until they had claimed all the land belonging to the Amorites, up to the borders of the Ammonites.

They followed the road and traveled another seventy miles north, putting them just east of the sea now known as the Sea of Galilee. This was the land called Bashan, and the king of that land also marched his entire army out to engage the Israelites in battle. But God encouraged them not to be afraid because He had already given them the victory just as He did when they fought the Amorites. So the Israelite army went out against the army of Bashan and conquered them, then claimed that land as their own too. They were now close to entering the land God had promised.

Chapter 5

The Moabites heard about the Israelites' battle victories and were terrified at what might happen to them. The king's son Balak sent a delegation to Midian, to a man they heard could tell the future. The Midianites were a community of people who were descendants of Abraham, born to the woman he married after Sarah died. The man in Midian they were looking for was named Balaam and their intent was to pay him to put a curse on the Israelites so they could be conquered in battle. But after hearing their offer, Balaam was instructed by God not to go with them because God had blessed these people.

The delegation returned home only to be sent back to offer Balaam anything he wanted if he would just put a curse on the Israelites. Because Balaam was tempted by their most generous offer, God allowed him to return with the delegation but was angry because he had given in to their temptation. God sent an angel with a sword to stand in the road in front of Balaam and when his donkey saw the angel, the donkey turned into a field and lay down. Balaam didn't see the angel and he tried to get the donkey to stand up and get back on the road by beating him. Then God opened his eyes to see the angel and he felt his shame towards God. He fell to the ground face down, pleaded with God for mercy, and then decided he would just go home. God told him to continue his journey but warned him to say only what He instructed him to say.

Balak came out to meet Balaam, and after offering sacrifices to honor God, Balaam walked to a private place to hear from God. He returned to report to Balak that God had not cursed the Israelites but blessed them. Out of frustration, Balak took Balaam to another location where he again offered sacrifices to honor God. Balaam went off to a private place to hear from God and returned giving Balak the same report, that the Israelites were not only blessed but would devour their enemies like a lion. Balak took him to a third location where they offered sacrifices to God again. Balaam returned to say the Israelites are beautiful in God's eyes and those who bless them will be blessed, and those who curse them will be cursed. Balak, furious that Balaam had not cursed them but instead blessed them three times, sent Balaam home with no reward. Before Balaam went home he prophesied that a "star" would come from the Israelites. The star Balaam foretold of was all part of the great plan God had to bless the world through the Israelites.

However, the Israelites were close to being conquered by their own hand. Balak sent Moabite women to entice the Israelite men into sexual affairs with the ultimate goal of getting them to worship their god, Baal of Peor. Because worship to this god was sensual in nature, they were seduced not only into worship but also offered sacrifices to this pagan god. God's anger burned hard against them and a plague started spreading through the camp. Their only hope of being spared was to kill those who had so defiantly worshipped the Baal of Peor. Even while Moses was instructing the leaders to kill those within their camps who had worshipped Baal, an Israelite man came to the front of the tabernacle with a Midianite woman arrogantly taunting them with his ludicrous behavior.

Phinehas, son of Eleazar the priest was cut to the heart over their behavior towards God and followed them to their tent. Out of absolute passion to honor God, Phinehas drove a spear through the Israelite into the woman, in their bed. His passion for God stopped the plague, but not before twenty-four thousand had died.

A lot had happened in the thirty-nine years since they left Mount Sinai, and God told Moses to take another census. Some tribes had increased and some had decreased, mostly due to their obedience or lack of obedience to God during their thirty-nine year journey. Overall, the total men available to fight in Israel's army had decreased from 603,550 to 601,730. The Promised Land would be distributed by lot based on this census.

Moses was one hundred twenty years old and had spent forty years in Pharaoh's house, forty years in Midian and his last forty years leading the Israelites through the desert. God told Moses they had to revenge the Midianites for seducing them, and when that was done, it would be time for Moses to die. Moses asked God to appoint someone to lead the Israelites into the Promised Land so they wouldn't be like sheep without a shepherd. God appointed Joshua to replace Moses because His Spirit was already with him. Eleazar the priest publicly anointed Joshua, then Moses laid his hands on Joshua and commissioned him. Moses immediately transferred some of his authority to Joshua so the Israelite community would honor him.

After this, one thousand men from each tribe were selected to fight against the Midianites, and Phinehas accompanied them to the battlefield bringing articles from the tabernacle. They were completely victorious in the battle, killing every male including that fox Balak. They then looted and burned their towns. Moses and the leaders went outside the camp to meet them only to discover they had taken the women and children captive, the very women that had seduced them into worshipping Baal of Peor. Moses was furious and demanded they kill all the boys and any woman that was not a virgin so they wouldn't be seduced again. Moses said even the goods they looted from the towns were defiled and had to be purified.

The total plunder included 675,000 sheep, 72,000 cattle and 61,000 donkeys, as well as 32,000 virgin women that were taken captive. A share of the spoils was given to the tabernacle and a portion to the Levites who serve in the tabernacle. Because not one Israelite perished in battle, they gave all 420 pounds of gold bracelets, rings, earrings, and necklaces that had been looted, to God as an offering.

When the battle was over, the tribes of Reuben, Gad and half of the tribe of Manasseh requested they be allowed to settle in the land on the east side of the Jordan River. At first Moses was angry that they might influence the rest of the tribes into settling for less than what God promised. But, when they vowed to join the other tribes in their conquest to take the Promised Land, Moses agreed and distributed the land among them according to the census he had taken.

The children of Israel had journeyed for forty years, camping in forty-one locations. The generation that was afraid to go into the Promised Land had all died. In the last year that Moses led them, he continually reviewed all the laws God had given them at Mount Sinai as well as the covenant they made with God. He reviewed with them the festivals God had asked them to celebrate and the details of how God wanted them to live to assure harmony and integrity among them.

Moses warned them against making treaties with the people in the Promised Land, against marrying them, and especially about worshipping their idols. He reminded them they had to destroy all the people in the Promised Land because they would eventually become a thorn in their side. If they did everything as God instructed, they would stand out as unique and distinctively different from any other people in the world. If they would keep their covenant with God; Moses promised that God would bless them and curse those who cursed them. Moses warned them that disobedience to God had consequences just as great as His blessings. If they chose to be disobedient, God would allow them to suffer hard and difficult times in attempts to draw them back to Himself.

All of the older generation was dead and there was so much to tell the younger generation. Stories going back to creation, to what God did in Egypt, how God parted the Red Sea, and all their experiences in the desert. These were stories that would help them understand how powerful God is and how much He loves them. They needed to know the laws, the covenant and all the instructions to be followed when they established their communities in the Promised Land. It was all important information needing to be passed on from generation to generation, so Moses recorded everything in books called the Torah, and then gave it to the priests and elders.

He told them it was extremely important they read the Torah in its entirety every seventh year to all the people of Israel when they gathered for the Feast of Tabernacles. They were also to write it on their hearts, teach it to their children, talk about it when sitting, standing or walking about, meditate on it, write it on the doorposts of their homes, tie it to their hands, and write it on their foreheads. They were to do whatever it took to remember it and live by it. They had to know their God was faithful and He would never forsake them or leave them.

Moses knew they were impulsive and unreliable people, prone to be swayed by any given situation of the moment. Try as he did to prepare them for their future, God told Moses they would fail to keep their covenant with Him. When everything becomes good for them and life is easy, they would forget Him and prostitute themselves to foreign gods and idols. They would get so wrapped up with the important things of life that they would eventually reject Him. But God would allow disasters in order to save them and would try over and over to draw them back to Himself and then heal them.

Moses did everything he could to encourage them to remain faithful. All that he recorded would be read and quoted by many people, from shepherd boys to kings. Even the Messiah that God would send to bless the world centuries later would quote from the words Moses wrote.

Moses climbed to the top of Mount Nebo across from Jericho. God allowed him to view the Promised Land, then Moses died.

THEY'RE IN
(Joshua 1–8)

After Moses died, the Israelites remained camped near a town named Shittim, which was about seven miles east of the Jordan

River just east of Jericho (see Illustration 5). God spoke to Joshua and told him to get ready because it was time to cross the Jordan River and enter the Promised Land. God described the territory He was giving them as the land from the desert of Lebanon to all the land belonging to the Hittites, and from the Euphrates River to the Mediterranean Sea. This was a sizeable area of land that stretched about two hundred and fifty miles from south to north; its width varied from one hundred and fifty miles to as little as eighty miles. Wherever they walked God would give them that land. God promised Joshua that He would be with him just as He had been with Moses, and he should remain strong and courageous because He would never leave him. Joshua was taking this one step at a time because he couldn't help but remember what happened when they explored the land thirty-nine years ago. He secretly selected two men to spy out their first city, the city of Jericho.

The two men traveled about thirteen miles to get to the city, but when the king heard they were there, they hid in the house of a prostitute. The prostitute was Rahab, who informed them that everyone in the whole land had heard all the stories of how their God intervened for them with amazing miracles over the last forty years. Rahab told them everyone was melting with fear especially now, after hearing of their most recent war victories. They heard God had promised their land to the Israelites and they all knew it was just a matter of time before they would be defeated by them. Rahab hid them on the condition that she and her family would be spared when the Israelites came to conquer Jericho. They agreed but she would have to hang a red rope outside her window to distinguish her home from the others, and all her family would have to be in her house.

When the king's men came to Rahab's house to find them, she told the soldiers the spies had already left. Late that night after the gates to the city had been shut, Rahab put a rope out a window so they could escape. Because Rahab's house was next to the city wall, they were able to escape out of the city. They hid in the hills for three days, then returned to tell Joshua they had no doubt that God has put that land into their hands.

The next morning Joshua led them out of Shittim and camped on the east banks of the Jordan River. The river was at flood stage and impossible to cross, but after three days Joshua instructed the priests to carry the ark into the river, assuring them God would stop the waters. They did what Joshua told them to do and sure enough, as they put their feet in the river the water stopped flowing and backed up into a heap twenty miles up river.

On the tenth day of the first month, the whole community crossed the Jordan River on dry ground into the Promised Land. They collected twelve large stones from the riverbed to establish a memorial so future generations would remember the day God stopped the Jordan River when they crossed over to enter the Promised Land. The priests holding the ark remained in the middle of the river until everyone had passed through, and when the priests stepped onto the banks on the west side, the river began to flow again. They continued on for about five miles until they were about a mile from the city of Jericho.

God told Joshua before going any further, they had to honor the covenant Abraham made and circumcise all the males. Because they were obedient to do this, God took away the shame of Egypt from them and they remained there until they were all healed. They named this place Gilgal and celebrated the Passover for the first time in the Promised Land. They also ate fruit and vegetables from the land and the next day, the manna stopped.

While at Gilgal, Joshua had an awesome experience when a man with a sword appeared to him saying he was the commander of Jehovah's army and had come to be with him. Even though Joshua couldn't see God's army, he knew they had come to fight for the Israelites. God told Joshua He has already given Jericho to them, they just needed to march around the city each day for six days, led by seven priests and the ark. On the seventh day they were to march around the city seven times, and when they blew the horns and shouted, the walls of the city would collapse.

Joshua had the army march around the city every day for the next six days as God instructed, and each night returned to their camp. On the seventh day Joshua announced this was the day they would take their first city in the Promised Land, and commanded that everything in the city be devoted to God. The silver, gold, and articles of bronze and iron would go into Jehovah's treasury, but everything else must be destroyed with the sword and fire. Only Rahab and her family would be spared because she hid the two spies.

They got up early and marched around the city, led by seven priests with seven trumpets and the ark. On the seventh time around Joshua commanded them to shout, so they blew the trumpets and shouted with a noise that would split your ears, and the city walls came tumbling down. The Israelite army stormed into the city, destroying everything as Joshua commanded except for Rahab's family. They saved only the silver, gold, bronze and iron, then burned the city of Jericho. Joshua declared a solemn oath that anyone who tried to rebuild Jericho would do it at the cost of their firstborn son.

Their victory would be short lived because a man named Achan from the tribe of Judah had not yet learned the importance of being obedient. He secretly took some of the booty from Jericho before it was burned. He had taken a beautiful robe in which he wrapped five pounds of silver and one and a quarter pounds of gold, then buried it in the ground inside his tent. As a result of this, God did not go with three thousand Israelite soldiers to conquer a place called Ai, and they were all massacred.

Joshua fell facedown on the ground before the ark and stayed there until evening. Finally, God told Joshua He had not gone with them because Israel had sinned by taking some of the devoted things from Jericho. They didn't realize how their disobedience played into Satan's plan to destroy the world and stop the Messiah from coming. After investigating and discovering it was Achan, they brought all his family and his belongings to a valley where they were stoned to death, then burned. They returned to the battlefield at Ai and God granted them victory. God allowed them to take the livestock and valuables for themselves, then they burned the city.

They traveled north about twenty miles to Mount Ebal where they built an altar and sacrificed burnt offerings and peace offerings to honor God. Half of the Israelites stood in front of Mount Gerizim and half in front of Mount Ebal with the ark between them. They waited quietly, perhaps reflecting on what had happened to Achan and his family. As they waited, Joshua copied the Law of Moses on stones then read aloud every word that Moses had written, reinforcing the importance of obeying all of God's commands.

CONQUERING THE PROMISED LAND
(Joshua 9–21)

There were six kings to the south of them who had heard about Israel's God and how He fought on their behalf. One of these kings, the king of Gibeon, came to meet Joshua at Gilgal with a caravan of donkeys disguised as people from a distant land. They dressed in old tattered clothes with worn out shoes, the sacks on their donkeys were old with holes, their wineskins were dry and cracked, and even their bread was moldy. They deceitfully came seeking a peace treaty because they too had heard about the Israelites' powerful God.

Joshua was reluctant to hear them because of God's command not to make any peace treaties with the people in the Promised

Land, but the king assured Joshua they were from a land far away. Joshua didn't ask God what to do and made a peace treaty with them, with the elders swearing to honor it. They soon discovered they were deceived by people who lived only fifteen miles from Gilgal. Joshua and the elders were afraid to break an oath they had sworn by God's name, so the king agreed that the people of Gibeon would become Israel's woodcutters and water carriers.

When the other four kings heard what the king of Gibeon had done, they were overwhelmed with fear for their own fate. But their anger at Gibeon for becoming traitors was greater than their fear, so the four kings joined forces and attacked them. When they attacked, the king of Gibeon sent word to Joshua at Gilgal to come save them from the armies of the four kings. God told Joshua He had already given him the victory over these four kings, so the whole Israelite army marched through the night and made a surprise attack. The four armies became confused and while many of them were slain at Gibeon, some fled north to Beth Horon and some south to Azekah. The four kings took refuge in a cave south at Makkedah (see Illustration 6).

Joshua prayed for God to stop the sun so they would have the time to pursue the enemy that was fleeing in several directions. God heard Joshua and held the sun in its place for a period equivalent to an entire day. The Israelite army pursued the enemy fleeing north and destroyed them before they got to Beth Horon, then they turned back to pursue those who fled south. When they caught up with them, they discovered God had intervened and many of them were already killed by a hailstorm. More soldiers were killed by hail that day than by Israel's sword.

They returned to their camp at Gilgal to rest and report on their great victory. Eventually, word got to Joshua that the four kings were hiding in a cave at Makkedah, and the king from Gibeon was with them. Israel pursued them and captured the kings as well as the city of Makkedah, and left no survivors.

Joshua and his army marched about six miles northwest from Makkedah and conquered a town called Libnah. From there they marched southwest and attacked Lachish. The king of Gezer and his army came from the north to help Lachish and after a two-day battle, Israel destroyed both armies. They continued to march southwest to Eglon and conquered that army in less than a day, then extended their campaign about twenty-five miles east to Hebron taking that city and its villages. About eight miles south was a town called Debir, which also fell to Israel's sword. In all their battles they never left survivors. Joshua's campaign through the southern region reached as far south as Kadesh Barnea and as far west as the Mediterranean Sea before they returned to their camp at Gilgal.

The kings of the north heard what was happening in the south and joined forces to fight against Israel. The king of Hazor had a controlling role over the northern kingdoms and organized the armies of Shimron, Madon, Acshaph, and Naphoth Dor to join him against Israel, as well as the armies of the Amorites, Hittites, Perizzites, and Jebusites. The king of Hazor met all these armies by the waters at Merom; together they were a massive army. They were absolutely so enormous they were like the sand on the seashore and were confident they would defeat the Israelites.

Now Israel's army had traveled north about seventy miles and were close to Merom. God told them not to worry about the northern armies because by tomorrow evening, He would give Israel victory over them. Joshua knew he could trust God and the next day made a surprise attack, with an unbelievable victory. Some fled north as far as twenty-five miles but Israel pursued and not one soldier from this unified army survived. Then Joshua led his army to Hazor and completely destroyed it with their swords and fire. They left no survivors in any of the towns or villages, just as God had instructed through Moses. Joshua victoriously led the army of Israel across the land of Canaan, claiming a good part of the land in an area that stretched north one hundred miles from Gilgal to below the Negev in the south.

Joshua had led the army of Israel in these campaigns for six years, but there still was a good amount of land to be conquered that God had promised to give them. Conquered or not, the land was allocated in size according to the census Moses had taken in the Valley of Moab. The tribes of Reuben, Gad, and the half tribe of Manasseh had taken their portions east of the Jordan River, but the remaining nine and a half tribes would take their portions on the west side of the river.

While the size of their lands had been decided based on the census, the locations were decided by casting lots which was done by Joshua, Eleazar the priest and the heads of the tribal clans (see Illustration 7). Beginning in the north, Asher was assigned land along the Mediterranean shoreline from Sidon in the north to Mt. Carmel on its south end. Naphtali's land was located between Asher's and the Sea of Galilee, stretching from Mount Hermon on its north edge down to the south shores of the Sea of Galilee. Zebulon was below Asher and Naphtali, with the Kishon River on the south border. Issachar was southeast of Zebulon, and extended south to Jezreel. While Zebulon and Issachar both had fairly small portions of land, it was fertile ground.

The half tribe of Manasseh was given the next portion south and held a large chunk extending from the Mediterranean Sea to the Jordan River. It ran south to the Jarkon River on the west part of the land but extended even further south on the east side, down to Gilgal. Just below the west side of this portion was Dan's land, a small piece on the Mediterranean Sea with the Sorek Valley on its south end. Ephraim was south of Manasseh with Dan to its left, extending south to Ai. Benjamin's land was a small piece nestled below Ephraim with Dan on its left and a small sliver of land extending to the Jordan River. Judah was south of Dan and Benjamin, covering a large area from the Mediterranean Sea on its left to the

Dead Sea on its right, and extended south to Kadesh Barnea. Because it was larger than what they needed, Simeon was allocated an oval-shaped piece of land within Judah from Ziklag to Ramah and south to the Negev.

In addition to dividing the land among the Israelites, cities within their borders were reassigned for varied reasons. Ephraim gave the city of Shiloh to the Levites and because the tabernacle was there, it would be viewed as the capital of Israel. For many years to come, the Israelites would gather at Shiloh to offer Jehovah sacrifices and celebrate the festivals.

Ephraim gave the town of Timnath Serah to Joshua, where he and his family settled. The city of Hebron was awarded to Caleb by Judah for trusting God after exploring the land of Canaan forty-five years ago. Several towns throughout the land were also given to the Levite families of Kohath, Gershon, and Merari, who carried the tabernacle and all its articles on their journey to the Promised Land.

A town in each of Naphtali's, Ephraim's and Judah's territories was designated as cities of refuge for those who killed someone unintentionally, without malice or premeditation. The accused had to stand trial at one of these cities and remain there until the current priest died, then was free to return home.

They had made tremendous progress in conquering and claiming the land, but the work of conquering wasn't finished. So much had been accomplished and even though they had a long way to go, it was good to be in the Promised Land.

Chapter 6

MISSING THE GOAL
(Joshua 22–Judges 2)

It had been seven years since they entered the Promised Land and it was time to disband their corporate army. This placed the responsibility for conquering any enemy remaining within their borders to each individual tribal army. Joshua gave his approval for the tribes of Reuben, Gad, and the half tribe of Manasseh to return to their lands on the east side of the Jordan, and encouraged them to keep God's laws and commands so they could live peacefully in their lands for a long time. They were returning home with a tremendous amount of livestock, silver, gold, bronze, iron, and clothing, which was their share of the bounty from seven years of fighting. Before they crossed over the Jordan River to return home, they built an altar to honor almighty Jehovah. This altar would also stand as a witness to future generations that even though they were not within the Promised Land, they were still Israel's brothers.

The war for Israel's corporate army may have ended but the battles for the tribal armies were just beginning. Fighting the enemy that remained scattered within their borders would continue on and off over the next seventeen years. The Israelites were not as aggressive when each tribe had to actually move into their allocated territories and deal independently with the few that remained within their boundaries. Yet, some instinctively knew they had to begin pursuing the destruction of these enemies or be destroyed by them.

Judah was the first to take the initiative and proposed a joint adventure with the tribe of Simeon to defeat the enemy living within both their boundaries. Together they successfully defeated the Canaanites and Perizzites in several cities, some of which were in Manasseh's and Benjamin's territories. They defeated enemies within their own borders, in the hills around the Negev and along the coast of the Mediterranean Sea. However, they did not defeat the enemy living in the plains of Judah east of the coast.

The army of Manasseh had a great victory when they defeated the fortified city of Bethel, but were never able to conquer the entire northern portion of their land. They didn't give up trying and at one point were able to force the enemy to become their servants, but never drove them out. They even complained to Joshua they needed more land, but Joshua insisted if they conquered their enemies they would have more than enough land.

Ephraim was not able to defeat the Canaanites in Gezer, a city on the southwestern edge of their land, so they learned to live among them. While Zebulun was also unable to defeat two of their cities, they conceded to forcing the Canaanites to work for them. Asher had seven cities and their surrounding areas they could not defeat, most of which were located on the coast of the Mediterranean Sea. But Asher was content to allow the Canaanites to remain in these most desirable cities rather than to fight them. Naphtali, like Zebulun, had two cities where the Canaanites were forced to work for them rather than driving them out of the land. The worst situation was the tribe of Dan which was confined by the Amorites to the hills, and were not allowed to come down to the fertile plains of their land.

When Joshua was one hundred and ten years old, he knew his time in life was coming to an end. He addressed the people one last time just as Moses did, with hopes it would make a difference in their loyalty to God after he was gone. It had been sixty-six years since they marched out of Egypt and a lot of Israel's younger generation hadn't even been born to witness the things God had done for them back there.

Joshua called a meeting with the elders, leaders, judges, and officials of Israel who gathered at Shechem, a town in the southern part of Manasseh. He reminded them of all their experiences and how God graciously intervened for them time after time, and recounted the occasions that God showed mercy to them. He urged them to have reverence and love for God, and follow His laws and commands. He emphasized the importance of not becoming allies with their enemies or worshipping their gods, because of the trouble this would bring them. The leaders recommitted themselves to wholly serving God, and God only. After they returned home, Joshua died.

Two years later the Israelites still had not destroyed the enemy as God instructed. Instead, they were content to live with them because in most cases they used their enemies as servants and slaves. They preferred to use their enemy to do their work rather than trust God for the promised victories spoken through Abraham, Isaac, Israel, Moses, and Joshua.

God sent an angel to speak to the Israelites at a place west of Jericho near Bethel, in the land of Ephraim. The angel reminded them that Jehovah had brought them into the land He had promised to give them, and even though God had promised He would never break His covenant with them, they had broken theirs. They had been warned many times not to make any covenants with the people of the land and also to break down their altars. Yet, they learned to live with their enemy and the gods they worshipped. Therefore God was giving them notice: He would not drive out any more of their enemies living among them and these enemies would be a thorn in their side and their gods would be a trap that destroys them.

The people wept bitterly when they heard all that the angel of God had to say, and offered sacrifices to Jehovah at that place. They were truly sorry they had been disobedient, but their repentive hearts and good intentions would not prevail. They would repeatedly become ensnared by the enemies living in their land as well as by their idols.

Over a period of about three hundred years they would run a cycle of being disobedient to God, which would result in being oppressed by their enemies, which would then cause them to realize their unfaithfulness to God, and finally repent and seek His help. When they would repent to God and ask for help against their enemies, God would always be there to hear them and provide a leader to rescue them.

But, in time they would come back full circle and repeat this cycle over and over. The battle for the land would seem insignificant in comparison to their battle to remain faithful to God. With each new generation, their understanding of God diminished, and the memory of what He did for their fathers faded. The daily routine tasks of life often overshadowed God's promise for the future, the promise that God would bless the world through them.

CAUGHT IN THE CYCLE

(Judges 3–5, 17–21 and Ruth)

The Israelites had been on their own for twenty-one years since Joshua died. The leaders that knew Joshua had also died as did Eleazar the priest, leaving his son Phinehas to become the next priest of a new generation. The Israelites didn't have anybody to lead them like Moses and Joshua, so many of them just didn't take the time or effort to observe all the customs and laws Moses gave them. The tabernacle was centrally located in Shiloh, but many of the Israelites in isolated areas preferred to worship in ways that were convenient for them, often far outside the scope God had commanded.

The Israelites had not been faithful to teach their children about God as instructed by Moses, so the new generation felt almost no obligation to the covenant their fathers had made. They didn't understand the benefits of being faithful to the God of their fathers, but even worse, didn't understand the disadvantages of being unfaithful.

Many Israelites embraced the gods of the land, and two primary gods commonly worshipped were the sun god Baal and Asherah the female counterpart to Baal. Even the Levites were not faithful to Jehovah, and often failed to challenge the people of Israel when they worshipped the gods of the land. There was one Levite who had migrated to Ephraim's territory and found an Israelite named Micah who owned several idols and carved images. The Levite overlooked Micah's idolatry because he was willing to support him as his personal priest; Micah even made an ephod for him.

A small group from the tribe of Dan met Micah's priest while on their way north of the Arabah to spy out land. They were tired of being forced by the Amorites to live in the hill country, and asked the priest to determine from God if they would be successful in finding better land. The priest assured them they would be, so they continued north to the east edge of Naphtali's land where they discovered a vulnerable town named Laish on the Jabbok River.

They traveled back home and returned with their families and an army of six hundred men to take Laish, but stopped at Micah's house on the way. They stole Micah's idols and convinced his priest it would be better to serve the tribe of Dan rather than one family. The Danites continued their journey with their new priest, stolen idols, and carved images, and conquered the town that would become known as the city of Dan.

Another Levite priest living in the territory of Ephraim had a mistress who left him. He traveled to Judah and found her, then convinced her to return with him. They left late in the afternoon, traveled about five miles into Benjamin and spent the night in the home of an old man who found them in the city square at Gibeah. During the night several men from the city came to their door, violently demanding to have sex with the Levite. The Levite, not knowing quite what to do, sent his mistress out who was raped and abused all night. She was able to make her way back to the house but died at the doorstep.

The Levite left the next morning and returned to Ephraim with the bruised body of his mistress. When he arrived home he cut her body into twelve pieces and sent one to each of the twelve tribes. All Israel was enraged and came with their armies to Mizpah, a town in northern Benjamin to take revenge on the men that had done this horrifying thing. Four hundred thousand Israelites came against the Benjamites, and after three days of fighting almost the entire tribe of Benjamin was nearly wiped out. All of Israel suffered for this, and it was by their own hand because they had forgotten God.

Their unfaithfulness also caused them to suffer at the hand of their enemies. When life became unbearable, they would cry out to God and God would always help them by giving them a leader to defeat their enemies. Several fronts were being attacked in Israel during this period. The king of Aram Naharaim came down from the extreme north and maintained control of Judah and the surrounding territories for eight years. When the Israelites humbled themselves and turned to God, He put His Spirit on Caleb's brother Othniel, who led a campaign against this king and won their freedom. Judah had peace during the forty years Othniel lived because he was able to influence their behavior towards God.

While Judah was struggling with the king from the north, the king of Moab made an alliance with the Ammonites and Amalekites, and they took possession of Jericho. After being under their authority for eighteen years, Ephraim turned to God for help. God gave them Ehud who personally killed the king then led Ephraim's army victoriously against the enemy. While Ehud was alive and able to influence their behavior towards God, they also had peace. During this same period there were conflicts with their enemies on a smaller scale throughout Israel. In a conflict with the Philistines, God rescued them through a farmer named Shamgar who killed six hundred soldiers with an ox goad.

Ninety years after God had sent Ehud to lead Ephraim's army, there was yet another new generation of Israelites living in the land. With each new generation, Israel became less and less knowledgeable about the God of their fathers. Just as the generation before them, this generation was also content to trade their worship to Jehovah for the gods and idols of the land. Because of their unfaithfulness, God did not protect them from their enemies and allowed persecution to be the tool to turn their hearts back to Him.

Jabin was king of the Canaanites and ruled from Hazor in Naphtali's territory, but his army was headquartered in the northern portion of Manasseh's territory. Their control stretched across the land; there wasn't a tribe or family in Israel that was free from their overbearing authority and cruelty.

There was a family from Judah who had abandoned their home in the Promised Land to live in Moab, because they were not able to get food. They were a true picture of Israel trading their inheritance for the crumbs of stronger nations, and the willingness of God to show mercy. Elimelech, who was named for strength, and his wife Naomi, left their town of Bethlehem which means *house of bread*. They moved away from Israel to find food in a land referred to as a "wash basin." They took with them their two sons whose names meant *sickly* and *weak*.

Within ten years Naomi found herself widowed, her sons had died and she was alone in a strange land with two Moabite daughter-in-laws, Orpah and Ruth. She decided to go home to Judah, but her daughter-in-law Ruth insisted on going with her. Ruth was determined to help her and vowed that Naomi's people would be her people and Jehovah would be her God. So, Ruth left her people in Moab and went to Judah with Naomi.

The laws given by Moses had provided a welfare system which allowed widows to harvest the corners of fields belonging to their relatives. If Naomi and Ruth wanted to eat, Ruth would have to take advantage of this law. Ruth faithfully went to work every day in a field belonging to Boaz, one of her father-in-law's relatives. When Boaz saw Ruth, he fell in love with her and married her. Boaz took Naomi into his home and treated her as if she were Ruth's own mother. God blessed Naomi because Ruth was better to her than any son could have been. Boaz and Ruth had a son, and Naomi lovingly cared for him as though he were her own grandson. One day this grandson would himself have a grandson who would become the greatest king in Israel's history (see Illustration 8). He would be King David, and would lead Israel with a passion for Jehovah.

By now Israel had suffered under the rule of King Jabin for ten years and would for another ten. There was a woman named Deborah who lived in the hill country of Ephraim who often called on God for the people, and got a reputation as a prophetess because she heard from God. When she sent for a fighting man named Barak from Naphtali, he came because of her reputation. She instructed him to gather an army of ten thousand from Naphtali and Zebulun, then go to Mount Tabor and defeat King Jabin's army because God had decided to give them victory.

Barak didn't know Jehovah enough to have the courage to do this on his own. Yet, he knew God was with Deborah, so he insisted she go with him to the battlefield. When they advanced on King Jabin's army, God's intervention was obvious by the noise and commotion among the enemy. Barak and his ten thousand men defeated them on the battlefield as well as on the road where some fled. Their commander also fled and was killed by a woman who agreed to hide him in her tent.

History credited this victory to Deborah because Barak lacked the faith to fight the enemy without her. Israel lived in peace for forty years after this victory.

DIMINISHED TO FEAR AND SLAVERY
(Judges 6–10 and 1 Samuel 1–3)

The forty years of peace was coming to an end because of their tendencies to prostitute themselves to worthless idols. Their indifference towards Jehovah brought a new enemy, the Midianites. They were gypsies who had no home and when they invaded the land of Israel, they consumed the crops like locusts and robbed Israel of their livestock. They oppressed the Israelites for seven years, forcing them to hide in the mountains, in caves, and strongholds. When Israel reached the point of being absolutely impoverished, they called out to the God of their fathers for help.

God would deliver them from this enemy using a young man named Gideon. He was a bit of a coward, which was evidenced by the fact that he threshed wheat while hiding in the winepress instead of at a high point where the wind could blow the chaff away. An angel of God came to him in the winepress, calling him a mighty warrior and informing him that Jehovah was with him. He had a hard time believing this because for one thing: he was the weakest one in his family and despite the stories he heard about Egypt, he was sure Jehovah had abandoned them. The angel was persistent and convinced Gideon that Jehovah had chosen him to lead Israel against the Midianites.

The Midianites had taken most of their livestock and flour, but Gideon sacrificed a young goat and made bread using more than a half bushel of flour, then presented it all to the angel as an offering to Jehovah. It was too much for Gideon to comprehend all this and with as much reverence as he could show, asked for a sign so he would know for certain he was a messenger from Jehovah. When the angel touched Gideon's sacrifice with the tip of his finger, it was consumed in fire, then the angel disappeared.

Gideon immediately built an altar to honor Jehovah Shalom, the God who would bring peace. That night God challenged Gideon to tear down his father's altar to Baal and to cut down the Asherah pole, then use the wood to offer a burnt offering to Jehovah. Gideon did this but in the cover of night because he was afraid of what the people would do to him. In the morning the people were enraged and demanded that his father turn him over to them so they could kill him in order to avenge Baal. When Gideon's father insisted Baal could defend himself, they consented and let Gideon go unpunished.

Gideon sent messengers to the people of Manasseh, Asher, Zebulun and Naphtali calling them to join him in the fight against the Midianites. Everything was coming together, but Gideon was still afraid and asked God for another sign just to be sure. He laid a fleece on the ground and asked God to wet it with enough water during the night, to fill a bowl. God heard his prayer and wanted to encourage him, so He did as Gideon asked. Again with absolute reverence he asked for another sign, the reverse of the first sign. He asked that the bowl be filled with water in the morning but for the fleece to remain dry. The Jehovah Shalom he was getting to know would honor his need for another sign, and God did as Gideon prayed.

The Midianite army was so massive it was impossible to count them. Gideon was able to assemble an army of thirty-two thousand, but God told him it was too many and Israel would boast it was their strength that gained the victory. So Gideon allowed those who were afraid of the Midianites to go home, and all but ten thousand did. But God told Gideon there was still too many and took him through a process that brought his army down to three hundred men.

It would be an impossible battle, but God encouraged Gideon by allowing him to overhear the enemy talking about a dream of a loaf of bread that rolled into their camp and collapsed a tent. The enemy interpreted this as being Gideon's sword that destroyed them with Jehovah's help. Gideon was encouraged and his three hundred men took their places around the camp and did exactly as God had instructed Gideon to do. They blew their trumpets, broke jars and waved their torches. Amazingly, the Midianites turned on each other and many were killed by their own sword. The Israelites from Manasseh, Asher, Zebulun, Naphtali, and Ephraim came out against all the Midianites and it was a tremendous victory.

Gideon became an esteemed man and after returning home to Ophrah, he married several wives and had seventy sons. Israel lived in peace for another forty years, but Gideon caused them to sin when he made an ephod of gold and they worshipped it. Besides worshipping the ephod, the people of Israel again prostituted themselves to Baal and Asherah, and forgot about Jehovah.

Gideon had a son named Abimelech by a mistress in Shechem twenty miles south of Ophrah. After Gideon died, Abimelech was determined to have the prestige his stepbrothers had so he convinced the people of Shechem to declare him their ruler. They gave him almost two pounds of silver from Baal's temple which he used to hire thugs to help murder his seventy brothers.

His youngest stepbrother escaped, and declared a curse on Abimelech and the town of Shechem. God honored that curse and within three years the people of Shechem turned against Abimelech. To avenge them, he and his men tried to kill them but the people ran to the temple of one of their gods and hid in a stronghold. Abimelech set fire to the stronghold and burned them to death.

He and his men left Shechem and went to another town that also refused to honor him. When the people barricaded themselves in a tower to hide from Abimelech, he decided to burn them too. While he was trying to set fire to the tower, a woman dropped a millstone on his head. Abimelech was dying and he knew it, but he didn't want history to say he was killed by a woman, so he commanded his servant to kill him with a sword.

After Abimelech was killed, a man named Tola from the tribe of Issachar led Israel for twenty-three years. When Tola died, a wealthy man named Jair who lived east of the Jordan River in Gilead led them for twenty-two years.

Despite the many who abandoned Jehovah for the gods of the land, there was a man named Elkanah from the hill country of Ephraim who faithfully traveled to Shiloh every year to offer sacrifices to God. He had two wives, one had children but Hannah had none. About twelve years after Jair began to lead Israel, Elkanah and his family were in Shiloh worshipping Jehovah. While there, Hannah wept bitterly before God and vowed if He would give her children, she would give her first born son to serve God all his life. Eli the priest thought she was drunk, but when he realized she was praying out of anguish and grief, he blessed her and prayed that God would grant what she asked for. After the family returned home, God blessed Hannah with a son and she named him Samuel.

Hannah loved Samuel and when he was able to eat solid foods, she brought him to Shiloh and dedicated him to Jehovah, then gave him to Eli the priest.

Eli was a descendant of Aaron but he rarely heard from God because they had not been faithful to serve God as the Law of Moses described. His two sons, Hophni and Phinehas, took advantage of their positions in the tabernacle and treated Jehovah disrespectfully. They ate choice portions of the sacrifices instead of the portions indicated in the law. In addition to having no regard for Jehovah, they defiled the women dedicated to working at the tabernacle by having sex with them. Eli had lost control of his sons and God rebuked him through a messenger saying his sons would both die on the same day. In addition, his descendants would all die in the prime of their life, and the priesthood would be taken from the Levites and given to a faithful servant who could know His heart and His mind. Eli knew this was a curse he would have to live with, a sin against God that could never be atoned for by sacrifices or offerings.

Samuel was six years old when he heard God's voice. He had gone to bed, and thinking Eli was calling him, immediately ran to see what he wanted. Eli hadn't called him and told him to go back to bed. Again Samuel thought he heard Eli calling him, and again Eli told him to go back to bed. When Samuel came to him a third time, Eli realized it was God calling him and instructed Samuel to answer God. Samuel went back to bed and waited to hear the voice call him again. God did call out to Samuel again, and Samuel answered saying he was listening. God told Samuel He was about to do something in Israel that would surprise everyone, and then confirmed his judgment against Eli and his sons. The next morning Samuel told Eli what God had said.

Eli could do nothing except resign himself to wait for the day of God's judgment against him and his sons. Four years later Jair died, ending his twenty-two year rule over Israel. During this long forty-five year period from Tola's leadership through Jair's, the Israelites had fallen back into their complacency and into worshipping idols. They not only went back to worshipping Baal and Asherah, but also chose to worship the gods of Aram, Sidon, Moab, Ammon, and the Philistines.

They worshipped the god Baal of Peor which involved obscene rituals, the god Molech which required the sacrificing of children, the god Chemosh who was believed to be a destroyer or subduer, the god Baalzebub who could tell the future, the god Baal-berith who was the god of a covenant Israel made with the Canaanites, the god Dagon who had the body of a fish but arms and head of a man, as well as other lesser significant gods. God became angry with them and their senseless need to believe that things made of stone and wood could possibly help them or defend them. So, God released them to their gods and turned them over to their enemies.

It wasn't long before the Philistines began oppressing the tribes along the west portion of Israel, and the Ammonites began oppressing the tribes living on the east side of the Jordan River. This oppression continued for eighteen years and when the Ammonites extended their cruel reign of oppression to the people of Judah, Benjamin, and Ephraim, they finally cried out to God for help.

They fully expected that God would send a leader to destroy their enemies just as He had every time over the last two hundred and sixty years since Joshua died. But this time they were utterly astounded when God told them no. God told them to cry out to all those gods they worshipped and relied on, that they should let those gods save them. But the people of Israel knew deep in their hearts there was no god like Jehovah, so they turned their backs to all the gods they had embraced and gave themselves wholeheartedly to God and His mercy.

While the Israelites held to their commitment to Jehovah and waited on His mercy, some of the leaders met on the east side of the Jordan River in Mizpah to discuss how they might conquer these enemies. The army of the Ammonites was camped only seven miles away at Gilead and the leaders from Gilead wanted them out. They proposed that if anyone was willing to lead Israel against the Ammonites, Gilead's highest position would be given to that person. Even with such a generous offer, everyone was afraid and there wasn't one person willing to step out and lead Israel against the Ammonites, nor the Philistines. So they endured their oppression and waited. They waited because they believed Jehovah would show mercy and send someone to lead them to victory.

DELIVERANCE BEGINS
(Judges 11–14 and 1 Samuel 4)

God saw Israel's misery and even though they didn't know it, He put a plan in place to begin their deliverance. On the southern edge of Dan in the town of Zorah, there was a woman who was not able to have children. God sent an angel to visit her, saying she would have a son and he would begin Israel's deliverance from the Philistines. God instructed her to stop drinking wine and eating unclean foods, and that they should never cut his hair because he was to be set apart for God from birth. The angel appeared a second time and confirmed this message to her and her husband.

They prepared a burnt offering and a grain offering to honor Jehovah, and as they presented it to God, the angel ascended into heaven in the flame that blazed upward from the offering. They never saw the angel again, but they believed what he said. They did have a son, and named him Samson.

While God had started their deliverance from the Philistines through the birth of Samson, on the other side of the Jordan River there was a young warrior named Jephthah from Gilead. He was the son of Gilead but because his mother was a prostitute, his step brothers drove him away so they wouldn't have to share any family inheritance with him. He moved north of Gilead to Mizpah with a group of men who were also unknown and unimportant in Gilead's society. When no one accepted Gilead's offer to lead their army against the Ammonites, the leaders of Gilead tried to hire Jephthah to do this by promising him the highest position they could give him, ruler of all Gilead. Jephthah had been faithful to God and knew that any battle he became involved in was not won by him but by Jehovah, so he accepted their offer.

Initially Jephthah tried reasoning with the Ammonites because they were descendants of Lot, Abraham's nephew. The Ammonites insisted Israel wrongfully took their land on the east side of the Jordan River when they came up from Egypt. But Jephthah had studied Israel's history and God's great miracles, and corrected the Ammonites in their accusation.

First he clarified that it was the Amorites who had taken the land away from them, then it was Jehovah who defeated the Amorites and gave it to Israel when they came up out of Egypt. Then Jephthah rebuked them and suggested they settle for what their god Chemosh was willing to give them, but the king of Ammon ignored him. Jephthah made a vow that if God would give him victory, he would in turn give God as an offering whatever came out the door of his home when he returned. Then Jephthah and his army went out and fought the Ammonites, and God gave them a huge victory by defeating them.

When Jephthah returned home, his daughter came out to meet him and he remembered his vow to God. So he kept his vow by offering her to God and she willingly accepted her destiny to remain a virgin for the rest of her life. The leaders also honored their word to make Jephthah ruler of Gilead, and he ruled that area for six years until he died. After he died, a man named Ibzan from Judah led Israel for seven years.

Even though Jephthah had defeated the Ammonites on the east side of Israel, they were still suffering persecution by the hand of the Philistines on the west side. A couple of years after Ibzan had led Israel, God began to stir a restlessness in Samson because it was time for him to confront the Philistines. Samson left home and found a Philistine woman he absolutely couldn't live without, in a town called Timnah about five miles away. When he returned home and informed his parents that he had chosen a Philistine woman to be his wife, they were disappointed. Based on what the angel had predicted, they expected Samson to fight the Philistines, not marry one.

Samson insisted on marrying this girl, so his parents went with him to Timnah to negotiate the marriage with her parents. While they were there, Samson went for a walk to a vineyard outside the city where a lion attacked him. He felt the power of God so strongly he was able to tear the lion apart with his bare hands. The experience was so unbelievable that he went back to the house and never said a word about the lion to anyone. The marriage details were worked out, and they returned home.

When they returned to Timnah for the wedding, Samson went back to the vineyard to rethink his awesome experience. He noticed that bees had built a hive in the carcass of the lion he had killed. He returned to be introduced to thirty male Philistine companions, hired to attend the wedding on his behalf. He decided to gamble with them and offered them each a linen garment and robe if they could answer the riddle: 'out of the eater something to eat, and out of the strong something sweet.'

The riddle was about his experience with the lion and the answer was honey. It was a sure bet because it was a stupid riddle about something he hadn't told anyone. By the fourth day of the celebration, the hired companions threatened to burn down the home and family of Samson's wife if she didn't get the answer to the riddle for them. She cried and begged Samson to tell her the answer, and nagged him up to the last day of the celebration. On the last day he finally told her and before the day was over, the thirty companions gave Samson the answer to his riddle.

Samson was furious that these Philistine men had convinced his bride to deceive him. He traveled almost twenty miles south to a town called Ashkelon, killed thirty Philistine men, stripped them of their clothes and returned to give the clothes to the thirty companions. He was still so angry that he went back home without his wife.

The Philistines and Israelites were camped and ready to engage in battle just twenty miles to the north of Samson. The Israelites were encouraged by the victory over the Ammonites and took a chance that God would help them fight the Philistines also. But God was not with them, and four thousand were killed on the battlefield.

They foolishly decided to force God's presence by bringing the ark to the battlefield, and it fell to Eli's son's Hophni and Phinehas to deliver the ark. When they entered the camp, the Israelites really believed Jehovah and the ark were one, so they began to shout just as loudly as their fathers did when they took the city of Jericho. But try as they might, they could not force a victory when God wasn't in it. They lost thirty thousand men in the battle that day, but even worse, the Philistines captured the ark.

A messenger was sent to Shiloh to report to Eli that his sons were killed in the battle and the ark was taken by the Philistines. Eli was ninety-eight years old and for twenty years he had anticipated the death of his sons because of what God had said, but the Philistines taking the ark was too much for him and he died. When Phinehas' pregnant wife heard the news, she went into labor and died giving birth to a son.

Samuel was twenty years old when he took over for Eli at the tabernacle, and was highly respected because everyone knew he heard from God.

DELIVERANCE DONE

(Judges 12, 15–16 and 1 Samuel 5–7)

The Philistines had captured Israel's symbol of power, carried it south to Ashdod and put it in the temple next to Dagon their fish god. During the night Dagon mysteriously fell face down in front of the ark, so they remounted him back on his stand. The next night the same thing happened but this time the head and arms had broken off his fish body. In addition to this, the town of Ashdod became infested with rats and the people developed tumors on their bodies. The leaders determined it was the God of Israel causing all this so they moved the ark east about seventeen miles to Gath. When Gath became infested with rats and the people plagued with tumors, they moved the ark north about five miles to Ekron. They too were plagued with rats and tumors, so their priests recommended they send the ark back to the Israelites.

Seven months after they captured the ark, it was being returned with a chest containing five gold rats and five gold tumors which they called a guilt offering. They hoped the guilt offering would influence Israel's God to stop the destruction that had spread across the land of the five Philistine rulers. They placed the ark and the chest on a cart and assumed Israel's God would lead the two cows pulling it. The cows traveled about ninety miles north to a town called Beth Shemesh, which was less than three miles from Samson's home.

The Levites from this town moved the ark onto a large rock, then using the wood from the cart and the cows that pulled it, sacrificed a burnt offering to Jehovah. These Levites were descendants of Kohath, the Levite tribe that carried the ark through the desert more than four hundred and fifty years ago. They had heard the stories about the things that happened in the desert, and about the stone tablets carved by God's hand that were placed in the ark.

Their curiosity prevailed over their fear of Jehovah and they opened the ark to look inside. Ninety Levites died that day because of their lack of respect. They were filled with fear of the ark and sent word to the people of Judah to come take it to Kiriath Jearim.

Even though the ark was being transported through the area where Samson lived, Samson chose to go the opposite direction to reclaim his wife. He went to Timnah only to discover that his father-in-law had given his wife to another man. Samson was furious and felt revenge was justified.

It was fall and the crops were ready to be harvested. Samson caught three hundred foxes, tied them in pairs by their tails, attached a torch to their tails, then lit the torches and sent them running through the fields. The damage done to the Philistines was almost immeasurable because their fields, vineyards, and olive groves all burned. The Philistines took revenge by going to his wife's home and burning her and her father to death. Samson went crazy and slaughtered several Philistines in that town, then escaped to a cave about twenty miles south in the hills of Judah.

The Philistine army went into Judah searching for Samson, but the people of Judah offered to find Samson for them in exchange for peace. Three thousand men of Judah's army found Samson in the cave and rebuked him because they were afraid of the Philistines. They had not been able to gain their freedom even with the ark in the battlefield, so Samson agreed to give himself up.

They tied his hands and arms with two strong ropes then turned him over to the Philistines. All of a sudden, Samson began to feel the power of God like he did with the lion; it was so intense that he broke the ropes that bound him as if they were straw. He then grabbed a donkey's jawbone from the ground and killed a thousand Philistine soldiers.

Samson not only experienced Jehovah's strength but later he also experienced God's compassion. After his amazing escape from the Philistines, Samson found himself weak and dying from thirst.

Chapter 6

God opened up the ground and gave him water, and Samson survived. For several years Samson led Israel, as did a man named Elon from Zebulon who led Israel for ten years and another named Abdon from Ephraim who led Israel for eight years.

Israel was still oppressed by the Philistines and God would use Samson one more time against them. Twenty years had gone by and the Philistines still wanted to arrest and punish Samson for the damage he'd done and the soldiers he'd killed. He tempted fate by traveling to a Philistine town on the Mediterranean shore called Gaza, about thirty miles from the safety of his home. He spent the night with a prostitute, but when he heard the Philistines plotted to arrest him at the city gates in the morning, he decided to leave in the middle of the night. He escaped through the locked and guarded gates with the strength God had given him, by pulling the gates loose and carrying them on his shoulders to the top of a hill.

Not long after that, he met and fell in love with a woman who lived to the west of him about twenty miles in the Sorek Valley. When the Philistine rulers discovered this, they offered this woman more than one hundred thirty pounds of silver to find out the secret of Samson's power. The woman's name was Delilah and she accepted their lucrative challenge.

Delilah asked Samson what his secret was, but he lied and told her if he were bound up with seven fresh bow strings he would be as weak as any other man. Delilah arranged for the Philistines to hide in her home during Samson's next visit. When he fell asleep, she tied him with the bow strings then started screaming that the Philistines were there. Samson broke loose from the bowstrings, and to Delilah's surprise, he escaped.

Samson really did love Delilah, but when she accused him of making a fool of her, he patronized her and said the secret was being tied with new ropes. She tried again with new ropes but he escaped. She continued to persist in knowing what the secret was so he told her if his long hair were braided with fabric he would lose his strength. Again she deceived him and again he escaped the grasp of the Philistines.

Delilah continued to nag Samson until he got so tired of it he told her the truth. His strength was in his long hair. Delilah convinced the Philistines to come back just one more time. After he fell asleep, she shaved his head then woke him up. The Philistines overpowered Samson and bound him with heavy bronze shackles. They gouged out his eyes and brought him to Gaza where they shackled him to a grinding stone in prison.

The five Philistine rulers came to Gaza to honor their god Dagon for delivering Samson into their hands. About three thousand people crowded into the temple as well as on the roof, all wanting to be a part of this historic celebration. The people were having the time of their life and in their zeal to celebrate, called for Samson to be brought out so they could be entertained by him. Samson was brought to the temple and humiliated by the crowd.

When they had finished having their fun with him, Samson asked the guard to allow him to rest against the pillars of the temple. The guard led him to the pillars where Samson prayed to God for the strength to avenge his enemies. With a hand on each of the center pillars, he pushed until they broke away and the temple collapsed on top of him. Samson died that day, but he killed more Philistines in his death than he did when he was alive.

When the Israelites saw the strength God had given Samson to destroy the Philistines, they realized Jehovah was their only hope. They cried out to God seeking His help but Samuel challenged their sincerity. If they truly were recommitting themselves wholly to God, they needed to forsake all their idols and gods, and serve Jehovah only. All of Israel withdrew from worshipping the other gods and came together at Mizpah where Samuel was going to intercede to God for them. But while they were at Mizpah fasting and confessing their sins, the Philistines came out to attack them. Samuel quickly sacrificed a young lamb as a burnt offering and out of anguish, publicly called out to God to save the people of Israel.

God's mercy for Israel against the Philistines started with Samson's birth, but now He would display His mercy through thunder. It was so loud that it literally weakened the Philistines and threw them into a panic. It was a miracle. It was Jehovah working on their behalf. The army of Israel boldly rushed out and pursued the Philistines. That day Jehovah turned the tables and it was now the Israelites who ruled the land.

Chapter 7

ISRAEL ASKS FOR A KING

(1 Samuel 8–12)

It had been about four hundred years since the Israelites left Egypt, and the only leader they recognized now was Samuel. His seventy-six years had been entirely dedicated to serving God, by serving Israel. He performed the priestly duties and judged Israel with integrity and with a heart for both God and Israel. After Eli and his sons died, Samuel assumed their responsibilities, which required him to travel a five-mile radius to Bethel, Mizpah, and Ramah, and also east to Gilgal nearly fifteen miles away.

His two sons Joel and Abijah helped with the priestly responsibilities, which included making a fifty-mile trip to serve at Beersheba. Samuel's sons weren't always honest in judging matters and they were known to accept bribes. The elders of Israel decided to ask Samuel to appoint a king like the other nations had, as a solution to the problem. In reality, it wasn't Samuel's dishonest sons that triggered their request, they wanted a king that would command an army to protect them so they could go about living their lives without worrying about any enemies.

Samuel took their request to have a king personal, but God assured him that it was Him they were rejecting. This solution would shift their trust in Jehovah for protection to an army led by a king. They were always so willing to put their trust in anything or anyone except Jehovah. God told Samuel they had been snubbing Him for the sake of other gods since the day they left Egypt. Yet God was gracious and told Samuel he needed to help them understand the consequences of their decision.

God warned that an appointed king would take their sons to serve in his army and to plow his fields. He would also take their daughters to serve as cooks and bakers in his house. He would require they donate the best of their fields, vineyards, olive groves, cattle, flocks and donkeys, as well as their servants. If they went forward with appointing a king and it all became too much of a burden, God would not help them when they cried out to Him for help. Samuel explained this to the leaders but their decision was final, they wanted a king. God accepted their decision because He would not deny them the freedom to make choices, whether they were good or bad.

Israel's leaders went home, but deciding to have a king did not change the fact that the Ammonites were regaining power and it would be just a matter of time before they would be oppressed by them again. But God would provide a commander to lead Israel's army. He told Samuel He would bring Israel's leader to him the next day and instructed Samuel to anoint him.

Two days prior to this, a young man and his servant went looking for his father's donkeys that had wandered off. After three days of searching, the servant suggested they ask the prophet Samuel about the donkeys. When they came into town they approached Samuel and asked him where they could find the prophet. Samuel knew instantly in his heart that this was the man God had chosen to lead their army.

His name was Saul and he was from the tribe of Benjamin. He was the tallest in his family, extremely good looking, and the son of a mighty warrior. Samuel invited him to be his guest, told him the donkeys had been found and in the same breath, told him he would be the desire and delight of all Israel. Saul was taken aback by this because he felt he was a nobody, the least important person in his family. After they ate, they talked privately for the rest of the visit and the next morning Samuel discreetly anointed Saul as leader of Jehovah's people.

To help Saul believe God was behind all of this, Samuel told him he would meet two men near Rachel's tomb who would tell him the donkeys were found and his father was worried about him. Samuel said three men would also meet him at Tabor and offer him three goats, three loaves, and some wine. He was to accept these gifts and go to Gibeah where he would run into a procession of men prophesying. When he joined them, the Spirit of Jehovah would come upon him and he would be changed. Everything happened just as Samuel said it would, but when Saul got home he didn't say a word to anyone about anything.

Samuel called the people of Israel to Mizpah where he would present Saul to them and publicly anoint him. When it was time to present Saul they couldn't find him because he was hiding among their traveling bags. Even though he was acting cowardly, the people didn't seem to care because they just wanted a king. Samuel eventually found him and presented him to the people who cheered and shouted, and gave him many gifts. There were a few who disagreed with the choice of Saul, but Saul never defended himself and remained quiet through the whole ordeal. When Samuel was finished, everyone went home, including Saul. Saul went back to plowing fields for his father, even though a group of valiant men who had been stirred by the Spirit of God followed him to his home.

The Ammonites made their move against the Israelites living on the east side of the Jordan River. They offered to spare them, but only if they would become their servants. In addition, they would also gouge out everyone's right eye because it was their intent to disgrace the people of Israel. The Israelites asked for a week to consider their proposal, then sent word to all the other tribes of Israel asking for their help. When Saul heard this, the power of God made him burn with anger and he cut up the oxen he had been plowing the field with, then sent a piece to each tribe threatening to do the same to their oxen if they didn't follow him in this battle against the Ammonites.

God caused a fear to come over the Israelites, which resulted in three hundred and thirty thousand men uniting as one to fight under Saul's command. After the Israelites east of the Jordan got word from Saul that their enemy would be conquered by noon the next day, they were ecstatic as well as deceptive by sending word to the Ammonites that they would surrender the next day. Saul strategically led Israel's army against the Ammonites for a quick and absolute victory. The people loved it and wanted to kill the few that had disagreed with choosing Saul as their king. But Saul said no because it was a good day, a day Israel was rescued by Jehovah. The people were delighted to have the commander they so desperately needed to protect them against their enemies, and would soon forget their real protector was Jehovah.

After the battle, Samuel had the people assemble at Gilgal where he sacrificed peace offerings to God and reaffirmed Saul as king of Israel. While they were there, Samuel poured out his heart to them, recounting the many times Israel had forsaken God for useless idols, yet when they were in trouble God always helped them. But now, when they saw the Ammonites were becoming a threat, their solution was to ask for a king when all along Jehovah was their king. To confirm that their decision to ask for a king was wrong, Samuel called on God to send thunder and rain. When the rain fell and the thunder rumbled through the sky, they felt an intense fear and reverence for both Samuel and God, then repented for adding to all their sin by asking for a king.

Samuel told them not to be afraid, just be obedient. He again reminded them that the idols and gods of the land could do nothing to help them because they are useless. Samuel had gone before God many times on behalf of the people and tried to express to them from his heart that God was pleased to choose them as His own special people, and He would not reject them. Samuel promised to teach them the good and upright way God wanted them to live. He counseled them to have reverence for God, to serve Him faithfully with their whole heart and never forget all the good things He has done for them.

GOD REJECTS ISRAEL'S KING
(1 Samuel 13–15)

After their victory with the Ammonites, Saul sent all the fighting men home except for three thousand. Two thousand were with him at Michmash and one thousand were with his son Jonathan at Gibeah. Both army posts were within five miles of Mizpah and Ramah, towns where the people of Israel often came because Samuel offered sacrifices to Jehovah in these towns. All these towns were within Benjamin's territory, which in itself was a hub of activity because of the access from east to west, as well as a main highway connecting the north territories to those in the south.

Jonathan decided to attack a Philistine outpost outside of Geba, which was in the heart of all these towns and activity. Saul instinctively knew it meant trouble so he recalled all the fighting men to join him at Gilgal, which was only ten miles east of his post at Michmash. Samuel told Saul he would meet him there in seven days to sacrifice a burnt offering and a peace offering on behalf of Israel.

The Philistine army converged at Michmash with three thousand chariots, and soldiers as many as the sand on the seashore. The army of Israel knew it was an impossible battle to win so most of them ran to the hills and hid wherever they could hide, and some of them even fled east to the other side of the Jordan River. Some stayed with Saul and waited the seven days for Samuel to arrive, but when he didn't show up on the seventh day, several more fled leaving Saul with only six hundred men.

Fear got the best of even Saul and he decided to sacrifice the offerings himself before everyone deserted him. Just as he finished the burnt offering, Samuel arrived and was stunned at what Saul had done. Saul was not chosen by God to present offerings, nor was he consecrated or anointed to offer sacrifices. By doing this himself, he minimized the significance of this sacred sacrament. Instead of the sacrifice being a sweet aroma to God, it was offensive.

The king of Israel should have led God's people to trust Jehovah, but instead he led them with an overpowering fear, a fear that caused him to break a most sacred command of God. Samuel informed him the kingship would not be handed down to his descendants but instead to someone who knows God's heart, then Samuel left. They did not go to war against the Philistines because they knew God would not be with them.

Instead, the Philistines reduced Israel's army to warriors without weapons, and in all Israel, only Saul and Jonathan had a sword. To keep them from making weapons, the Philistines would not allow any blacksmithing in Israel and even forced the farmers to go to the Philistines if they needed their tools sharpened. The six hundred men that had remained faithful to Saul at Gilgal were still with him, but the rest of Israel's army continued to hide. For a few, their fear was so great they became traitors and joined the Philistine army. Eli's great grandson joined Saul in his camp at Gibeah, bringing with him an ephod and the ark.

Chapter 7

It had been about six years since the incident at Gilgal when Jonathan decided he wanted to scout out a Philistine detachment camped about five miles away. Not only did he convince his armor bearer to go with him, but also that the two of them could defeat this detachment of Philistines if God chose to be with them. The Philistines were camped at the top of a cliff overlooking Michmash. Jonathan's plan was to climb up the cliff, and if the Philistines called them to come up into their camp, that would be their sign that God was with them.

Without telling Saul, the two went to Michmash and began climbing to the top of the cliff. When the Philistines saw them climbing up the cliff, they laughed and accused them of crawling out of their holes, then challenged the two to continue climbing so they could teach them a lesson. With that, the two were convinced God had decided to give them victory, so they climbed to the top of the cliff and entered the Philistine camp. The two killed more than twenty soldiers within a space of an acre with only one sword.

God shook the ground and sent panic among the Philistines in the camp, and fear among those in the outposts and raiding parties. Saul's men at the lookout posts reported that the Philistine army was breaking apart and running away in every direction. Saul turned to the priest for advice but when the noise from the Philistines got louder, he impatiently left the priest and led his men out. They found the Philistines killing each other out of total confusion, and the Israelite soldiers that had previously joined the Philistines out of fear had now joined Jonathan in the battle against them. The Israelite soldiers who had been hiding in the mountains and caves were also surfacing to join the battle. God was with Israel and the Philistines were on the run.

Saul took the lead of Israel's army away from Jonathan that day and forced the Philistines to retreat to their own land. In the months and years to come, Saul would victoriously lead Israel's army against Moab, the Ammonites, Edom, and the kings of Zobah, but his battle against the Philistines would continue for as long as he lived. Saul appointed his cousin Abner to the position of army commander while Saul took his place as their king. As king, he imposed his authority on every brave or strong man he found in Israel to fight in his army.

A year after this unexpected turn of events, Samuel instructed Saul to destroy the Amalekites because God wanted to avenge them for attacking Israel in the desert when they had returned from exploring the land. Saul and his army were to destroy the Amalekites just as their fathers destroyed Jericho when they came into the Promised Land. Absolutely nothing was to be spared, not even an animal. Saul and his commander led their army of one hundred and ten thousand against the Amalekites and destroyed them, except they spared the king. In addition to this, Saul kept the best of their cattle and flocks and then established a monument to honor himself.

Samuel went to see Saul after God told him how grieved He was over Saul's disobedience, but Saul excused himself by insisting he saved the sheep to offer sacrifices to God. Samuel informed Saul that God prefers obedience over a sacrifice and his arrogance was just as bad as the sin of idolatry. Samuel killed the Amalekite king himself, then reminded Saul that God would take the title of king from his family and give it to a neighboring tribe, one better than him. Saul realized he messed up but thinking only of his honor, begged Samuel to return with him and make an appearance with him before the elders. Samuel graciously accommodated Saul, then went home to Ramah. God was grieved over Saul, and so was Samuel. Even though Samuel never stopped praying for Saul, he never went to see him again.

Chapter 7

God Selects a Shepherd Boy
(1 Samuel 16–20)

Samuel was now ninety-two years old and God had allowed him to mourn Saul for sixteen years. But now it was time for him to take his anointing oil and go to Judah, to Jesse's house in Bethlehem because God had chosen one of his sons to be Israel's next king. Samuel was obedient and went to Bethlehem, bringing the anointing oil and a calf for a sacrificial offering.

There he met Jesse's seven sons and he assumed the oldest and courageous son was the one God had chosen. God told Samuel, man looks on the outward appearance but God looks at the heart. Jesse's youngest son David was in the field tending the sheep and when they called him in, Samuel knew he was the one God had chosen to be king of Israel. In front of his family, Samuel anointed this young handsome man with red hair. Then the Spirit of God came over David in power just as it had for Saul when he was anointed. Samuel returned home to Ramah and David returned to the fields to tend his father's sheep.

The Spirit of God had left Saul because of his disobedience, and was replaced by an evil spirit that occasionally tormented him. Soothing harp music was one of the few things that would relieve him of the torment, and ironically enough, David was selected to play for Saul because of his reputation with the harp.

They found themselves at war again against the Philistines about ten miles west of Bethlehem. While David's three older brothers joined the army to fight the Philistines, David traveled the ten miles to the battlefield only when he was needed to play the harp. The battle had continued for almost two months, so David's father sent him with cheese and bread to the battlefield to find out how his brothers were doing.

The soldiers were just going out to line up for battle when David arrived, so he joined them. Out of the Philistine's battle line came a giant of a man named Goliath who was over nine feet tall, and wore a bronze helmet and armor weighing more than a hundred pounds. He defiantly challenged Israel's army to settle this battle by sending someone out to fight him; the loser's army would become the slaves of the one who won.

Saul and his soldiers were terrified of the giant and retreated to their camp out of fear. David couldn't understand their lack of faith and after inquiring, discovered this has gone on every morning and evening for forty days. While Saul was willing to pay a huge reward to anyone who killed Goliath, which included his daughter's hand in marriage and exemption from taxes, there were no volunteers.

David's curiosity over all this got his brothers angry and they told him to go back to his sheep. But word about David got to Saul, and hoping this person might have the potential to fight Goliath, he sent for David. Saul was so preoccupied with how to destroy Goliath and win the battle that he didn't even recognize David as his harp player.

When David offered to fight Goliath, all Saul could see was a young boy and judged his ability based on his appearance rather than his faith in Jehovah. David convinced Saul that if Jehovah could help him slay a bear and a lion to protect the sheep, He would certainly help him slay a Philistine who defied Israel's army. Saul was persuaded but insisted David wear his armor and carry his sword. David tried the armor on but couldn't walk in it, so he went to the battlefield with only a sling and five smooth stones.

When Goliath saw David, he was insulted that they would send a young boy out with sticks and stones. David assured Goliath he came out to fight in the name of Jehovah, the God of the armies Goliath had defied. Goliath began to approach David but was struck down by a stone that hit his forehead, thrown by David with his sling. David approached Goliath on the ground and killed him with his own sword. When the Philistines saw Goliath was dead, they ran. The army of Israel pursued them west to Gath and north to Ekron leaving a wake of dead Philistine soldiers along a route of about thirteen miles. They returned to plunder the abandoned camp, but Goliath's sword was placed in the tabernacle at the city of Nob.

Saul's son Jonathan loved David because he trusted Jehovah so wholeheartedly, almost child like. Jonathan couldn't do enough for David and gave him his robe, tunic, sword, bow, and his belt. Saul wouldn't let David go home because he wanted him to serve in his army. It didn't matter what mission or battle Saul sent David on, he was always successful and built a reputation around that. When they returned home after their battle with Goliath and the Philistines, women came from all over Israel to sing and dance in the streets in honor of Saul for killing thousands. But, they honored David for killing tens of thousands.

Saul's jealousy got the best of him and tried to kill David twice while he was playing his harp for Saul. Both times David dodged his deadly spear. Saul feared David because he knew God was with him and all of Israel loved him. Saul offered David his oldest daughter in marriage if he would serve him in their battles against the Philistines. Saul's only motive was the hope that David would die at the hand of the enemy. David didn't feel worthy to be the son-in-law of a king so Saul gave his daughter to someone else. When Saul found out his other daughter Michal was in love with David, again with the same motive offered her to David for the price of one hundred Philistine foreskins. To Saul's surprise, David returned with two hundred foreskins and accepted Michal as his wife.

In the course of a year, Saul's fear of David had become so intense that he ordered David's death, but Jonathan interceded for him and convinced his father that David was not his enemy. It didn't last long because when war broke out against the Philistines again, Saul's jealousy and fear of David returned. Saul made another attempt to kill David with his spear, but failed. On the advice of his wife Michal, David fled from Saul. In order to give David the time he needed to get out of Saul's reach, Michal fixed their bed to appear as though David were sleeping in it. When the soldiers came to find David, she told them to come back later because he was ill.

David fled to Ramah to see Samuel because he thought he was the only one who could help him. Samuel took David to a settlement outside of Ramah but somehow word got to Saul that he was there. When Saul and his army pursued David at the settlement, he escaped and went to Jonathan for help. Jonathan made an oath with David to determine whether Saul had plans to kill him or if he was just trying to find him. Jonathan promised to let him know so he could escape with his life. In return, David made an oath to forever treat Jonathan and his descendants with kindness.

When Jonathan returned home, he saw his father's fear and uncontrolled anger for David when he tried to defend him, and realized without a doubt his father was determined to kill David. Jonathan sent the signal for David to escape, but was able to see him before he fled. They embraced and wept as brothers, then repeated their vow to remain friends. It was a vow they swore by the name of Jehovah.

David was in his mid twenties and even though he had been anointed to be king of Israel, he was now a fugitive instead.

THE LIFE OF A FUGITIVE
(1 Samuel 21–27, Psalm 56)

David would remain a fugitive for the next six years. After leaving Jonathan he fled south two miles to the city of Nob where the tabernacle was (see Illustration 9). Even though the ark was not in the tabernacle anymore, many of Aaron's descendants still served in the temple. David was given help from the priest Ahimelech who gave him bread from the temple and also Goliath's sword. An Edomite named Doeg who worked for Saul saw David with

Ahimelech, and because David knew he would tell Saul, fled as quickly as he could, traveling west twenty-five miles until he arrived at Gath.

By the time he realized Gath was Goliath's hometown and headquarters for the Philistines, it was too late and he was arrested almost immediately. They brought him to the king but David acted like a mad man with saliva drooling down his chin. The king felt there was absolutely no honor in capturing a madman even if it was David, and commanded they release him.

David turned his fear into praise for God and wrote a psalm acknowledging that man can do nothing to him because his trust is in Jehovah. David saw Jehovah in every situation he was confronted with, and would write many psalms of praise and deliverance throughout his days of running from Saul.

After David escaped from Gath, he hid in a cave at Adullam where his brothers and parents joined him. He was also joined by about four hundred men who were either in trouble, in debt, or suffering from bad situations, all of whom could relate to David and his situation. David left the safety of the cave and traveled east to Moab, and arranged for his parents to remain there in safety until he could work things out with Saul. When a prophet advised David not to go back to the cave at Adullam, he hid in a forest at Hereth.

While in the forest, a priest from Nob named Abiathar came to David and reported that Saul killed his father Ahimelech because he had given David Goliath's sword and bread from the tabernacle. Doeg the Edomite had informed Saul that they had helped David, then returned on Saul's orders to kill them. He not only killed Abiathar's father but also eighty-four other priests, every woman, child and infant, then killed all the animals as well. David felt responsible for their deaths and invited the priest to stay with him in the safety of his camp.

David got word that the Philistines had attacked the town of Keilah, which was close to where they were. After seeking advice from God, David and his men went to Keilah and defeated the Philistines. Saul heard about David's victory and immediately left for Keilah with the intent to kill David. When he arrived, David and his men had already fled south about twelve miles to the Desert of Ziph and hid in the hills. Saul continued his pursuit and followed David into the desert.

Jonathan was also pursuing David and after finding him, encouraged him to keep on trusting God. He told David he believed that his father would never kill him because God wanted to make him the king of Israel and Saul couldn't change that. David was encouraged by his words, then Jonathan went home. After days of unsuccessful searching, Saul and his army returned to Gibeah also.

The Ziphites that lived in the desert of Ziph went to Saul at Gibeah saying they knew the general area David was hiding, so Saul hired them to be his spies. Saul and his army followed the Ziphites into the desert and when David heard he was getting close, he and his men fled further south into the Desert of Maon. Saul was informed that David had gone further south, so he and his army also went south and came close to capturing David. He was literally on one side of a mountain with David on the other side when he got word that the Philistines had attacked Israel. Saul was so close but had to give it up for the moment, and return to defend Israel. David was able to escape Saul's grasp one more time, and fled east to live in the caves at En Gedi which was near the coast of the Dead Sea.

After Saul's battle with the Philistines, he found out David was in the Desert of En Gedi and pursued him with three thousand men. They searched the desert and when they arrived at the area of the caves, Saul entered one for the privacy of relieving himself. Of all the caves in the desert, Saul entered the one David and his men were hiding in. But because they were hiding deep in the cave,

Saul didn't know they were there. David's men wanted to kill Saul, but instead David quietly cut off a piece of Saul's robe that he had temporarily thrown on a rock.

After Saul returned to his men, David called out to him and showed him the piece of robe he had cut off, testifying that he could have killed him but chose not to. He pleaded with Saul, saying he was not guilty of any wrongs against him, vowing he would never bring harm to Saul and invited God to be their judge in this matter. Saul wept because he realized how close he had come to being killed, but was spared by the one he called his enemy. He also knew without a doubt that God had given the kingship of Israel to David, and asked David to swear by Jehovah that he would never destroy him or his family. When David gave him his word on that, Saul took his army and went home. But David had learned not to trust Saul and returned to his life as a fugitive.

David had been on the run for two years when he heard Samuel had died. All of Israel came to Ramah to bury him, but David and his men headed south back to the Desert of Maon. There was a wealthy man living just north of the desert at Carmel, and because David had protected his shepherds in the past, he sent ten men to ask for whatever provisions he might be able to share with them. He was quite rude in his refusal to help David, but when his wife Abigail heard what he did, she loaded provisions on donkeys and brought them to David herself without saying a word to her husband. When she returned and told her husband what she had done, he had a heart attack and ten days later he died.

David heard Abigail's husband had died so he sent for her to join him. Eventually, David married Abigail and also married a third wife named Ahinoam. Even though his first wife Michal loved David dearly, Saul had given her away to be the wife of a man named Paltiel.

The Ziphites sent word to Saul that David was hiding in a specific hill in the desert of Ziph, so Saul and his three thousand men immediately left to capture David. After Saul and his army had made camp at the bottom of the hill and fell asleep for the night, David and Abishai snuck into their camp and took Saul's spear and water jug. When David had put a fair amount of distance between him and Saul, he called out to Saul from the top of a hill. He showed him the spear and water jug, saying God had given him another opportunity to kill him but he chose not to. He pleaded again with Saul insisting he was not guilty of any wrongs against him, and declared God would reward him for his righteousness and faithfulness.

Saul realized that David would prevail no matter what, and acknowledged to David that he would in fact do great things. Saul conceded by taking his army and going home, but David still wasn't ready to trust Saul yet.

David had been on the run for more than four years and was tired of it. He now had six hundred men who went with him to Gath to seek safety from the king of the Philistines. Even though this same king had wanted to punish David in the past for killing Goliath, God gave David favor with him and he let them live in Ziklag. Because this town was within the Philistine territory, Saul gave up his pursuit of David.

Eventually, all the families were able to join David and his men, and they lived there in peace for a year and four months. Achish, the king of the Philistines, came to trust David and was convinced of David's never ending loyalty to him.

DAVID BECOMES KING
(1 Samuel 28–2 Samuel 5, 1 Chronicles 10–12)

Achish and his Philistine army were preparing to attack Israel, and he wanted David and his men to fight with him. He completely trusted David and for his loyalty, promised to award him a position as his personal bodyguard for life. However, the king's command-ers didn't share his trust for David and after three days into their journey to the battlefield, insisted David and his men return to Ziklag.

They returned only to discover that the Amalekites had burned the city and taken all their women and children hostage. For the first time, David's men became bitter toward him but as always, he turned to God for strength and God encouraged David to pursue the Amalekites. The men were exhausted from their three-day trip back to Ziklag and even though two hundred abandoned the pur-suit, David and his remaining four hundred men successfully over-took the Amalekites and recovered every person and item that was taken. In addition to this, they plundered the camp and returned with so much wealth, they were able to share it with all the people that had helped him while he was on the run over the last six years.

Saul was in Gilboa and heard the Philistines were organizing about thirty miles south of him in Aphek, with plans to head north to fight him (see Illustration 9). Saul was terrified and went to a fortune-teller hoping she could reach Samuel in his grave to ask what their fate would be. She was able to talk to Samuel's dead spirit, who confirmed what he had told Saul more than twenty years ago. She told Saul that God was taking the kingdom away from him and by tomorrow he and his sons would be dead. Saul fell to the ground in fear and refused to get up, but his soldiers convinced him to get himself together and they returned to the army post that night.

The next day the Philistines attacked Saul and his army at Gilboa, and many Israelite soldiers were killed. Those that were not killed fled for their lives leaving Saul critically wounded and his sons dead. Saul commanded his armor bearer to kill him before the enemy found him, but when he refused, Saul fell on his own sword and died. His armor bearer chose to do the same and died by his own sword next to Saul and his sons.

The Philistines found Saul and stripped him of his armor then cut off his head. They fastened his body and the bodies of his sons to a wall in Beth Shan east of the battlefield. Saul's armor was hung in the temple of Ashtoroth and displayed as a trophy. The men from Jabesh Gilead heard what they had done and traveled through the night more than twenty miles to take their bodies from the wall. These brave men returned home, burned the bodies and buried the ashes under a tree.

The third day after David had been back in Ziklag, a man who had escaped from the battlefield came to David to report that Saul and his sons were dead. The man bragged it was him who had killed Saul, and proved it by giving him Saul's crown and the band he wore on his arm. Instead of honoring the man, David had him killed because Saul was God's anointed servant. David mourned the death of Saul but even more so, the death of Jonathan.

David left Ziklag and returned to Judah, to the town of Hebron where the people anointed him and declared him king of Judah. He sent word to the men of Jabesh Gilead that he was pleased they would honor Saul and his sons by doing what they did. But the tribe of Benjamin did not view David as their friend but rather as their enemy and declared Saul's son Ish-Bosheth king of Israel. Abner had survived the battle with the Philistines and was still the commander of Israel's army.

David had chosen Joab to be the commander of his army. The armies of Abner and Joab came against each other at Gibeon, but the two commanders agreed to fight with a dozen strong men in lieu of their armies fighting. Not one of these strong men survived to declare a victor, so the two armies engaged in a fierce battle. When it became obvious to Abner that Israel would be defeated by Judah's army, they retreated from the battlefield. But Joab's brother Abishai who was a runner more than a fighter, ran on foot after Abner, determined to kill him. Abner warned him to quit following them, but when he refused Abner felt compelled to kill him.

Chapter 7

Joab and his army came across his body lying on the roadside, but continued their pursuit of Abner into the hills of the wilderness. By the time they caught up with Abner, several fighting men from the Benjamites had rallied together and joined Abner's army. Abner didn't want to see any more soldiers of Israel or Judah killed, so he proposed a truce. As embittered as Joab was because of his brother's death, he preferred a truce instead of fighting Israelites.

Abner crossed over the Jordan River and returned to Mahanaim with a loss of three hundred and sixty men. Joab lost only twenty men but one of the twenty was his brother. He buried his brother in Bethlehem then returned to Hebron by the next morning to report to David. Even though Abner and Joab agreed to a truce, the war between the house of Saul and the house of David continued for several years.

Abner remained faithful to Saul's son but when Ish-Bosheth rebuked him for sleeping with one of Saul's concubines, Abner became so angry that he swore his allegiance to David. Abner immediately sent word to David proposing an alliance. David agreed to the alliance on the condition that he get his first wife Michal back. Abner sold the idea to the elders of Israel and also the people of Benjamin, then went to David with only twenty men and informed him the whole house of Israel wanted to make him king. It was something to celebrate, so David threw a feast then sent Abner home in peace.

Joab was just returning from a raid when Abner was leaving, and confronted David immediately after finding out what had happened. Even though Joab could not be convinced that Abner could be trusted, David was not willing to change his decision. What Joab really wanted was to avenge his brother, so he secretly arranged for Abner to be killed. When David heard what had happened he mourned Abner's death and refused to eat or be comforted.

Through it all, Israel's soldiers realized David was a man of integrity, and more than three hundred thousand came to Hebron to swear their allegiance to him as king. Two men from the tribe of Benjamin were a bit too enthusiastic about the change and killed Ish-Bosheth, then brought his head to David. David was taken aback, not only because they would commit such a crime, but amazed at their ignorance to think he would reward them. David ordered that they be killed for their crime.

The elders of Israel also came to Hebron acknowledging David as the one that God had chosen to lead Israel. David went from shepherd boy to fugitive, then to king of Judah, and now king of Israel. He was thirty-eight years old and the most important thing he learned in all his experiences was that he could always trust Jehovah. He went on from Hebron and conquered Jerusalem, making it his headquarters and the heart of Israel.

It seemed a lifetime ago that Samuel had anointed him when he was just a shepherd boy tending his father's sheep. But now, fifteen years later he was the shepherd of God's people, he was King David—king of all Israel.

Chapter 8

THE KING AS A LEADER OF ISRAEL

(2 Samuel 6–10, 1 Chronicles 13–19)

David knew that God's presence rested above the ark and was determined in his heart to have it moved and permanently placed in Jerusalem. He made the necessary preparations for the move by having people join the procession with dancing, singing, and praising, but instead of carrying the ark as it was through the desert, he had it transported on a cart pulled by oxen. When the cart bounced and one of the men put his hand on the ark to steady it, he was struck down on the spot and died. This scared the people so much that they stopped where they were and left the ark in the home of a man named Obed-Edom.

News about David and his rise to power was spreading fast. Some liked it and some did not. When the king of Tyre heard, he sent materials and workers to build David a palace within Jerusalem in an area referred to as the city of David. When the Philistines heard, they tried to dethrone David by sending their army to defeat him but were not successful. God was with David and as his fame spread, nations grew to fear him.

When David's palace was completed, he prepared a tent covering for the ark, then summoned all of Israel and the descendants of Aaron to join him in bringing the ark to Jerusalem. This time he ordered the Levites to consecrate themselves in order to carry the ark as instructed by Moses, and accompany it with music, dancing, and praise to honor Jehovah. He also made arrangements for the care of the ark after it arrived by appointing Levites to varied positions. Some would make petitions, some would give thanks and praise to Jehovah with harps, cymbals, and trumpets every day, and some would just simply guard the gates and doors.

When the ark entered the city, David was among them dancing as passionately as he could because Jehovah was coming to reside at Jerusalem. They offered burnt offerings and fellowship offerings before God, then David blessed the people and gave them gifts. David wrote a poem of worship which emphasized God's faithfulness to His people for a thousand generations. The poetry encouraged the people to declare God's glory among all the nations because His love endures forever. It was a wonderful celebration when all Israel gathered together to worship and praise God, and then they returned home.

David wanted to build a spectacular temple for the ark but God spoke through a prophet named Nathan saying He didn't want David to build a home for Him. God told David it would be his son who would build a house for His name, and promised David his kingdom would be established forever through his descendants. David was humbled by this promise because he did want his kingdom to last forever, but for God's glory—not his.

Over the next eight years, David subdued the Philistines and took control of their capital as well as its surrounding villages. After he defeated the Moabites, they regularly brought tributes to David. He defeated the king of Zobah as far north as Hamath, which was way beyond the Promised Land their forefathers claimed. He defeated the Arameans who became subject to David and also brought tribute. From his victories in the north, David was able to establish a huge treasury of gold and bronze reserved solely for the building of God's temple. Wherever David went, Jehovah gave him victory, even against Edom, the Ammonites, and Amalekites.

David didn't even have to go to war for Jehovah to give him victory over his enemies. When the king of Hamath heard of David's successful battles around his territories, he donated several articles of gold, silver, and bronze to David's treasury. Whether the victory came through battle or submission, all the spoils from every victory as well as any donations were dedicated to Jehovah.

David organized the management of his kingdom from every aspect. He chose Joab to command his army, Jehoshaphat to keep records, Zadok and Ahimelech to serve as priests, and Seraiah to be his secretary. He also appointed Benaiah to manage the guards and messengers, and his sons to be royal advisors.

The six years David spent as a fugitive were becoming less significant compared to his sixteen years of being king over Judah and now Israel. But time didn't dull his memory of Jonathan, nor the significance of the oath he made to him. He sent for one of Saul's servants named Ziba, and asked if any of Saul's descendants had survived because he wanted to show God's kindness to them. When Ziba told him Jonathan's crippled son Mephibosheth was still living, David immediately had him and his family brought to his palace to live with him and eat at his table. He couldn't do enough for Jonathan's son. David ordered that all of Saul's property be transferred to Mephibosheth then instructed Ziba and his fifteen sons to farm the land.

David's throne was well established, but three years later, the king of the Ammonites died and his son Hanun succeeded him as king. David sent men to express his sympathy but Hanun's advisors convinced him they were there to spy on him for the purpose of overthrowing their government. Hanun disgraced the men by shaving half their beards and cutting off their garments to expose their buttocks. When they returned, David advised them to stay at Jericho until their beards had grown back.

When Hanun realized he had made a mistake, he hired thirty-three thousand soldiers from among several nations to defend him. Joab led Israel against the Ammonites' hired army and fought until they fled, then returned to Jerusalem. A regiment of the hired army were Arameans, who would not accept defeat because they were considered leaders among the nations. The Arameans regrouped to fight Israel again, but after forty thousand seven hundred soldiers were killed, they had no choice but to submit.

As king of Israel, David would have enemies throughout his entire reign, and the battles would continue on and off for years to come.

THE KING AS A FATHER
(2 Samuel 11–14)

Joab returned to the battlefield with Israel's army to fight the Ammonites, but David remained in Jerusalem. One evening when David was walking on the roof of the palace, he caught sight of a beautiful woman taking a bath and recognized her as Bathsheba. She was the wife of a Hittite soldier named Uriah, but David had her brought to him and slept with her. In just a few short months, Bathsheba sent word to David that she was pregnant. Instead of facing his guilt, David decided to bring her husband back from the battlefield so he could sleep with her. Uriah would think it was his baby and David's sin would remain a secret.

Uriah did return home to Jerusalem but refused to even sleep in his house because his fellow comrades were all sleeping in the field. David got him drunk but he still refused to go home and sleep with his wife. Because David was still unwilling to expose his sin, he sent a sealed note with Uriah instructing Joab to place him in a vulnerable battle position. Joab did as David requested and Uriah was killed in battle just as David hoped he would be. After Bathsheba mourned her husband's death, David married her and brought her to his palace where she gave birth to a son.

God was angry with David for what he did and sent the prophet Nathan to rebuke him. God had given David everything including Israel and Judah, but he killed Uriah to have more. To punish David, God was going to cause tragedy to come to his household. Even though David had defiled Uriah's wife in private, God was going to give his women to someone close to him who would defile them in public. In addition to this, the son born to Bathsheba would die. David interceded for the child with seven days of fasting and lying on the ground, but the child still died. Bathsheba mourned for her baby, but it wasn't long and God blessed her and she became pregnant again.

Joab and the army were east of the Jordan River at the royal city of Rabbah where the king of the Ammonites resided. Joab was successful in taking control of their water supply and victory was close. He sent word to David to gather his men and come take the city so the credit wouldn't fall to himself. David took the remaining army in Jerusalem and went to Rabbah where he attacked the city and captured it. The bounty from Rabbah was tremendous and the king's crown alone was made of precious stones set in seventy pounds of gold. Joab showed respect to David by placing the crown on his head. David continued the battle into the surrounding towns, taking the people captive and forcing them into hard labor. Then David and the entire army returned to Jerusalem.

Bathsheba gave birth to David's seventh son when he was just over fifty years old. It was customary for a king to have several wives, and David had eight. David's first six sons were born when he was in his early thirties while he was king of Judah and living in

Hebron. Saul's daughter Michal was his first wife but she had no children. The two wives David married when he was a fugitive were Ahinoam, who gave David his first son Amnon, and Abigail, who gave David his second son Kileab. His wife Maacah was the daughter of King Talmai of Geshur and she gave David his third son Absalom and also a beautiful daughter named Tamar. Three other wives each had sons; Adonijah was David's fourth son, Shephatiah his fifth and Ithream his sixth son. David's seventh son was born to Bathsheba and God instructed David to name him Solomon, which means *loved by Jehovah.*

Solomon was still a toddler but his brothers and sisters were in their late teens to upper twenties. His oldest brother Amnon was obsessed with his half sister Tamar. Following his cousin's advice, he told his father he was sick and asked that he send Tamar to bake bread for him. David sent Tamar as Amnon requested but when she finished baking the bread, Amnon sent everyone away then raped her. She begged him to stop but he wouldn't and when he finished raping her, she wept bitterly. Amnon's obsession turned from desire to hatred, and he threw her out of his house.

David found out and was furious, but did nothing to punish Amnon. Tamar's brother Absalom didn't say anything but he hated Amnon for what he did to his sister. Two years later when it was time to shear the sheep, Absalom arranged a celebration more than twenty miles north of Jerusalem. All his brothers were there when he gave the signal to kill Amnon, the king's first son. His brothers fled back to Jerusalem where they joined David in mourning Amnon, but Absalom fled north to Geshur to stay with his grandfather, King Talmai.

David missed Absalom even more than he missed Amnon, but couldn't find it in his heart to go see him. It took five years, but Joab was finally able to convince David to allow Absalom to return to Jerusalem. Joab personally went to Gesher to escort him back. Absalom came home, but with a wife, three sons, and a beautiful daughter he named after his sister Tamar. It wasn't the homecoming he had expected because David refused to see him or his children.

After being home for two years, Absalom decided life in Gesher or even death was better than being shunned by his father. He sent word to Joab to arrange a meeting with his father, but Joab ignored his message. Absalom was so frustrated he didn't care what it took, and burned Joab's field to get his attention. It worked, and for the first time in seven years Absalom was finally going to meet with his father.

The two were reunited with kissing and hugging, but when the meeting was over their relationship fell short of Absalom's expectations. Absalom turned bitter and decided he wanted more, he wanted to be king of Israel.

GREAT DISAPPOINTMENTS
(2 Samuel 15–24, 1 Chronicles 20–21)

Over the next four years, Absalom deceitfully won the people's hearts by meeting them outside of Jerusalem and telling them King David wasn't available to judge their disputes. His deception always included the suggestion that if he were the one deciding the disputes, he would be available to them. At the end of four years he told King David he was going to Hebron to offer sacrifices to God, when he really had plans to overthrow David's kingship. Absalom had sent word to all the tribes in Israel of his plans, and at Hebron he declared himself king of Israel.

When a messenger informed David what Absalom had done, he fled out of Jerusalem to save his life and avoid a massacre. He fled with his family, the guards, messengers, the priests Zadok and Abiathar who brought the ark, and the six hundred men who were faithful to him when he was a fugitive. David left his concubines to take care of the palace, and after going a short distance decided to send the priests back with the ark so they could keep him informed. David also asked a good friend named Hushai to go back to Jerusalem and be a spy for him among Absalom's advisors. Hushai agreed and returned immediately.

Ziba and his sons joined David with provisions, but his motive was to own Saul's property and he lied to David, saying Mephibosheth stayed in Jerusalem with hopes of becoming king. Ziba's plan worked and David gave Saul's property to him. He also encountered a man named Shimei from Saul's family, who threw stones as they passed by and cursed David. It was an unexpected and hard day for David. He was exhausted and would never have believed he would be on the run again, but he realized this was the punishment the prophet Nathan spoke of because of what he had done to Bathsheba's husband. He pressed on and they camped south of Jerusalem.

While David was fleeing, Absalom and all those who supported him made their way into Jerusalem. David's counselor Ahithophel was among Absalom's supporters, and advised Absalom to pitch a tent on the roof of the palace and rape David's concubines. Ahithophel further advised him to send twelve thousand men to pursue David and attack him while he was tired and weak, but to kill only David because those following him would come back and be loyal to Absalom. David's spy Hushai was also there and advised against this and suggested they wait until all of Israel was united as one army, then attack. Absalom took Ahithophel's advise to rape David's concubines, but took Hushai's advise to postpone their pursuit of David. Ahithophel felt betrayed and went home and hung himself.

Hushai secretly sent word to the priests asking them to send their sons Jonathan and Ahimaaz to find David and warn him. The two were almost captured but were able to escape and inform David of the plans. As a result, David and all those traveling with him crossed the Jordan River and traveled north for more than thirty miles to Mahanaim, where the people came out to him with provisions (see Illustration 9).

Israel's army had gathered and Absalom appointed Joab's second cousin Amasa to be the commander. They crossed the Jordan River to pursue David and camped in the land of Gilead. David's spies knew where they were and he sent his army to attack them, but instructed them to be gentle with his son Absalom. David's men defeated Israel's army, killing twenty thousand soldiers. It was Joab who unquestionably and deliberately killed Absalom, despite David's orders. After Absalom was dead, Joab sounded a trumpet and commanded his men to stop fighting Israel, then buried Absalom under a pile of rocks. When King David found out Absalom had been killed, he mourned so bitterly his army returned from the battlefield feeling shame instead of victory.

David sent word to his brothers in Judah to escort him back to Jerusalem and they were honored to do what he asked. They met him at the Jordan River as did others, including a thousand Benjamites, Ziba and his sons, and even the Benjamite who had cursed him was there repenting. David discovered Ziba's deceitfulness when Mephibosheth came out to meet him, but Mephibosheth was so happy to have David back that he allowed Ziba to keep all of Saul's properties.

Even people from all the tribes of Israel had come to escort King David to Jerusalem but when they discovered he chose Judah to escort him back, they became quite annoyed. A Benjamite named Sheba blew a trumpet and convinced the other tribes of Israel to abandon King David and follow him. While they all followed Sheba, Judah remained faithful to David and escorted him back to Jerusalem.

The first thing David did after he returned was to move the concubines that Absalom had raped into a protective shelter where they lived as widows. His second order of business was to regain the loyalty of the people of Israel that Sheba led away. David had not forgotten it was Joab who killed Absalom, so he sent Amasa to summon the army of Judah instead of Joab. When Amasa failed to do what he had asked, David sent his army out under the command of Joab's brother Abishai. His orders were to pursue and defeat Sheba. Joab went with them and when they were about ten miles out, Amasa finally caught up with them. When he did, Joab killed him because he was a traitor who had chosen to lead Absalom's army out against David.

Joab led them as they continued their pursuit about one hundred miles north to a town called Abel Beth Maacah where Sheba was hiding. They surrounded the town and began battering the wall to break through, but a wise woman from town offered to give them Sheba if they would spare the people. After she convinced the people to give up Sheba, they threw his head over the wall. With that, Joab blew the trumpet to retreat and they returned to Jerusalem. David was almost sixty-five years old when he reestablished his kingship among Israel, and it included Joab as his commander.

David was getting too old to go to the battlefield but when they fought the Philistines, he went with his army. When he became exhausted at a battle and was nearly killed, the men in his army convinced him he was too valuable to Israel to take the risk of being killed in battle. He never went to the battlefield again, but stayed in Jerusalem to be king and to worship God by writing poetry that honored Him.

Life seemed so much easier for David when he was a shepherd boy watching his father's sheep, even when confronted by bears and lions. He had time in the field to study what Moses had written in Deuteronomy, and those writings became the basis of his understanding of Jehovah, which was often reflected in his poetry. When he left the sheep in the field and confronted Goliath, God gave him victory with a sling and stone. When he fled from Saul and became a fugitive, God gave him comfort by providing six hundred men to protect him. When he became a king, God gave him an army of mighty men to fight the enemy.

But now David wasn't going to the battlefield anymore to witness the strength of his army, and the temptation to trust the size of his army rather than God was too much. David ordered a census to determine just how big his army was even though he knew it was wrong. When the census was done, God would punish David but graciously offered him three choices of punishment. He chose three days of plague by God's hand, over three years of famine or three months of fleeing from his enemies because he knew he could trust God's mercy.

Life never seemed to stop offering opportunities for him to realize God's love and faithfulness. God not only showed faithfulness when his own family disappointed him, but also when he himself disappointed God. David spent hours writing poetry and songs that expressed what he had learned about God.

The one thing David knew with absolute certainty was that people would not always be faithful, nor would he always be faithful, but Jehovah always was.

SOLOMON BECOMES KING
(1 Kings 1–2:12, 1 Chronicles 22–29)

As much as David wanted to build a temple in Jerusalem for Jehovah, he had shed too much blood among Israel's enemies and God would not allow him to build His sacred house. But God did instruct David what to build and how to build it, and gave the honor of building the temple to his son Solomon. God also told David that Solomon was to be the next king of Israel and promised he would reign in peace, and that the throne of his kingdom would be established forever. God had been so gracious to David his entire life and now he was so humbled by God's promise to give his descendants the kingship forever. David knew it was a huge honor but felt so undeserving of it.

David adored and worshipped God, and wanted to make sure his inexperienced son was ready and able to do the task God had chosen him to do. David appointed stonecutters to prepare stones and provided large quantities of iron for the hardware to be used on the doors and gateways. He arranged for the Sidonians and Tyrians to deliver a huge supply of cedar logs, more than could be counted. David worked hard and made sacrifices to reserve three thousand seven hundred and fifty tons of gold, thirty-seven thousand five hundred tons of silver, and more bronze than could be weighed. He sought out people who were skilled in stonecutting, masonry, and carpentry, as well as men skilled in working with gold, silver, and bronze.

David wasn't just concerned about building the temple, but was also concerned about the loyalty of his son and the people towards Jehovah. He told his son what God had promised, but emphasized the importance of observing the laws God gave to Moses for Israel. It was a huge responsibility for Solomon who was in his early twenties, but David told him not to be afraid; rather, be strong and courageous because God would never leave him or forsake him. David also ordered the leaders of Israel to help Solomon, and to devote their hearts and souls to seeking Jehovah their God.

David was about seventy years old and loved by the people, but he was now confined to his bed and needed help. A young girl dedicated herself to serving him, and even when David couldn't keep warm, she would lay beside him. David had always been quite liberal with his children and his son Adonijah didn't respect his decision to make Solomon king. He plotted with David's commander Joab and the priest Abiathar, to go with him to the south part of Jerusalem to offer sacrifices and declare him king of Israel. He also invited his brothers to go with him, but not Solomon nor anyone that was loyal to his father.

Bathsheba and those who were loyal to David informed him, so he ordered Zadok the priest to immediately anoint Solomon king over Israel. They went to Zadok on the east side of Jerusalem where Solomon was anointed, and returned with the sound of trumpets and people shouting "long live King Solomon." The celebrating and shouting was so loud that the ground shook. All the royal officials were in the palace when King Solomon took his place on the throne.

Adonijah and his invited guests were enjoying their feast when they heard the noise of the people, then Abiathar's son came with the news about Solomon. Everyone fled including Adonijah who went to the temple and clung to the horns of the altar, refusing to let go until King Solomon promised he would not kill him. Solomon promised if he was found to be a worthy man he would be spared, but if he was found to be evil he would die. Adonijah went to King Solomon and bowed to him out of respect, then was allowed to go home.

David had served Israel nearly forty years and wanted to start Solomon out on the right foot. He counted thirty-eight thousand Levites and assigned twenty-four thousand to supervise the work of the temple, six thousand to be officials and judges, four thousand to be gatekeepers and four thousand to praise Jehovah with musical instruments. He also assigned descendants of Aaron to serve as priests. In addition, David made provisions among the twelve tribes of Israel to each provide twenty-four thousand soldiers and commanders for one month every year, and Joab would continue to be the royal commander. He organized people to manage the royal storehouses and supervise the workers that tended his vineyards, olive groves, fig trees, herds, camels, donkeys, and sheep.

David was still concerned about the people's loyalty to Jehovah so he summoned all the tribal officers, commanders, and officials to Jerusalem. One last time, David repeated all of God's promises. He commanded them to follow all of God's laws so they could live in the land and pass it on as an inheritance to their descendants forever. Then he commanded Solomon to serve God with whole-hearted devotion and a willing mind because God understands every motive behind our thoughts. He assured Solomon that if he would seek God he would find Him, but if he ever forsakes God, God would forsake him. David had documented all the building plans and all the organizing he had done, and handed it to Solomon.

David reviewed with all those gathered there, the treasures he had stored away for the building of the temple. David also announced he was donating his personal treasures which consisted of one hundred and ten tons of gold and two hundred and sixty tons of silver. Then he invited them to give whatever they were willing to give to Jehovah. The leaders donated more than one hundred ninety tons of gold, three hundred seventy-five tons of silver, six hundred seventy-five tons of bronze, and three thousand seven hundred fifty tons of iron.

David was absolutely so touched by their generosity and willingness to give from their hearts, that it inspired him to write another psalm of praise. He sang this song to Jehovah acknowledging they were giving back to God what He had generously given to them Himself. David prayed that God would keep the people's hearts loyal to Him, and that his son would have wholehearted devotion for God's laws and commands. David's heart was so filled with compassion and love for Jehovah that when he asked the people to praise God, they dropped to their knees and bent prostrate to the ground praising God.

The next day they offered three thousand burnt offerings to God along with drink offerings and other sacrifices. They ate and drank with great joy in the presence of Jehovah then for the second time, anointed and acknowledged Solomon the king of Israel. They pledged their obedience to King Solomon and after all the celebrations were over, went back to their homes.

Shortly after, David died.

SOLOMON BUILDS A TEMPLE AND AN EMPIRE
(1 Kings 2:13–9:9, 2 Chronicles 1–7)

David had not been dead long when Adonijah came to Bathsheba requesting she ask the king to give him the young virgin girl who had dedicated herself to David during his last days. King Solomon was exhausted by Adonijah's persistent disrespect shown not only to him but to David, and ordered he be put to death that day. King Solomon also gave orders regarding Abiathar and Joab who supported Adonijah in his attempt to steal the kingship. For Abiathar, he was removed as priest and retired to the country but Joab the commander of David's army was put to death. Benaiah, who had been David's commander over the guards and messengers was given charge over Israel's army.

King Solomon also gave one last order to take care of old business, which was for Shimei the Benjamite who cursed David as he fled from Absalom. Solomon put Shimei's fate in his own hands by ordering him to remain in Jerusalem with the promise of death if he ever left the city. However, after three years he chose to leave the city to hunt down servants that had fled from him. When he returned he was brought before King Solomon who ordered his execution because he had defied the orders to remain in the city. All the unfinished business against David was done, and the kingdom of Israel was now firmly established in Solomon's hands.

The Egyptian kingdom was still considered a world power. Even though Israel's ancestors had broken free from their bondage almost a half century earlier, King Solomon made an alliance with them by marrying Pharaoh's daughter. Pharaoh sent his army to Gezer just west of Jerusalem and defeated the Canaanites living there, then gave the city to Solomon as a dowry for his daughter. Until King Solomon finished building his palace, Pharaoh's daughter would live in the city of David.

The ark of the covenant was in the city of David but the tabernacle remained in Gibeon. While many of the people went to Gibeon to offer sacrifices, some chose to offer sacrifices on elevated locations more convenient to them. King Solomon went to Gibeon and offered one thousand sacrifices to Jehovah because he was feeling absolutely too young and inadequate to rule God's chosen people. At Gibeon he humbled himself before Jehovah and asked for a heart to govern God's people and the ability to distinguish between right and wrong.

God was pleased that he would ask for wisdom instead of wealth, fame, or a long life, and promised there would never be anyone wiser than Solomon. In addition, God promised He would give him all those things he didn't ask for. King Solomon would be honored, wealthy, and famous with nobody equal to him, and promised he would have a long life if he would be faithful to God's commands.

Solomon returned to Jerusalem and his wealth began to accumulate quickly, as did his reputation for wisdom. When two prostitutes came to King Solomon, each claiming to be the mother of a baby, he chose to settle the dispute by suggesting that the child be cut in half. The true mother was given custody when she forfeited her claim to the child in order to save it. Not only Israel, but people of every nation were amazed at the wisdom, insight, and understanding God had given Solomon. He spoke three thousand proverbs, wrote one thousand and five songs, became an expert on plant life, animals, birds, reptiles, and fish, and received visitors from every corner of the world who desired to hear his wisdom.

Chapter 8

The people of Israel enjoyed prosperity and wealth during Solomon's reign and were tolerant of the cost to keep Solomon's kingdom operating. Daily he required one hundred eighty-five bushels of flour, three hundred seventy-five bushels of meal, ten stall-fed cattle, twenty pasture-fed cattle, one hundred sheep and goats, as well as deer and fowl. The twelve tribes of Israel would take turns providing the king's daily needs for a month, as well as the barley and straw needed for the king's more than fifty thousand horses.

Solomon began the task of building the temple. He paid a yearly fee of one hundred and twenty-five thousand bushels of wheat and one hundred and fifteen gallons of pressed olive oil to the king of Tyre in exchange for cedar trees from Lebanon. He also required Israel to provide one thousand men each month to work in Lebanon, seventy thousand men to be carriers and eighty thousand to cut stones, all of which required three thousand six hundred men to supervise.

Four years after Solomon became king of Israel, work on the temple began. It was a magnificent piece of architecture made of stone measuring ninety feet long, thirty feet wide and forty-five feet high with three levels. The porch in front of the temple was the width of the building and extended fifteen feet. The inside walls and ceiling were paneled with carved cedar boards overlaid with gold, and the floor was covered with pine overlaid with gold. A wall of blue, purple, and red fine linen curtains sectioned off thirty feet at the end of the building for the Most Holy Place. Two golden angels with wings that spanned from wall to wall were in the Most Holy Place where the ark of the covenant would reside. The gold used just for the Most Holy Place weighed twenty-three tons. In addition to the palm tree, chain and angel designs, the temple was also adorned with precious stones. Huge doors were made of carved olive wood overlaid with gold, and two fifty-foot pillars were on each side of the front entrance.

The courtyard had doors overlaid with bronze. A bronze altar was built thirty feet square and fifteen feet high, then placed in the courtyard. Also in the courtyard between the altar and the temple was a round washbasin for the priests, which measured fifteen feet wide and almost eight feet high. The washbasin rested on the backs of bulls made from bronze. Ten other washbasins were placed at the north and south ends for the people to use. There was also a bronze platform in the courtyard measuring almost eight feet square and nearly five feet high.

Inside the temple were ten tables with a hundred gold bowls, and ten lamp stands made of solid gold placed on the north and south sides. All the silver and gold furnishings dedicated by David were brought into the temple and placed in the temple treasury. After seven years of building, the last thing Solomon did was bring the ark of the covenant into the Most Holy Place.

King Solomon summoned all the elders of Israel, the heads of the tribes, and the chiefs of the families to join him in the procession to bring the ark from the City of David into the temple. They offered so many sacrifices it was impossible to count them; then the Levites placed the ark under the wings of the angels in the Most Holy Place. The only items in the ark were the stone tablets placed there by Moses. There was singing, dancing, and musicians playing instruments, including one hundred and twenty priests blowing trumpets. They were all united in giving praise and thanks to Jehovah.

Solomon knelt on the bronze platform in the courtyard and spreading his hands to heaven, acknowledged there was no God in heaven or on earth like Jehovah. He prayed a humble but diligent prayer pleading with God to hear His people when they prayed towards the temple, and to have mercy on them. When Solomon finished praying, a fire came down from heaven and consumed the burnt offerings on the altar; then a cloud filled the temple. There wasn't a person there that didn't instinctively drop to their knees and fall prostrate before the glory of the Lord.

They continued to offer twenty-two thousand cattle and a hundred and twenty thousand sheep and goats. All the Levites took their positions appointed to them by King David as musicians and worshippers, and continually gave thanks chanting 'God's love endures forever.' After about three weeks of offering sacrifices, worship, and celebrating, Solomon sent the people of Israel home.

Solomon spent the next thirteen years building a showcase palace that all of Israel could be proud of. He had been king of Israel twenty-two years when he finally moved into it. When it was finished, God appeared and spoke to Solomon a second time, promising that His eyes and heart would always be on the temple they built for Him, but only if he walked with integrity of heart and was faithful to His commands.

God warned Solomon that if he or his sons turned away from Him and didn't observe His commands, He would not only cut them off from the land, but would reject the temple they built for Him. Solomon's passion for God wasn't the same as it was when he first became king. As his daily life got more comfortable, his need for God diminished.

INTEGRITY COMPROMISED
(1 Kings 9:10–14:20, 2 Chronicles 8–11)

After all the building was done, King Solomon compensated the king of Tyre for all the cedar and pine by giving him twenty towns in Galilee, but the towns were good for nothing. Solomon knew it and he could have been more generous in his compensation because Israel had a huge treasury. In addition to the several tons of gold given as gifts from the neighboring countries, he had also built a fleet of ships that returned from their expeditions with about sixteen tons of gold. Even though God had blessed Israel with great wealth, Solomon only felt obliged to honor Jehovah as required by the Law of Moses and went to the temple just three times a year to offer sacrifices.

Despite King Solomon's lack of passion, God continued to bless him with wealth and wisdom as He said He would. The Queen of Sheba was one of many dignitaries that traveled to Israel with gold and gifts for the wisest and wealthiest king in the world. He sat on a throne made of ivory and gold with statues of lions as his arm-rests and twelve on the six steps leading up to the throne. All the dishes and goblets in his palace were made of pure gold. There wasn't a kingdom in the world that was more wealthy than Israel. In addition to the revenue from merchants, traders, and the gifts given by visitors, his annual income was about twenty-five tons of gold.

Solomon was the greatest king on earth but it cost him his in-tegrity. He adopted the traditions of other kings by having seven hundred wives and three hundred concubines. These women came mostly from other countries and brought with them their idol wor-ship of pagan gods and idols. King Solomon not only patronized their requests to worship their foreign gods, but participated in the ceremonies. He worshipped Ashtoreth, Molech, and Chemosh, burned incense to honor them and built shrines and altars for them on high places.

The first time Solomon heard God's voice he was a humble man seeking God's help. The second time he heard God's voice he wasn't really looking to hear from God at all. Now he was hearing God's voice for a third time and probably wished he hadn't. God told Solomon He was going to tear the kingdom of Israel from his son, but for David's sake and for the sake of Jerusalem, He would allow his son to rule over one tribe. God also promised Solomon He would not do this during his lifetime, but God did give him two adversaries, an Edomite named Hadad and a rebel group led by Rezon from Damascus.

God also spoke through a prophet to an Israelite from Ephraim named Jeroboam. The prophet told Jeroboam that because Solomon was disobedient to God's commands, God was going to tear away ten tribes of Israel from Solomon's son and make Jeroboam leader over them. Even though God was doing this to humble David's descendants, God promised Jeroboam an enduring dynasty if he remained faithful to His commands. When Solomon heard about God's promise to Jeroboam he tried to kill him, but Jeroboam fled to Egypt where Pharaoh gave him refuge.

Solomon was the wisest king the world would ever know, but after ruling forty years, he died. His son Rehoboam was designated to inherit his throne and went to Shechem to be anointed king of Israel. Jeroboam was representing the people and asked the new king to consider lightening the heavy requirements Solomon placed on them. But after consulting his young advisors, Rehoboam informed the people he would not only require more than Solomon did but he would be even harsher.

The people returned to their homes but rebelled against King Rehoboam by refusing to do any labor for him. In order to regain control of his kingdom, the young king organized an army of one hundred and eighty thousand men from the tribes of Benjamin and Judah to fight Israel. But, before going out to battle, a prophet warned Rehoboam not to fight Israel because this was God's doing. Rehoboam feared God enough to cancel his plans and did not go to war against Israel.

Jeroboam wasn't as confident as Rehoboam was about God's power, and became insecure about the loyalty of the people towards himself. Even though it was God who made Jeroboam leader of ten tribes of Israel, he was sure they would desert him when they went to Jerusalem to offer sacrifices and celebrate the festivals.

Convinced of this, he drew them away from Jehovah and established a new religion.

Jeroboam told the people of Israel it was too much to expect them to travel all the way to Jerusalem to worship so he presented two golden calves as their new gods. He conveniently placed one at Bethel and the other in Dan, then built shrines on tops of hills and appointed men from among the people to be priests. He instituted festivals similar to those celebrated in Jerusalem and required sacrifices be made on altars to honor their new gods.

The priests and Levites who were faithful to God left their homes in Israel and moved to Jerusalem where they were free to worship Jehovah. God sent a man to tell Jeroboam that someday a king from Judah named Josiah would sacrifice their priests on the altar, and to prove it God would split their altar in half. When Jeroboam pointed at the man of God and furiously demanded they seize him, his arm turned white with leprosy and the altar exploded, splitting it down the middle. He pleaded with the man of God to intercede for him. Even though God graciously restored his arm, it didn't change his behavior, and he continued to deliberately lead ten tribes of Israel away from Jehovah. Jeroboam's legacy would be that he did more evil than any person since the beginning of creation.

Judah was not without sin either because Rehoboam continued to worship idols just as his father Solomon did. He also allowed male prostitutes to lead the people into detestable rituals. Time would prove over and over that people follow the behavior of their leaders. God had chosen this people to accomplish His plan, but without godly leaders, God would do what was necessary to bring salvation to the world.

Chapter 9

SETTING THE PACE

(1 Kings 14:21–16:28, 2 Chronicles 12–16,
Reference Books)

After Israel split into two nations, neither the northern kingdom named Israel nor the southern kingdom named Judah were faithful to the covenant their forefathers had made with God. As the people withdrew more and more from God, it lessened their ability to hear Him speak, so God would speak to them by sending faithful servants who could still hear His voice. These servants often carried a message the people didn't want to hear and almost always were persecuted and sometimes killed. These servants were called prophets of God.

God would also try drawing them back to Himself by using powerful nations to humble them. The kingdom of Syria was northeast of the Mediterranean Sea and on occasion would partner with one or both of the split nations against a stronger world power. However, for the most part Syria was an enemy to both Israel and

Judah. God used Egypt to intermittently become a friend and foe of the Israelites.

The nation of Assyria extended to the Persian Gulf area east of Syria and rose to the status of world power shortly after the Israelites settled into the Promised Land. Just a few years before Saul was anointed king of Israel, the nation of Assyria began to decline as a world power but regained its status about twenty years after the nation of Israel split. While Assyria would represent an occasional threat to Judah, God would allow Assyria to defeat the northern kingdom of Israel because of their stubborn hearts. Babylon also dates back to Abraham's day, but in the days of Israel and Judah, it was under the control and influence of Assyria. The Israelites never considered Babylon a threat until the last years of Judah. God would allow Babylon to defeat Judah because of their sin.

God even used Israel and Judah against one another to soften their hearts. God was gracious in that He kept on trying to draw them back, over and over. Early in Rehoboam's reign, God allowed Egypt to attack Judah and carry off all the treasures in the temple and royal palace, but didn't allow them to destroy Judah because Rehoboam humbled himself and turned his heart back to God. Rehoboam died and his son Abijah became king of Judah (see Illustration 10). During Abijah's three-year reign he fought against Jeroboam's army of eight hundred thousand with an army half that size. God allowed Abijah and his small army to defeat Jeroboam because Abijah chose to trust God for the victory. When Abijah died his son Asa became king of Judah.

The land was in turmoil because God was troubling them with every kind of distress to draw them back to Himself. After a prophet encouraged King Asa to seek God, he commanded the people of Judah to seek God with all their heart and soul, and those who refused would be put to death. The people followed the example of Asa because he served God with a passion like David did. The male shrine prostitutes were expelled from the land, all the idols were destroyed and even Asa's grandmother lost her position as queen because she insisted on worshipping Asherah.

Because King Asa wholeheartedly committed himself to God all his life, the people did also. Even when the Cushites came up against Judah with a massive army, God gave Judah victory because they trusted Him for it. When the people of Israel saw how God had blessed Judah because of their faithfulness, several left Jeroboam and his man-made gods, and relocated to Judah with a determination to re-commit their hearts to God.

Asa had been king of Judah for two years when Jeroboam died and his son Nadab succeeded him. Jeroboam had reigned twenty-two years, but his son Nadab would reign only two because Baasha from the tribe of Issachar assassinated him and claimed the throne. Baasha was ruthless and after claiming the throne, killed Jeroboam's entire family. King Baasha also led Israel's army against Judah by piling stones and timber around the city of Ramah to prevent anyone from going in or out of Judah. Ramah was strategically located on a main artery leading in and out of Judah and it was enough to cause Asa's faith in God to waiver. Asa chose to trust an enemy to save him by paying Syria to distract the army of King Baasha. After Syria attacked and claimed several of Israel's cities, King Baasha and his army abandoned the siege at Ramah to defend themselves against Syria.

Now Asa had been king of Judah for more than thirty years when this happened, and obviously his view of God's power and grace had gotten clouded through the years of peace. God sent a prophet who told Asa that because he had chosen to put his trust in an enemy to save Judah, Judah would not be blessed with peace anymore. Asa was so angry with the message, he threw the prophet in prison.

God was also angry with Baasha for the evil he committed against the family of Jeroboam, and because he led the people to sin throughout his entire twenty-four-year reign. Before he died, God sent a prophet named Jehu to tell Baasha that his family was cursed because of his sin, and would be slaughtered as he did to Jeroboam's family. After he died, his son Elah was king for two years when one of his officials named Zimri assassinated him and killed Baasha's entire family. Zimri resided at the royal palace for only one week when Israel's army pursued him for what he had done, but rather than be captured, Zimri set fire to the palace and died in the fire.

Israel was split in that they had two candidates for the position of king, Tibni and Omri. It would be Omri who emerged as the next king of Israel, probably because he was the commander of Israel's army. During Omri's eight-year reign, he built a city on a hill that would become Israel's capital, and called it Samaria. He led God's people to sin just as Jeroboam did, and when he died, his son Ahab became the next king of Israel.

Three years after Ahab became king of Israel, Asa died, leaving the throne of Judah to his son Jehoshaphat. These two kings were absolute opposites in that Jehoshaphat led Judah towards God but Ahab led Israel away from God.

THE STAND-OFF
(1 Kings 16:29–19)

King Ahab married the daughter of a Sidonian king, and her name was Jezebel. In addition to worshipping the gods introduced by Jeroboam, he built a temple in Samaria for Israel to worship the Sidonian god Baal. Ahab also supported the effort by Hiel of Bethel to rebuild Jericho, the first city God destroyed for Israel when they came into the Promised Land. God honored the curse Joshua declared for anyone who would attempt to rebuild Jericho, which cost Hiel the lives of his oldest and youngest sons. Ahab did more to provoke God to anger than all the kings before him. Because Ahab led the ten tribes of Israel to trust in worthless gods, God revealed Himself to the people in a way that no one could deny Him.

God sent a prophet named Elijah to tell Ahab He was holding back the rain for the next few years, and it would only rain when He allowed it to. God knew Ahab and Jezebel would want to kill Elijah because of his message, so He instructed him to hide and sent ravens to bring him food. After some time when everyone was feeling the affects of the drought, God sent Elijah to stay with a widow in Zarephath. Even though she only had enough flour and oil for one more meal, she was willing to take Elijah into her home and God rewarded her for it. Throughout the entire drought she never ran out of flour or oil, but even more miraculously, when her son died God restored him back to life.

Ahab never stopped looking for Elijah and made every possible attempt to find him. There wasn't one neighboring nation that would even consider harboring him. As powerful as Ahab was and as hard as he tried, he could not find Elijah because it was God that had hidden him. Ahab had no sympathy for any of God's prophets and tolerated random mass killings of prophets by his wife Jezebel. The man in charge of Ahab's palace was Obadiah and despite the risk, remained faithful to Jehovah by hiding a hundred prophets in two caves. He continued to risk his life throughout the drought by providing them with food and water.

After three years of drought, God instructed Elijah to go present himself to Ahab and on his way, ran into Obadiah. Obadiah was delighted to see Elijah but when he asked Obadiah to tell Ahab he wanted to see him, Obadiah felt cursed. After all the risk he had taken to save God's prophets, there was no doubt in his mind Ahab would have him killed if Elijah disappeared again. Elijah gave him his word he would not disappear, so Obadiah brought his message to Ahab. When Ahab came to meet him, Elijah challenged him to prove who was more mighty, Baal or Jehovah.

The people of Israel gathered to watch the stand off as Jezebel's four hundred and fifty prophets of Baal and four hundred prophets of Asherah came to discredit Jehovah. A bull was sacrificed for Baal and placed on an altar. All morning the hundreds of prophets danced and called on Baal to consume their sacrifice with fire but nothing happened. By noon Elijah began to taunt them by suggesting they pray louder, perhaps Baal was sleeping or busy traveling. They shouted louder and began to shed their own blood by slashing themselves with swords and spears to invoke the power of Baal, but still nothing happened.

Elijah built an altar with stones, laid a sacrificed bull on it and instructed the people to pour twelve large jars of water over the sacrifice until it filled the trench around the altar. Elijah then called out to Jehovah to prove He was their God, the God of Abraham, Isaac, and Israel. Immediately, fire came down from heaven and consumed the sacrifice, the altar, the soil, and even licked up the water that was in the trench. With that Elijah told the people to seize Jezebel's prophets, and they took them to a valley and killed them. Elijah told Ahab to go home because it was going to rain, and it did.

When Ahab went home and told Jezebel everything that had happened, she was furious and vowed to kill Elijah. Elijah heard about Jezebel's threat and ran for his life into the desert, but then stopped and realized how pathetically he reacted. He felt horrible as well as tired and weak, and asked God to just let him die. He collapsed, but an angel woke him and gave him food and water. After he ate and drank he collapsed a second time, and again the angel brought him something to eat and drink. The food strengthened him and he got up and traveled for forty days and nights until he reached the mountain of God at Horeb.

While he was in a cave on the mountain, God told him a man named Hazael would become king of Syria, an Israelite named Jehu would become king of Israel, and a man named Elisha would become a prophet to eventually replace him. It was difficult for Elijah to think about the future or even hope for a future when all Israel had turned their backs to Jehovah. God tried to encourage Elijah by assuring him there was hope, because in all of the northern nation among the ten tribes of Israel, there were still seven thousand who had not prostituted themselves to other gods. Elijah went home strengthened and encouraged, and Elisha became his attendant.

ISRAEL INFECTS JUDAH
(1 Kings 20–2 Kings 1, 2 Chronicles 17–21)

Ben-Hadad, the current king of Syria, organized a coalition of thirty-two kings to attack Samaria. He took Ahab's wives, children, and treasures but Jezebel was not among them because she lived at the palace in Jezreel. When Ben-Hadad sent word to Ahab he was returning to plunder the homes of Israel's officials, the leaders and people of Israel told Ahab not to agree to his demands. It was an impossible situation, but God wanted to show them His mercy, so He sent a prophet to tell Ahab He would provide for them to defeat this army. With only seven thousand men, Israel successfully won the battle against the coalition in the hill country. The coalition was convinced they lost because Jehovah was a god of the hills, so they regrouped to attack them in the valley.

God sent the prophet back to tell Israel He would give them victory once more to prove He was not just a god of the hills. When it became evident to Ben-Hadad that he was defeated once more, he negotiated a treaty with Ahab by giving back the cities they took when Nadab was king of Israel. God was angry that Ahab spared the enemy instead of trusting Him for complete victory. The prophet told Ahab it would cost him his life for sparing Ben-Hadad's life, and his people for sparing their people. Ahab missed a tremendous opportunity to demonstrate to the people how they could trust

Jehovah. As a result, they experienced God's wrath instead of His grace.

Ahab proved over and over his inability to lead the people with integrity. There was a vineyard Ahab wanted next to his palace in Jezreel that belonged to a man named Naboth. Naboth refused to sell his vineyard under any circumstances, and it didn't matter who wanted to buy it. When Jezebel got tired of Ahab pouting over it, she took care of it by plotting to have Naboth falsely accused and stoned. Ahab was willing to spare the life of his enemy but allowed an innocent man to be intentionally killed just to have his garden.

There had never been anyone as despicable as Ahab, and God was angry with him. He sent Elijah to tell him that his family was cursed because of him and would be slaughtered like Baasha and Jeroboam's were. As for him and his wife Jezebel, not only would they be killed, but the dogs would lick up their blood. The prophetic words from Elijah were too much for Ahab and it humbled him tremendously. Because he humbled himself, God sent Elijah back to tell him the disaster to his family would not happen as long as he was alive.

Jehoshaphat, on the other hand, had a passion for God and by example led the people of Judah to know and trust Jehovah. He also sent officials throughout Judah to teach the people the Law of Moses. God was pleased with Jehoshaphat and blessed Judah by giving them favor with all the surrounding nations who honored Judah with extravagant gifts and tributes. Judah's wealth increased tremendously and was able to support an army of more than a million soldiers.

Jehoshaphat seemed to be doing everything right except he invited trouble when he allied himself with Israel through the marriage of his son Jehoram to Ahab's daughter. God was not pleased with this partnership because even though Israel and Judah were brothers, Jehoshaphat willingly embraced people who hated God. Ahab and Jehoshaphat collectively built a fleet of ships through this partnership but they never set sail. This partnership also led Jehoshaphat and his army into a battle with Israel against Syria. When a prophet of God warned them they would be defeated, Ahab threw the prophet in jail and they went out to fight Syria anyway. Jehoshaphat barely escaped with his life but Ahab was killed, leaving the throne of Israel to his son Ahaziah (see Illustration 10).

Some time later, the Moabites, Ammonites, and Meunites joined forces and came with a huge army to fight Judah. Jehoshaphat chose to trust Jehovah and called for all of Judah to fast and pray. God saw their hearts and instructed Judah to stand in the battlefield and just watch. The battle was not theirs to fight because Jehovah would fight the battle for them. The next day while Judah's army stood in the battlefield and sang praise to Jehovah, the enemy fought among themselves until they were destroyed. It was an amazing victory given to them by Jehovah's army, and all the nations feared Judah because of it.

Israel was being led by Ahab's son Ahaziah, who chose to put his trust in Baal instead of God. After he consulted Baal to determine his fate from an accident, Elijah sent word he would die in his bed because he put his trust in Baal. King Ahaziah became angry at Elijah's message and sent a troop of soldiers to arrest him, but fire came down from heaven and consumed them. The king sent another troop of soldiers and they too were consumed with fire. When the captain of the third troop asked Elijah for mercy, God told Elijah to go with them to King Ahaziah to confirm his fate. Ahaziah was king for only two years when he died and because he had no son, his brother Joram, who was Ahab's second son, became king of Israel.

Jehoshaphat also died after twenty-five years of reign, and his son Jehoram, who was still married to Ahab's daughter, became the next king of Judah. Israel's influence on Judah as a result of the partnership Jehoshaphat made with them was fatal. Johoram was not going to allow any of his brothers to take his throne as Ahaziah's brother did, so he killed them. He and his wife also introduced Judah to Israel's evil culture and idol worship.

God was angry and sent Elijah to tell King Johoram that because of all he had done, Judah and his family would all suffer, and he too would suffer from a horrible fatal disease. God allowed nations to rise up against him and they took Judah's treasures. They also killed all his wives and sons except for his youngest son Ahaziah. After ruling for only eight years he died from a disease, and his only son Ahaziah became king of Judah. There was no honor shown him at his funeral nor did anyone in all of Judah regret his death.

GOD SPEAKS CHANGE THROUGH ELISHA
(2 Kings 2–10, 2 Chronicles 22:1–22:9)

When Elijah knew his life on earth was over, he asked Elisha what he could do for him before he was taken away. Elisha asked for a double portion of his spirit and with that, a chariot and horses of fire separated them. Elijah dropped his cloak on the ground as he was taken up in a whirlwind. Elijah was gone and it was a stunning experience. When the reality set in that Elijah was not coming back, Elisha picked up Elijah's cloak and went on his way.

Incident after incident, Elisha began to realize God did bless him with a double portion of the spirit just as he had asked Elijah. When he came to a river, he struck the river with Elijah's cloak and it parted so he could cross over on dry ground. The drinking water at Jericho where Elisha was staying was bad but when Elisha threw salt in it, God healed it. When he was on his way to Bethel, he cursed some young kids who were harassing him and two bears came out of the woods and killed them.

Elisha used the double portion to serve God's people. When a widow told him a creditor was going to take her sons as slaves, he instructed her to collect as many jars as she could then take the little oil she had and pour it into the jars. She did what he told her to do and her small amount of oil didn't run out until she filled the last jar. She sold the oil, paid off the creditor and still had enough money to live on.

Another family who had opened their home to him while he traveled was blessed with a son after many years of not being able to have children. When the son died, Elisha prayed for him and as he lay over the boy, life slowly came back into his body. Elisha went to Gilgal where there was a famine and when the people cooked a pot of stew from poisonous vines, he was able to neutralize the poison by throwing flour in the stew. He also fed a hundred men with only twenty loaves of bread and still had bread left over. Elisha even performed miracles in what might be considered unimportant, like making an ax head float that was lost in a river.

Many were able to witness the power of God through the prophet Elisha, even the commander of Syria's army. Elisha told him his leprosy would be healed if he washed himself in the Jordan seven times. He was repulsed at the idea of washing in the Jordan because it was dirty water. But the commander of Syria's army humbled himself and did what Elisha instructed him to do, and he was healed of his leprosy.

God also used Elisha against the commander of Syria's army by warning Israel several times where Syria's army was located. It happened often enough that the king of Syria became convinced he had a traitor in his camp. When they discovered it was Elisha, the king of Syria ordered his commander to lead Syria's army out to capture him.

They surrounded the city where Elisha lived but he wasn't afraid because he could see the hills were filled with God's horses and chariots of fire. God blinded Syria's army, and Elisha led them away under the pretense of taking them to the man they were looking for. When God opened their eyes, they were in Samaria surrounded by Israel's army. Elisha ordered Israel not to kill them but to serve them a feast. After the feast, the Syrian troops returned home and stopped raiding Israel.

A short time later the king of Syria marched his entire army against Israel and lay siege to Samaria. The siege lasted so long the people ran out of food and resorted to cannibalism. The king blamed Jehovah for their problems and sent a messenger to kill Elisha, but Elisha informed the king they would have plenty of food by the next day. When God caused the Syrian army to hear chariots and horses, they abandoned the siege for fear it might be a hired army coming to kill them. What they left behind in their camp was more than enough to feed everyone living in Samaria.

Elisha went to Syria to see King Ben-Hadad who was ill, but was greeted by an official named Hazael instead, the very man Elijah prophesied would become king of Syria. After Hazael gave gifts to Elisha and asked if Ben-Hadad would recover from his illness, Elisha informed him that Ben-Hadad would die, then wept as he told Hazael he would become the next king of Syria and mercilessly kill the men, women, and children of Israel. Hazael listened in amazement then returned to King Ben-Hadad. After assuring King Ben-Hadad that he would recover, he smothered him in his bed then declared himself king of Syria.

Ahaziah was king of Judah but he was coached by his mother Athaliah, Ahab's daughter. Ahaziah not only united with Ahab's son Joram in Israel's battle against Hazael, he went to visit Joram at Jezreel where he was recuperating from a battle injury. While Joram was recuperating, Elisha remembered Elijah's prophesy about Jehu becoming king of Israel and sent a prophet to anoint Jehu. He also sent instructions for Jehu to kill all of Ahab's descendants in order to avenge the many servants and prophets that were killed by Jezebel.

The army accepted Jehu as king of Israel and followed him to Jezreel where he killed both King Joram of Israel and King Ahaziah of Judah. Jehu then led Israel's army to Jezebel's palace and at his command, her servants threw her out of a window and she died in the street. Everything God told Elijah He would do, He did.

SPIRALING OUT OF CONTROL
(2 Kings 11–16, 2 Chronicles 22:10–28)

When word reached Judah that Ahaziah had been killed, Athaliah quickly had all his children killed in order to claim the throne of Judah for herself. Yet, there was a baby named Joash the Levites were able to hide from Athaliah. While Athaliah was on her killing rampage in Judah, Jehu was in Israel killing all of Ahab's family and all the priests of Baal. Because Athaliah was in Judah, she was the only descendant of Ahab that Jehu did not kill. She ruled Judah for seven years in the wicked style of her father Ahab, but when Joash turned seven years old, Jehoiada the priest declared him king of Judah and Athaliah was put to death for treason.

Jehu was king of Israel and even though he discontinued the worship of Baal, they continued to worship the golden calves Jeroboam created. Israel seemed determined to prostitute themselves to worthless and powerless gods. During Jehu's twenty-eight-year reign, God slowly reduced the size of Israel by giving it over to King Hazael of Syria, bit by bit. When Jehu died, his son Jehoahaz succeeded him as king of Israel.

Jehoahaz also led Israel to worship the gods introduced by Jeroboam, and they continued to be severely oppressed by Syria. When it got bad enough for Jehoahaz to humble himself and cry out to Jehovah for help, God graciously provided deliverance. Despite God's deliverance, Jehoahaz never stopped worshipping powerless gods, and he died after ruling seventeen years. His son Jehoash became the next king of Israel and by now its army had been pathetically reduced to fifty horsemen, ten chariots, and ten thousand soldiers.

King Joash of Judah remained faithful to God and had been king for about thirty-seven years when Jehoash became king of Israel. King Joash not only led Judah towards God, but initiated the necessary work to repair the tabernacle. Yet after Jehoiada the priest died, so did Joash's loyalty to God. He was persuaded by the people to abandon worship at the tabernacle and allow them to worship Asherah poles and idols instead. God sent Jehoiada's son Zechariah to speak to King Joash and the people of Judah, but Joash ordered him stoned to death.

Within a year the army of Syria marched against Judah and Jerusalem, killing all the leaders, but King Joash refused to turn to Jehovah for help. Instead, King Joash stripped the tabernacle and palace of all its treasures and paid Syria to retreat. Even though King Joash had been severely wounded in the attack by Syria, the people of Judah conspired and killed him in his bed. He had been king of Judah for forty years, but now his son Amaziah would succeed him as king (see Illustration 10).

Jehoash had been king of Israel for about two years when Amaziah became king of Judah. One of the first things Amaziah did was execute those who assassinated his father Joash; then he drafted all the available young men for his army which totaled three hundred thousand. He also hired one hundred thousand soldiers from Israel to help fight against the Edomites, but a prophet told him to send them home because God would give him victory without them. Amaziah did as the prophet instructed and God gave them an amazing victory, but they sinned against God when they brought the gods of the Edomites home to worship them.

God was angry and sent a prophet to speak to Amaziah, but the king was too arrogant and proud over his victory to listen to the prophet. Instead, Amaziah challenged Israel to a battle because they had the audacity to be angry for not being allowed to fight with Judah. The king of Israel tried to talk Amaziah out of fighting with them, but he wouldn't listen. Amaziah went to battle against Israel but in the end, Judah was defeated. Amaziah was taken captive on the battlefield and they brought him back to Jerusalem to watch Israel tear down part of the wall and rob the tabernacle and palace of its few remaining treasures. Israel also took some of the people hostage to Samaria.

When King Jehoash died, his son Jeroboam II became king of Israel. Amaziah outlived Jehoash by fifteen years, but from the day he turned his heart away from God, the people of Judah conspired against him. He fled south to Lachish where he was assassinated and his son Uzziah was declared king of Judah.

Uzziah became king of Judah when he was sixteen and reigned for fifty-two years. Zechariah taught him to honor God and as long as he was faithful to lead the people to have faith in God, God gave him success. King Uzziah's fame spread throughout the country and many nations brought tribute to him. More than a quarter-million men were in Judah's army and they became a powerful nation once again.

Not so with Israel. Jeroboam II was the king of Israel and continued to lead the people into sin just as the first Jeroboam did. Even though Jeroboam II had several military accomplishments throughout his forty-one year reign, God was not with them. God was tired of the many years and generations of Israel that had prostituted themselves to trust false gods and idols. When he died, his son Zechariah succeeded him as king of Israel and reigned a mere six months. He was assassinated by a man named Shallum who would become Israel's next king.

Evil was raging in Israel and after one month, Shallum was also assassinated by Menahem who ruled ruthlessly for ten years. When the king of Assyria invaded them, Menahem taxed the people to pay Assyria thirty-seven tons of silver in order to keep his position as king of Israel. He led Israel to sin and when he died, his son Pekahiah succeeded him. Pekahiah was king for only two years when a man named Pekah assassinated him and became king of Israel.

Israel was in tremendous turmoil and getting weaker while Judah was getting stronger. King Uzziah had led Judah to trust Jehovah but the fame and power was getting the best of him. Out of pride, he decided to assume the priestly duties of offering incense to Jehovah and was enraged that the priests would dare challenge him. God ended the controversy by causing leprosy to break out on his forehead and he spent the rest of his days in solitude because of the leprosy. Uzziah died during Pekah's second year as king of Israel, and his son Jotham became the next king of Judah. Jotham led the people to honor God for sixteen years and when he died, his son Ahaz became the next king of Judah.

Pekah had been king of Israel for seventeen years when Ahaz became king of Judah. Israel as a nation was deteriorating because the king of Assyria was invading their territory over and over, and every invasion resulted in the deportation of citizens to Assyria. Even though Israel was deteriorating, God allowed Israel to partner with Syria against Judah because Ahaz was leading the people of Judah into terrible sin. He led them to worship the false gods and idols Israel had worshipped, even to the extent of burning his sons in fire to honor the false gods.

When Israel and Syria came to war against Judah, Ahaz turned to Assyria for help instead of Jehovah. After Judah was saved by the Assyrian army, Ahaz went to Damascus to express his gratitude to the king of Assyria and returned with orders that the altar used to honor Jehovah be moved to the side in order to make room for an altar that would honor the Assyrian god.

Because Ahaz was leading the people to sin, God tried to turn the people's hearts back to Himself by allowing the Philistines to raid the perimeters of Judah. Ahaz still refused to put his trust in God and went to Assyria for assistance again, but they refused to help. He tried to bribe the king of Assyria with gifts, but they still refused to help. Ahaz knew his problems were because of Jehovah so he set up altars to false gods on every street corner in Jerusalem and closed the tabernacle.

Ahaz had been king for twelve years when Pekah was killed. He was assassinated by Hoshea who became the next king of Israel, and would be the last king of Israel. Israel had turned their back on God too many times, and now God would finally turn His back to them. Ahaz was leading Judah down the same deadly path Israel had taken, the path that would lead them away from Jehovah. He was king of Judah for sixteen years and when he died, his son Hezekiah became king.

Pleading Through Prophets
(Isaiah, Hosea, Joel, Amos, Jonah, Micah, Nahum, Zephaniah)

Despite Israel's persistent worship of idols and false gods, God's grace was amazing and He often reached out to them by sending prophets to warn about the destructive path they were on. God used a prophet named Hosea to emphasize to Israel they had prostituted themselves to worthless gods and filled the land with the vilest adultery.

God asked Hosea to marry a prostitute so he could understand in his heart what it meant to God when Israel prostituted themselves to idols and false gods. Hosea willingly married a prostitute and she gave Hosea three children. Hosea's wife was not faithful to him and as difficult as it was, Hosea returned her unfaithfulness with love. When Hosea warned Israel about their lack of faithfulness to God, he truly spoke with conviction from his heart. He tried to tell them that God would not show mercy for their unfaithfulness forever. Just as Hosea dearly loved his wife but hated her unfaithfulness, he tried hard to express God's love for them, and His incredible desire for them to return to Him with their hearts.

God sent a prophet named Amos to help them understand what it meant to turn their backs to Him and His laws. Amos was not a timid prophet, but strong like a lion; he relayed to Israel how detestable their sins were to God. He accused them of using bribes to deprive justice, selling out the needy people for their own gain, trampling on the heads of poor people, denying justice to the oppressed, sharing the same woman between a father and son, profaning God's holy name, and so on. Amos warned them that their life style contradicted God's covenant so much that their nation was as good as dead already. Despite all this, Amos pleaded with them that God's mercy and love for them was beyond what they could understand and if they humbled themselves and turned from their sin, He would forgive them and heal their corrupted nation. Yet the people refused to listen and like sheep, followed their leaders into sin.

God had a plan and He kept his eye not only on His chosen people, but on the other nations that He would use to accomplish His plan. He sent a prophet named Jonah to speak to the Assyrian people of Nineveh because of their extreme wickedness. Jonah resisted this calling because after all, they were the enemy, a pagan people he felt were beyond hope. Yet, after God miraculously saved him from the belly of a whale, he decided to go to Nineveh as God asked. To his surprise, the people overwhelmingly humbled themselves and were not destroyed by their wickedness.

God also sent prophets to the people of Judah to try and turn their hearts so they didn't get lost down the same road Israel had taken. Through a prophet named Joel, God pleaded with Judah to humble themselves and confess their sins because they were in danger of the plague of destruction. Joel described this plague as a destruction that impacts not just them but His whole creation. Judah had seen God pour out His vengeance many times on their enemies, and Joel warned Judah they were not exempt from God's vengeance. He pleaded with them to repent and return to God, promising that God had a plan, a plan for salvation.

The prophet Micah primarily spoke to the people of Judah but some of his messages were also directed to the people of Israel. Either way, his messages rebuked the rich for how unfairly they treated the poor and how they manipulated the weak to increase their own wealth. He warned them that their obligation to the covenant was much more than just offering sacrifices to God, they had to live it. Micah prophesied they would eventually face God's judgment, but also promised that in the end, God would save a remnant to accomplish His plan. The prophets Nahum and Zephaniah also had similar messages for the people of Judah.

Another prophet was Isaiah who had a magnificent vision of God on His throne in all His glory. God told Isaiah His chosen people heard but didn't understand, and could see but they could not perceive. God opened Isaiah's eyes to see Judah's sin and he anxiously volunteered to speak to the people of Judah about their sinful rebellious hearts that prevented them from hearing God. Isaiah accused Judah of being evil, defiant, and corrupt people who talked religion but didn't live it. Isaiah had many harsh words for the people of Judah but also emphasized God's desire to save them from the darkness they were walking in.

In many ways God tried to reveal His plan for sending a Savior to redeem them, a Messiah that would save the world. It was a promise God made to Abraham, Isaac, and Jacob, something God had planned from the beginning of time. Satan wanted to rule the world through his kingdom of darkness, but Isaiah told the people that God was going to send a light into the world to draw people out of that darkness.

God began to reveal more and more of His plan to the people. Isaiah told them a virgin would give birth to a child and He would be called Wonderful Counselor, Mighty God, Everlasting Father and Prince of Peace. This child would reign on David's throne and establish justice and righteousness forever, not just for them but for all of God's creation. The Spirit of God would give Him wisdom, understanding, and knowledge, and He would wear righteousness like a belt and faithfulness like a sash around His waist. He would open the eyes of the blind, free captives from prison, and release those who sit in darkness.

God also revealed that they would slaughter the Messiah like a lamb, but He would willingly be led to the slaughter to suffer the punishment for sin. The Messiah would be the perfect sacrifice, and by shedding His blood would pay the price required to redeem the world from sin.

God promised He would redeem them, that deep waters would not sweep over them, nor would fires consume them because they were precious to Him and He loved them. In the end He would gather them from every corner of the earth and bring them back because they were created for His glory, and through them the Messiah would come.

God knew this was a difficult thing for them to grasp because their entire religion was centered on atoning their sin through the sacrifice of a lamb, a system not offered to the Gentile world. The descendants of Israel were the people God had chosen out of all the nations on the earth and blessed them, but God's intent was to bless the whole world through them. God told them His thoughts are higher than their thoughts just as the heavens are higher than the earth.

Despite what they thought or did, whether they turned their hearts back to Him or chose to follow the path Israel walked, He would accomplish what He has desired to do since before the beginning of creation. Redemption will come to both Israel and Gentiles alike, to any and all who look to the Messiah and repent of their sins.

Chapter 9

A NATION FALLEN

(2 Kings 17–20, 2 Chronicles 29–32)

Hoshea was king of Israel and like kings before him, chose not to listen to the prophets. He discontinued paying his annual tribute to the Assyrians and conspired with Egypt against Assyria. When the king of Assyria discovered he was a traitor, he had King Hoshea arrested and thrown into prison. There wasn't a bit of land left in Israel that the Assyrians hadn't marched on and their final conquest was to take Israel's capital, the city of Samaria. All the Israelites remaining from the eleven tribes of Israel were deported and dispersed among the Assyrian towns in central Asia, and the nation of Israel was no more.

After more than two hundred years of worshipping golden calves, Asherah poles, stars, and Baal, after sacrificing sons and daughters in fire, practicing divination, fortune telling, and witchcraft, turning their backs on widows and the needy, denying justice and all the other countless evil they did, God could no longer bless them but let them go. God had entrusted His people, eleven tribes of Israel, into the hands of their first king Jeroboam who willfully and intentionally led them astray, away from Jehovah. No one except Ahab sinned more than Jeroboam, because he set a fatal course for Israel and an evil standard for every king after him.

Hezekiah became king of Judah three years after Hoshea had become king of Israel. He watched from his royal position in Judah as Assyria broke down the nation of Israel and carried away all their brothers. Perhaps it had an impact on Hezekiah because he trusted God with all his heart like David did, and there were no kings of Judah either before him or after that were more faithful to God's commands and laws than Hezekiah. The first thing he did was open the temple to reestablish worship to Jehovah. Hezekiah ordered the Levites to consecrate themselves, remove any unclean thing from the temple, then repair and re-consecrate the temple. He also had all the places of worship on the hills removed, the sacred stones smashed, and Asherah poles cut down. He even broke the bronze snake Moses had made because the people were burning incense to honor it.

When the temple repairs were completed and it was time to rededicate the temple, the people brought so many sacrifices that the priests had to look to their fellow Levites for help. Hezekiah also sent word to people far and near that they were going to celebrate the Passover. The response was phenomenal and Jerusalem was filled with people who came with thousands of offerings, singing shouts of praise to Jehovah. The celebration was so wonderful that Hezekiah extended it for another week and almost twenty thousand more offerings were sacrificed to Jehovah. When it was over, the people went home and destroyed all the sacred stones, Asherah poles, and altars with a passion. All of Judah followed Hezekiah's lead and wholeheartedly committed themselves to Jehovah. God provided for Hezekiah to prosper in everything he did because of his faithfulness.

It was customary to pay tribute to the strong world powers, but Hezekiah had refused to pay any tribute. The king of Assyria was pressuring him to pay tribute by attacking and capturing several cities within Judah. After the attacks, Hezekiah humbled himself to the king of Assyria and paid him eleven tons of silver and one ton of gold. He had to strip the temple walls and doors of all its gold and empty the treasuries of all their silver to make the payment. It wasn't enough for the king of Assyria and they camped outside Jerusalem and tormented the people of Judah with insults against Jehovah.

Hezekiah went to the temple and cried out to God for help. God answered him through the prophet Isaiah saying, Assyria would not shoot even one arrow in the city nor build a siege ramp against it. God Himself would defend Jerusalem and save it. That night the angel of God went among the Assyrian camp and by morning one hundred eighty-five thousand soldiers were dead. The Assyrians retreated and while the king of Assyria was worshipping in the temple of his god Nisroch, his own sons assassinated him.

Shortly after this, Hezekiah became ill and called out to God for mercy when he realized he was dying. God sent Isaiah to tell Hezekiah He would heal him and give him fifteen more years. Meanwhile, the king of Babylon sent messengers to Judah with a letter and gifts because he had heard Hezekiah was ill. Babylon was just another small nation and certainly not considered a threat to Judah, so Hezekiah proudly gave the messengers a tour of his kingdom showing them every treasure Judah had.

When Isaiah learned what Hezekiah had done, he knew in his heart that just as Israel had crumbled under Assyria, Judah would crumble at the hands of Babylon. Even though he revealed this to Hezekiah, Hezekiah didn't show concern because it would not happen in his time, but rather in the days of his sons. Hezekiah did live for another fifteen years and when he died, his son Manasseh became king of Judah.

LIMPING TO THE END
(2 Kings 21–24, 2 Chronicles 33–36:11, Jeremiah, Zephaniah, Habakkuk and Ezekiel)

Manasseh was twelve years old when he became king of Judah, and the reality of Israel's sin and fall to Assyria was just a history story to him that happened fourteen years before he was born. Manasseh had no fear of God and erected altars and poles within the temple of God to reestablish worship to Baal and Asherah. He worshipped the stars, practiced sorcery and divination, consulted mediums and spiritists, sacrificed his children in fire, and shed so much innocent blood it filled Jerusalem from end to end. The people of Judah followed his lead into sin so God sent prophets to say He was going to bring disaster on Judah just like He did Israel, and they would be looted and plundered by their enemies.

The warnings from the prophets were ignored so God invoked Assyria against Judah who bound Manasseh with bronze shackles, put a hook in his nose, and took him prisoner. In his distress, he truly humbled himself and called out to God for help. When God showed mercy by bringing him back to Jerusalem and restoring his kingdom, it convinced Manasseh of God's power and strength and he reversed everything he had done. Yet, he had set a precedent for the people to worship on the hill tops that he was never able to reverse. Manasseh reigned for fifty-five years and when he died, his son Amon became king of Judah (see Illustration 10).

Amon was twenty-two years old and didn't agree with his father's conversion to Jehovah, and led the people of Judah back into sin. He reigned only two years when his officials assassinated him. The people of the land killed his assassinators and declared his son Josiah king of Judah, even though he was only eight years old. Josiah did what he thought was right in the eyes of God and eighteen years into his reign a book containing the Law of Moses was found in the temple walls during restoration efforts. After reading the book, Josiah realized the magnitude of their sin and how far they had wandered away from the covenant their fathers made with God. He was humbled and feared God's wrath towards the people of Judah because they had certainly sinned grievously.

God sent a prophetess named Huldah to confirm that the disaster Josiah suspected would in fact come to Judah, but because Josiah had humbled himself before God, the disaster would not come in his days. Josiah called all the elders and people together and read the entire book to the people at the temple. Josiah made a commitment to follow all the decrees and laws with his whole heart, and the people followed his lead by also pledging themselves to the covenant.

Once more, everything pertaining to worship of the stars, Baal, or Asherah was removed from the temple and destroyed, and worship on the hills was discontinued. Quarters for the male shrine prostitutes had been established in the temple of God and these were also eliminated. The altars used to sacrifice their sons and daughters were destroyed and the chariots dedicated to the sun were burned. A death sentence was proclaimed for any priest that served false gods or idols.

Josiah ordered a celebration for the Passover, which could not have been equaled since the early days when Israel entered the Promised Land. Josiah turned to the Lord with all his heart, soul, and strength as commanded in the Law of Moses like no other king had. He reigned thirty-one years then was killed in a battle against Egypt. When he died, a prophet named Jeremiah wrote poetry to lament his death, and through the years it became a tradition among the people of Judah to sing these laments to commemorate Josiah. His son Jehoahaz succeeded him as king of Judah.

Even though Jehoahaz was king for only three months, he led the people of Judah back into sin. He was captured by Pharaoh on the battlefield, put in chains and brought to Egypt where he died. Pharaoh declared his brother Jehoiakim king of Judah and demanded a tribute of almost four tons of silver and seventy-five pounds of gold. Jehoiakim was king of Judah for eleven years and led the people down the same road Israel had taken.

God sent a prophet to say He was going to destroy Judah and Jerusalem, leaving them desolate and deserted, but would spare them if they repented. Jehoiakim tried to kill the prophet for his message but he escaped to Egypt, only to be killed later after they hunted him down. Another prophet called Jeremiah brought the same message and the priests and officials wanted to kill him too, but his life was spared because one temple official named Ahikam supported him.

God instructed Jeremiah to write all the words he had prophesied on a scroll so the people would have an opportunity to read the words and perhaps turn from their wicked ways. Jeremiah dictated everything to a scribe named Baruch, and sent him to the temple to read the scroll to the people. Word about Jeremiah's writings spread quickly and royal officials took possession of the scroll, read it, and decided to show it to King Jehoiakim.

Jehoiakim had been king for four years by now, and not only arrogantly burned the scroll, but demanded Jeremiah and his scribe be arrested. God hid them so they couldn't be arrested and instructed Jeremiah to write the words again, but this time he was to be specific. It would be the Babylonians that would destroy Judah.

It was during Jehoiakim's reign that the world power shifted from Egypt to Babylon, and Jehoiakim was now required to pay his tribute to Nebuchadnezzar, king of Babylon instead of Egypt. Jehoiakim decided to quit paying tribute to Babylon in his last three years as king, so King Nebuchadnezzar had him bound with bronze shackles and brought to Babylon. While in Jerusalem, King Nebuchadnezzar helped himself to some of Judah's temple treasures as payment for Judah's tribute.

Jehoiakim's son Jehoiachin was an evil man who took over the role as king of Judah. He had only been king for a mere three months when King Nebuchadnezzar marched against Judah again, and took him along with his mother, his wives, and children to Babylon. All his officials, Judah's army, the young educated men, the blacksmiths and any people trained in a craft were brought to Babylon. Nebuchadnezzar left only the common and poorest people in the land, and declared Josiah's son Zedekiah king of Judah.

Zedekiah, like Josiah's other sons, led the people who remained in Judah into sin. During his eleven-year reign, even the priests followed his lead. God sent another prophet named Zephaniah, who was appalled when he saw the travesties that had been done in the temple. Zephaniah condemned their sin and warned about the day of destruction that God would bring upon them. Even though he condemned them, he also encouraged them with the hope that in the end, God would remove their shame and bring them home with honor.

Habakkuk was another prophet who recognized the evil that prevailed among the people of Judah and continually prayed for them before God. He was stunned when God informed him that He was going to use the Babylonians against Judah. He couldn't believe God would use such an evil nation to punish them because for sure, Judah was more righteous than the Babylonians. God helped Habakkuk to understand that it wasn't about who was more righteous. The righteous live by faith and Judah had put their faith in useless false gods and idols. Habakkuk knew more than anything that God was a God above all gods. No matter what God might allow to happen to the people of Judah, he would always rejoice and remain faithful to Jehovah.

Zedekiah had been king of Judah for five years when God tried to plead with the few people that had been exiled to Babylon. This time it would be through a prophet named Ezekiel. When God opened his eyes to the immensity of their horrible, sinful lifestyles and their stubbornness towards God, Ezekiel sat by a river for a week in a state of being overwhelmed. God strengthened and encouraged Ezekiel to speak to the people, whether they chose to listen or not. Not all the money in Judah could save them from God's sword, and his sword would be Babylon. God pleaded with them through Ezekiel, saying He has no pleasure in the death of the wicked, but would rather have them turn from their evil ways and live.

Over and over God pleaded with them through Ezekiel, acknowledging they were like sheep with bad shepherds. God promised that one day He would seek them out from every place they had been scattered, and bring them back to Zion. He would give them a shepherd who would lead them in righteousness forever.

God declared they were His sheep, His people, and He was their God. One day there would be a new Jerusalem, and every nation would come to understand that the God of Israel is holy and His sanctuary would be among them forever.

ANOTHER NATION FALLEN
(2 Kings 25, 2 Chronicles 36:12–36:23, Jeremiah and Obadiah)

The battle Satan waged against God's people was coming to a climax. The people were confused with false prophets who took advantage of the opportunities to tell leaders and officials what they wanted to hear. Despite what they were saying, Jeremiah boldly contradicted them with a message not only for Judah but also for the kings of Edom, Moab, Ammon, Tyre, and Sidon. He informed them that God would hand their nations over to His servant Nebuchadnezzar, but God would allow them to remain in their countries if they willingly subjected themselves to Babylon. If they refused to yield to Babylon, God would punish them by the sword, famine, and plagues.

Jeremiah warned King Zedekiah not to listen to the prophets who told him what he wanted to hear. Especially those who said Babylon would let the people in captivity come home with the temple treasures. A false prophet named Hananiah challenged Jeremiah saying that God was going to break Nebuchadnezzar's hold on all the nations within two years. Jeremiah told him he would die within the year because he was advocating rebellion against God; seven months later he died.

Jeremiah even sent letters to the people held captive in Babylon telling them to build homes and make the best of it because they would be there for seventy years. No one would listen to Jeremiah: not the people, not the officials of Judah and certainly not King

Zedekiah. Yet, Zedekiah did send word to Jeremiah, asking him to pray for Judah when Egypt indicated they would support Judah against Babylon. Jeremiah sent back a harsh message from God saying Egypt would return home and Babylon would prevail over Judah. Jeremiah said that even if Judah destroyed Babylon's entire army, their wounded would burn the city of Jerusalem.

Shortly after, Jeremiah was arrested as a deserter when he left for the territory of Benjamin to claim a share of property that belonged to him. Despite his arguments, he was beaten and thrown into a vaulted cell in the prison dungeon. He had been there for a long time when Zedekiah brought him out to secretly ask if there was any word from God. Even though Jeremiah's response was still firm about all he had prophesied, Zedekiah ordered Jeremiah be confined to the prison courtyard instead of the dungeon.

Even from the prison courtyard, Jeremiah continued to tell the people they should surrender to the Babylonians and live, rather than rebel and die by the sword, famine, or plagues. Officials reported this to the king, suggesting Jeremiah be sentenced to death because he was discouraging the people as well as the few soldiers left in Jerusalem. The king allowed them to do what they wanted with Jeremiah so they lowered him into a deep, dark, muddy well in the middle of the prison courtyard, where no one could hear him.

An official from the palace heard what they had done to Jeremiah and convinced the king to have him taken out of the well. The official was deeply concerned for the now weak and frail Jeremiah, and lowered rags to pad his armpits so the ropes wouldn't hurt him as they pulled him up. He was still confined to the prison courtyard, but it was a blessing compared to the wet mud in the cold, dark well.

Zedekiah refused to listen to Jeremiah and his despairing prophesies, but chose to rebel against King Nebuchadnezzar instead. Babylon responded by marching their entire army to Jerusalem and kept it under siege by camping around the city. After six months, food was scarce and Jeremiah's prophesy about suffering by the sword, famine, and plagues was unfolding before their eyes. Neither the leaders nor the people wanted to hear from Jeremiah anymore, but the king did and had him secretly brought to him from the prison courtyard one more time. Jeremiah pleaded with the king to surrender to Babylon in order to save himself and Jerusalem, warning if he didn't they would take him prisoner and burn the city. Zedekiah again rejected what Jeremiah said and returned him to the prison courtyard.

Everyone in the city was affected by the famine, and nations who were friends of Judah turned their backs to them. God stirred the heart of a prophet named Obadiah who cursed Edom because they willingly abandoned Judah in the face of the enemy. God was angry with Judah but He still loved them. God tried to encourage them through Jeremiah by assuring the people He would bring them back and make them prosper. He would make Judah and the servants of Levi as countless as the stars in the sky, and as vast as the sand on the seashore. God absolutely would accomplish His plan for salvation, and the Messiah would come from David's descendants and reign forever. The people didn't want to hear it; they were too consumed with just surviving each day.

Zedekiah had been king for eleven years but it was time to abandon Judah because the famine in the city had become just too severe. The few soldiers that remained in Judah's army broke through the wall and escaped with King Zedekiah in the night, but they weren't able to escape the army of Babylon and were captured. Zedekiah watched as his sons were killed one by one, then they put out his eyes, bound him in bronze shackles and took him to Babylon where he remained a prisoner until he died.

The magnificent temple built by Solomon was being invaded by Nebuchadnezzar's army. They broke the huge tall bronze pillars at the entrance in order to carry off all the bronze, including the bronze sea and its bull-shaped stands. They took the pots, shovels, wick trimmers, sprinkling bowls, dishes, and all the articles made of precious metals that were used in the temple service. After stripping the temple of all its valuables, they burned it.

They also looted the king's palace and burned it as well, and all the large homes within Jerusalem. Before leaving the city, they tore down the walls that had protected Jerusalem, then gathered and executed the commander, the chief officer, royal advisors, leaders, and priests. The seven hundred and forty-five people that survived Babylon's sword that day lived only to see the beautiful city of Jerusalem destroyed, then were taken to Babylon. Jerusalem was the capital of Judah and had been the pride of all Israel. But, Judah chose to follow their leaders into sin just as Israel did, and the nation of Judah was no more.

Chapter 10

LIFE IN EXILE

(Jeremiah, Lamentations, Daniel)

All those that had been captured were bound in chains and taken to Babylon, leaving only a few of the poor in Judah. Before they had left the borders of Judah, the commander of the imperial guard discovered Jeremiah was among the prisoners and released him. Jeremiah was allowed to go wherever he pleased and found a handful of soldiers and some people from Judah that had scattered in their escape from the Babylonians. Wanting to flee to Egypt to get beyond the reach of the Babylonians, they decided to ask Jeremiah to seek God to determine if this was the right thing to do before they left. They assured Jeremiah they would do whatever God wanted.

After Jeremiah sought God for them, he advised them to stay in Judah where Jehovah would protect and flourish them. They rejected Jeremiah's advice, and accused him of being a traitor by conspiring with the Babylonians. Once more they refused to trust the

God of their fathers and fled to Egypt out of fear. Despite all their worship and commitment to false gods, there was none that could save them from the fate of death awaiting them in Egypt. Jeremiah was faithful to serve God's people even to following them to their fate, and expressed his grief by writing poetry that lamented Jerusalem, once a queen but now a slave.

Of those taken prisoner to Babylon, most of the officers and leaders were executed, the educated and skilled people were taken to the royal palace to serve the king, and the common people were permitted to live freely in the city. They lived among people who had also been exiled from other nations that Babylon had conquered, and because they had come from the land of Judah, they became known throughout the land as Jews.

Among the few that were taken to the royal palace was Daniel and three others whose names were changed to Shadrach, Meshach, and Abednego. They would receive three years of intense training in the Babylonian language and literature, for the sole purpose of being assigned to serve the king. They were given food and wine every day from the king's table, but Daniel and his three friends refused to be defiled by eating their food. God gave them favor with the royal guards who agreed to test their vegetarian diet for ten days. When they ended up looking much healthier and nourished than the ones eating the royal food, the royal guards put all the men on Daniel's vegetarian diet. When the three years of training were finished, Nebuchadnezzar found Daniel, Shadrach, Meshach, and Abednego to have ten times the wisdom and understanding of all the wise men and magicians in his kingdom.

Early in his reign, King Nebuchadnezzar had a dream about a statue with a head made of gold, arms and chest of silver, belly and thighs of bronze, legs of iron and the feet a mixture of iron and clay. A rock cut out by non-human hands was hurled at the statue causing it to crumble and blow away like dust, but the rock remained and became a huge mountain that filled the whole earth.

The king was so traumatized by the dream that he searched throughout all of Babylon to find a wise man or magician who could not only interpret what it meant, but first tell him what his dream was.

When no one could be found to do what the king asked, God enabled Daniel to describe the king's dream in detail and explain what it meant. Babylon was the golden head that would eventually fall to a stronger empire represented by silver, which would fall to a stronger empire represented by bronze, which would fall by yet another represented by iron, which would become weak as represented by the mixture of clay and iron. Ultimately, the kingdom of God, as represented by the rock, would prevail forever.

It would take more than six hundred years for time to reveal these subsequent kingdoms as the Persian, Greek, and Roman Empires, but for the moment King Nebuchadnezzar was so pleased to understand his dream that he assigned Daniel to the third highest position in all his kingdom. At Daniel's request, King Nebuchadnezzar also made his three friends Shadrach, Meshach, and Abednego administrators over the province of Babylon.

Shadrach, Meshach, and Abednego attended a ceremony where a ninety-foot-high gold statue of King Nebuchadnezzar was unveiled. When they refused to bow down and worship it, the king didn't care that they were friends of Daniel and threatened to throw them into a furnace. They were sure God would save them, but vowed that whether God was willing to save them or not, they would not worship anyone or anything except Jehovah. King Nebuchadnezzar was so annoyed at their arrogance that he ordered the furnace be heated seven times hotter than usual. Even the men that bound the three and threw them into the furnace died from the heat.

To the king's amazement, he saw four men walking around in the furnace and one of them looked like a god. The king called for them to come out, and Shadrach, Meshach, and Abednego came out unscathed, without even so much as a singed hair or the smell of fire on them. King Nebuchadnezzar was so amazed that any god could save anyone from the fiery furnace, that he felt compelled to declare severe penalties for anyone in his kingdom who spoke anything against the God of Shadrach, Meshach, and Abednego.

Daniel and his three friends served King Nebuchadnezzar for more than thirty years. When King Nebuchadnezzar died, his evil son Merodach became king of Babylon (see Illustration 11). He ruled for less than two years, then Neriglissar ruled for less than three years, then Labashi-Marduck for less than one year. Nabonidus became king of Babylon and reigned for sixteen years, but left his son Belshazzar in charge for the last ten while he lived in the desert south of Babylon.

When Darius the Mede marched into Babylon and took over the Babylonian kingdom, Belshazzar was killed. Darius ruled for two years on behalf of Cyrus, the king of Persia. He organized this newly acquired kingdom by appointing one hundred and twenty men to govern the districts throughout the kingdom, and made them accountable to three administrators, one of whom was Daniel.

Despite any of the honored positions Daniel had been given throughout his fifty years, he always prayed three times a day. He would kneel and pray from a window facing the direction of Jerusalem, hoping Jehovah would hear his prayer from the land of Judah. Daniel had heard what God spoke through Jeremiah about them being in exile for seventy years, but he also remembered what Moses had written about God's mercy if they would humble themselves and pray. So Daniel faithfully and earnestly prayed every day for God's mercy, repenting on behalf of the people over and over, always acknowledging God's righteousness. He knew Judah deserved to be exiled, but he pleaded with God not because of Judah's righteousness, but because he knew God was a God of mercy.

Daniel was relentless in his prayers and faithfulness to God, and it was because of his faithfulness that God blessed him and distinguished him above all the leaders. But when rumors circulated among the governors and administrators that Darius planned to appoint Daniel ruler over the entire kingdom, they became jealous and conspired to destroy him. The governors and administrators knew Daniel's habit of praying every day without exception. They convinced Darius that Babylon should honor him with worship for thirty days, and anyone who willfully prayed to any god during that period should be thrown into the lions den.

Even after Darius put the decree in writing, Daniel didn't hide his prayers, but continued to pray to Jehovah through his window so Jehovah would hear him. He was arrested immediately and thrown into the lions den. Darius realized he had been used by a few for their own selfish gain, but couldn't help Daniel because Daniel had broken a law that he himself had signed. Through the night Darius couldn't eat or sleep for worrying, hoping that the God Daniel was so committed to would somehow rescue him. At daybreak, Darius ordered the cover removed from the lions den and found Daniel still alive without even a scratch. After pulling him out, Darius ordered Daniel's accusers and their families be thrown into the lions den.

As Daniel continued to pray and intercede for the people that they might return home and rebuild Jerusalem, his desire was not embraced by all. It was a new generation now called Jews, who were financially established and flourishing in the country they considered home.

GOING HOME
(Ezra 1–6, Haggai, Zechariah)

It had been almost two years since Darius marched the Persian army into Babylon, but now Cyrus had arrived to take his place as their new king (see Illustration 12). God allowed this Persian king to rise in power because it was time for the children of Israel to return home. The people willingly embraced the Persian Empire and King Cyrus as a welcome replacement to the unstable leadership they had been under after the death of King Nebuchadnezzar. One of the first things Cyrus did was announce to the Jews they could go back to their beloved land of Judah, back to Jerusalem to rebuild their temple. At last they were allowed their freedom, but because many of the Jews had established successful businesses in Babylon, less than fifty thousand chose to go home.

It was the intent of King Cyrus that the Jews' return was for the purpose of rebuilding the temple for the God of Israel, the God who was in Jerusalem. Cyrus ordered all the Jews in Babylon to provide silver, gold, goods, and livestock for the rebuilding of the temple. While few were willing to go back, many were willing to make donations and a total of eleven hundred pounds of gold and three tons of silver were donated for the rebuilding of the temple. For those willing to go back to Judah, Cyrus also gave them more than five thousand gold and silver articles that had been taken from the temple by Nebuchadnezzar's army.

Going home was an historic event, and they were led by Jeshua the priest and his associate Zerubbabel. At first, everyone went to their home towns, but after seven months they all gathered at Jerusalem where Jeshua and Zerubbabel had built an altar to God. Even though they celebrated the Feast of Tabernacles with burnt offerings and freewill offerings to the Lord, it was kind of sad because the temple had been completely destroyed, even down to its foundation. They hired masons and carpenters, then contracted Sidon and Tyre to bring cedar logs by sea. After two years when they completed the foundation, there were shouts of joy and celebration, but there was also the sound of weeping. For those old enough to remember, there were tears for the temple that once was the pride of Jerusalem and all of Judah.

The people living in the communities surrounding Judah weren't happy that the Jews had returned, and desperately tried to discourage the rebuilding efforts. King Cyrus had died so they sent a letter to his son the new king, hoping they could convince him to stop the rebuilding in Jerusalem. Their letter accused the Jews of being rebellious people and given the chance, they would rebel against the Persian Empire. Their recommendation of course was to stop any rebuilding efforts in Jerusalem to minimize their strength. The king had his advisors research their accusations against the Jews and history confirmed it: the Jews had rebelled against Babylon. The king responded with a letter that demanded the Jews cease all rebuilding in Jerusalem, and the work on the temple stopped.

In the absence of pressure to get the temple rebuilt, for more than fifteen years the people were content to work on building themselves fine homes instead. Eventually, God sent a prophet named Haggai to scold them for being content to live in their fine homes while God's house remained in ruins. There was no denying what they had done was wrong and the people felt ashamed. Their hearts were so stirred by God with a passion to finish the temple, they resumed the rebuilding efforts despite the opposition from their enemies. Haggai continued to encourage them and reassured them that the new temple would be filled with a greater glory than was seen in the old temple.

Because of their obedience, God blessed them even through their enemies. Cyrus' son who demanded the rebuilding be stopped had died, and his son Darius was now king of Persia. King Darius also did his own review of the historical records and discovered his grandfather Cyrus was not only generous to the Jews in allowing them to go home, but had encouraged them to rebuild the temple. King Darius decided to be equally as generous and commanded Judah's accusers, who caused the rebuilding to be stopped, provide whatever was needed by the Jews to finish rebuilding the temple. In only four years the temple was completed.

God also sent the prophet Zechariah to speak to the people in Judah. His message from God wasn't so much like other prophets who tried to turn them from their evil ways back to God, rather he spoke mostly about future events. Even though Zechariah assured them that their towns would again overflow with prosperity, they needed to give true and sound judgments in their courts and not plot evil against one another. Zechariah told them marvelous things like someday, many powerful nations would come to Jerusalem seeking their God. He also said people of different languages and nations would be so desperate to know their God that ten men would grab hold of the robe of one Jew just because they knew God was with him.

Even though the people were back home, they were still under the rule and thumb of Persia. But, Zechariah promised that God would send them a king who would be righteous and bring them salvation. This king would be gentle and come riding on the foal of a donkey. He would be from the descendants of Judah, and even though they were no longer a nation now, this king would rule from sea to sea and even to the ends of the earth. They didn't know when God would send this king, but it would be about five hundred years before the time would be right for the Messiah to come.

But for now their king was Darius and he reigned for thirty-seven years. When he died, Xerxes, also known as Ahasuerus, succeeded him as king of Persia (see Illustration 12).

SAVED THROUGH A QUEEN
(Esther)

King Xerxes preferred to live in the winter capital of Susa which was southeast of Babylon about two hundred miles. Three years after he had been crowned king of Persia, he threw a celebration that lasted about six months. All the officials, military leaders of both Persia and Media, princes, nobles from the provinces, and notable wealthy citizens attended this first class celebration. King Xerxes was enamored by his wealth and power and wanted everyone else to be also, so he displayed all the wealth of his entire kingdom for his guests to view.

When the king had probably too much wine, he sent orders for his queen to put on her royal crown and display her beauty to all his honored guests. The king was humiliated when Queen Vashti refused to come, and in his rage turned to seven close nobles for advice on what to do regarding her behavior. Concerned that other women in the Persian Empire would follow the example of Queen Vashti's behavior, they advised the king to strip the queen of her crown and never allow her to come into his presence again.

The king accepted their advice, but because the queen had humiliated him so much, he also declared that no one was allowed to come to him without his invitation. Anyone breaking this law would be executed with only a few exceptions. The law was written and proclaimed throughout the entire Persian Empire in every language, emphasizing that every man should be the ruler of his household.

When the search for a new queen began, a young girl named Esther was taken, along with many other girls, to be considered for the position of queen. Esther was raised by her cousin Mordecai from the tribe of Benjamin, and at his advice, never let on that she was a Jew. Every day Mordecai would pace back and forth in the courtyard near the house where Esther was kept, hoping he would hear some news about her. At the end of twelve months of beauty treatments, it became a cruel process of elimination as one of the girls would be brought to the king each evening, and in the morning be sent to another house where the king's concubines were kept.

It had been almost two years since the king had his celebration, and it was now Esther's turn to go into King Xerxes. God gave Esther favor with the king and he placed a crown on her head, declaring her the queen of Persia. The king was so pleased with his new queen that he threw a banquet to celebrate the occasion, and even declared it a holiday.

Shortly after, Mordecai was able to help Queen Esther reinforce her position as queen and ensure the king's commitment towards her. Every day Mordecai would sit at the city gate hoping to overhear some news about Esther and how she was doing. He happened to overhear two of the king's officials angrily talking about killing the king. He was able to get a message to Queen Esther regarding the conversation, and after reporting it to the king, an investigation confirmed the conspiracy to assassinate him. The two officials were hung on the gallows, and the matter was recorded in the palace logs as reported to Queen Esther by Mordecai.

Less than five years later King Xerxes promoted a man named Haman to one of the highest positions in his kingdom. Everyone honored and bowed down to him at the city gate except Mordecai, and this infuriated Haman. Because Mordecai was in the habit of sitting at the city gate every day to hear news about Esther, his insolence was a daily reminder to Haman which made him despise Mordecai.

When Haman discovered Mordecai was a Jew, he decided to take revenge on him by annihilating his entire race. He convinced the king it would be good for Persia to be rid of all the Jews in his empire and proposed that men, women, and children, including the elderly, be killed in one day throughout all of Persia. He declared this glorious day would be the thirteenth day of the twelfth month, and those who did the killing could claim all their goods and properties as a reward.

The orders were written in every language, signed by the king and distributed immediately. Even the Jews that had accepted Cyrus' offer to return to Judah weren't exempt from this order, and thousands of thousands were facing the reality of being massacred by friends and neighbors in less than a year. All of Persia was in shock at what the king had ordered, and Mordecai sent word to Esther that she must go to the king and intercede for the Jews. Esther knew that even as queen, she could be executed for violating the law of going to the king uninvited. Yet she was a Jew, and even though the king didn't know it, she probably would not be exempt from Haman's day of execution. After all the Jews including Esther had fasted three days and nights, Esther went to the courtyard to see the king.

When King Xerxes saw Esther, he not only spared her life, but offered her whatever she wanted up to half his kingdom. She simply asked that he and Haman attend a banquet she had prepared especially for Haman, and she would reveal her request to the king at the banquet. When Haman heard about the banquet being planned by the queen that only he and the king were invited to, his arrogant pride got the best of him and he went home boasting of his achievements to family and friends. But, embarrassed by Mordecai's refusal to honor him, his family and friends encouraged him to do something immediately. Haman demanded a gallows be built that day with plans to ask the king to hang Mordecai in the morning before the banquet.

That night when the king couldn't sleep, he began reading palace records and discovered that the man responsible for exposing the conspiracy and saving him from being assassinated had not been rewarded. The next morning Haman came to the king to request Mordecai be hung, but the king first asked what would he suggest be done for a man that the king chooses to honor. Haman of course assumed it was himself the king wanted to honor, so he suggested he be led through the streets on the king's horse, wearing one of the king's robes and crown, with a prince declaring "this is what is done for the man the king chooses to honor." The king liked his suggestion and ordered Haman to immediately do this for Mordecai. Haman wanted to hang Mordecai but instead was forced to honor him. It was the most grievous and humiliating thing he ever did, but finished in time to attend Esther's banquet.

At the banquet, the king insisted Queen Esther tell him her request and reassured her he was still willing to give her up to half his kingdom. She humbly requested her life and the life of her people, apologizing that if her fate had instead been to be sold as a slave she would not have bothered the king with her request. The king was furious and when he realized Queen Esther's death would come through Haman's plot to kill the Jews, he stormed out of the banquet hall in a rage and ordered Haman be hung. Ironically, Haman was hung on the gallows he had built for Mordecai.

The king gave all of Haman's possessions to Esther, who in turn appointed Mordecai to manage the estate. King Xerxes then rewrote the orders written by Haman, to allow the Jews to protect themselves by destroying, killing, or annihilating any armed forces or nationality or province that might attack them. The king also gave them the right to plunder their enemies' property and possessions, and do it on the day Haman had declared as the day of execution. These orders were written in every language and distributed throughout all of the Persian provinces. With nine months to go before the day of execution, many people converted to Judaism out of fear of what the Jews could do to them.

When the day of execution arrived, the king approved the queen's request to extend it into the next day. The Jews attacked all those who had been seeking their destruction but did not lay a hand on any of their possessions. After two days of executions, more than eight hundred were killed in the capital city of Susa, and seventy-five thousand among the provinces of Persia.

The king promoted Mordecai to a position second only to himself, and Mordecai gained the respect of every Jew because he worked for the good of his people and spoke up for the welfare of all the Jews. The Jews celebrate their Persian victory every year on the fourteenth and fifteenth of March, and they call this celebration the Feast of Purim.

STRUGGLING TO REMAIN FAITHFUL
(Ezra 7–10, Nehemiah, Malachi)

King Xerxes reigned for almost twenty-two years and when he died, Artaxerxes became the next king of Persia (see Illustration 12). There was a Levite priest named Ezra who was an expert in the Law of Moses, and was determined to help those who had returned to Judah get reconnected with Jehovah. King Artaxerxes committed to giving Ezra whatever he needed in order to do whatever it was he had in his heart to do. Ezra's view of getting them reconnected was to teach them the Law of Moses, instruct them in celebrating the Festivals, and make sure the necessary offerings were being sacrificed. King Artaxerxes and his top advisors made a donation of silver and gold, and also authorized Ezra to receive donations from Jews in the province of Babylon.

In King Artaxerxes' seventh year, Ezra and less than two thousand Jews went home to Judah, taking with them more than twenty-five tons of silver and almost four tons of gold. When they arrived in Jerusalem, all the donations were given to the priests and placed in the temple treasuries. Ezra was pleased with the temple they had rebuilt and they offered almost two hundred sacrifices to Jehovah on the altar. But when Ezra realized that some of the Jews had intermarried with their neighbors and were defiled by pagan cultures, the celebration came to an abrupt end.

Ezra ached to the core of his soul and fell before God in repentance. It was the mixed marriages that King Solomon entered into that led Judah into worshipping idols, which ultimately split the nation of Israel. Ezra felt too ashamed and disgraced to even lift his face towards God because the remnant God had chosen to rescue had started the process that would cause history to repeat itself. As Ezra wept and cried before the Lord, a large crowd gathered and they too wept bitterly before God. Those that were gathered in Jerusalem agreed that the only possible solution would be to send the foreign women and children away.

Ezra sent a proclamation throughout Judah calling all the Jews to come to Jerusalem. He also vowed that the Jews who refused to come would forfeit their property. When they arrived, Ezra demanded they make a confession to the Lord, then separate themselves from the foreign people they had married. The entire community agreed to what Ezra was asking with no exceptions. Within two weeks, one hundred and eleven men had been identified as having sinned through intermarriage. Among these men included leaders, priests, Levites, singers, and gatekeepers, many of whom set the standards among God's people.

Ezra had been in Judah for fourteen years. The temple had been rebuilt and the people were following God's laws, but no one had done anything to repair the walls or gates around Jerusalem. A Jew named Nehemiah was working as a cupbearer for King Artaxerxes, and he heard that the walls and gates were still broken and burned. He viewed this as a disgrace because the walls around a city were extremely important for protection. The people of Jerusalem were vulnerable to any enemy that might choose to invade them.

God gave Nehemiah a passion for Jerusalem and he went through stages of weeping, then fasting, then praying. Nehemiah found an opportunity to ask the king for permission to return to Jerusalem to oversee the rebuilding of the walls and gates. King Artaxerxes not only approved a leave for Nehemiah, but declared him governor of Judah. He gave Nehemiah a letter to assure his safe journey, a second letter to provide timber for rebuilding the gates and walls, and a third letter to provide a place for Nehemiah to stay while in Jerusalem.

Chapter 10

Judah's enemies found out about Nehemiah's business before he arrived in Jerusalem. Two men named Sanballat and Tobiah were extremely upset when they heard he was coming to promote the welfare of the Israelites. Despite their rejection, Nehemiah was determined to go back to Judah, but when he arrived he was dismayed at the condition of Jerusalem.

After three days he secretly gathered a small party of men to go with him to inspect the walls. They went out in the middle of the night so no one would know what he was doing. He went through the Valley Gate and passed the Jackal Well, Dung Gate, Fountain Gate and the King's Pool. He wasn't able to go any further on horseback because of the rubble, so he returned and reentered the city through the Valley Gate.

The next day he told the people he had returned to Jerusalem to rebuild the walls and gates, and they all became enthusiastic about helping with the effort. Sanballat and Tobiah, along with an Arab named Geshem, tried desperately to stop them, but Nehemiah refused to be discouraged. Instead, he encouraged the people by declaring with confidence that the God of heaven would give them success.

More than forty individual groups joined in the effort, each working on their own section of the walls, which included eleven gates and three towers. Those working to rebuild the walls were rulers, goldsmiths, perfumers, priests, temple servants, guards, merchants, and even women. Everyone worked no matter what their background or social position was, and the walls began to rise around Jerusalem.

When the gaps in the wall were closed and it had been rebuilt to half its height, Sanballat and Tobiah realized their discouraging words were not going to stop the Jews. They conspired with the Arabs to attack Judah and Jerusalem, but God frustrated their plans. The Jews were encouraged when God came to their rescue and the work continued, but with a tool in one hand and a weapon in the other. The walls were almost done when Sanballat and Tobiah tried one more time to stop the work through a plot to assassinate Nehemiah. Because Nehemiah realized their plans to assassinate him, they were not successful in stopping the work. At the end of fifty-two hard days, the doors and gates were hung and the wall was finished.

Nehemiah assigned Levites to be gatekeepers and singers, just as King David did when the wall was initially built more than six hundred years ago. He instructed the gatekeepers to have the gates opened at noon but to shut them before the end of their watch. He also authorized some of the residents who had homes connected to the wall to act as guards.

Most of the exiles that had returned to Judah had returned to their homes among the smaller towns and rural areas of Judah. There were few people who actually resided in Jerusalem, and Nehemiah recognized the need to increase the population within the city for its own protection. Nehemiah ordered ten percent of the descendants of Judah and ten percent from Benjamin to move into the city. As the people moved into the city, ten percent of the priests and Levites moved also.

Nehemiah was in Jerusalem for twelve years and during that time, he was an example to the people of how they should live and respect one another. He ruled from a heart that was committed to Jehovah, and wanted the people to not only live according to God's covenant, but to know and love their God. He supported Ezra in his efforts to teach the people God's law, and stood by him when he read the Law of Moses to all the people of Judah when they assembled in Jerusalem. Ezra not only read the law, but explained it so they could fully understand it. It was as though they were all hearing it clearly for the first time in their lives, and it touched their hearts so much that they began to weep.

Nehemiah was overjoyed when they heard the words and embraced God's law with their hearts. Without a doubt in his mind, it was a day that would be special to God and he commanded them not to weep but to rejoice and celebrate instead. They celebrated for more than three weeks and also dedicated the wall to God. They marched around the city on top of the wall singing praises to Jehovah, then went to the temple and offered many sacrifices to God. Their rejoicing and praise could be heard for miles. At the end of their celebrations, they humbled themselves before God and confessed their sins, then reaffirmed their commitment to God's covenant.

After spending twelve years in Jerusalem, Nehemiah returned to serve King Artaxerxes as his cupbearer. Nehemiah served the king for about a year then returned to Jerusalem. He arrived to find that the Levites had left Jerusalem to go back to their homes, and not only had the Sabbath become a work day but their enemy Tobiah was living in the temple. Even worse, Nehemiah was stunned to discover the men had married foreign women and their children weren't even being taught the language of the Jews.

Nehemiah was infuriated and rebuked them with a fierceness that was fueled by his passion for God. A prophet named Malachi was the last prophet God sent to speak to the people, and he also rebuked them for the same reasons Nehemiah did.

In the short time that Nehemiah had left them to go back to serve King Artaxerxes, the Jews had failed to keep their covenant with God. Ezra could teach them and Nehemiah could rebuke them, but what they needed was a leader who had a heart for God. It was difficult being different, and far too easy to fall into the routine lifestyles of the pagan cultures. Sometimes just surviving was overwhelming and they had no energy left to hope for the tomorrows or the promises Jehovah kept repeating through the prophets.

It had been approximately fifteen hundred years since God had chosen Abraham and promised to bless the world through his descendants. God had taken the Israelites out of their bondage in Egypt and made them a nation, so large they were like the sand on the sea shore, as numerous as the stars in the sky. But now those who were back in Judah were so few and only a handful of them held to their commitment to remain faithful to God.

It seemed evident that Satan and his destructive plans would emerge as the victor. But, one of the last things Malachi emphasized was that God did have a plan and no matter what, the Messiah would come.

Chapter 11

SURVIVING THE PTOLEMICS AND SELEUCIDS

(1 Maccabees 1–4:35, 2 Maccabees 1–9,
Reference Books)

The Persian Empire would survive for almost another hundred years under the succeeding kings Xerxes II, Darius II, Artaxerxes II and III, Arses, then Darius III (see Illustration 12). It was during the reign of Artaxerxes II that Persia signed a treaty with Greece, but Artaxerxes III ignored the treaty by successfully conquering Egypt and ruling them ruthlessly. Ten years later, a Greek named Alexander the Great liberated Egypt, then marched into Babylon to defeat the Persian Empire.

What was once the Persian Empire, extending from Asia Minor and Egypt to India, was now the empire of Alexander the Great. Alexander imposed the Greek language and customs on the people, which became known as the Hellenistic culture. Less than ten years later he died of a fever resulting from a wild lifestyle.

Alexander had no sons to bequeath his empire to, so it was divided among his four generals, two of whom emerged to split the empire between themselves less than twenty years later (see Illustration 13). One general was Ptolemy who ruled Egypt; the other was Seleucus who ruled Mesopotamia, Syria, and Asia Minor. The land of Israel, as it was known at its peak, was now called Palestine. Except for the Jews that had returned to Judah, Palestine was primarily inhabited by outsiders who settled there after Israel was deported. Both generals wanted to control Palestine because of its strategic location, and their successors would continue to fight over Palestine for more than a hundred years. The Ptolemics maintained control of it most of the time, but as a result of the fighting back and forth among them, the Jews were often in a state of devastation.

The Jews were free to pursue their religious obligations, but suffered economically because of the Hellenistic culture imposed on them. This culture introduced tax farming, which allowed tax rights for sections of land to be sold to the highest bidder, who would in turn be allowed to collect as much tax as they could. It was a lucrative business sanctioned by the government because they consistently received the property tax, but the tax collectors became wealthy by it. Throughout the reigns of Ptolemy I, II, III, IV and V, tax farming established two classes of people; the rich who got richer, and the poor who got poorer.

After a little more than a hundred years, the Seleucids were able to take possession of Palestine when Antiochus III became their ruler. It was 198 B.C., and because the majority of Jews had been living in poverty, they embraced Antiochus III in hopes that life would change under his rule. He allowed the Jews to do restoration work in Jerusalem, gave them tax exemptions, and also allowed them to live by their old religious laws. Unfortunately, the Jews would soon discover the Seleucids were rooted deeper in the Hellenistic culture than the Ptolemics.

The strength of the Greek Empire was beginning to decline and another world power was on the rise. Within ten years, Antiochus III signed a treaty transferring most of Asia Minor to Rome. He also agreed to pay an enormous tribute, which drained the treasuries and forced him to rob from the temples. In the end, he resorted to selling the poor people as slaves in order to raise the funds to pay the tribute.

Two years later his son Seleucus IV became the new ruler, then within thirteen years his second son Antiochus IV became the ruler. Antiochus IV continued to impose tax farming and established a precedence for government to appoint priests. The priestly office had become a politically lucrative position, and when a Levite named Jason offered a large sum of money for the appointment, Antiochus IV awarded it to him.

Jason had Jerusalem incorporated as a Greek city, then had a Greek gymnasium built next to the temple and introduced nudity among the athletes. The Jews were appalled at what Jason did, but Antiochus IV would prove to be their real nightmare. Antiochus IV would eventually become known as the madman.

After a less than successful attack against the Ptolemics to take Egypt, Antiochus IV returned to Jerusalem in a rage, determined to either turn the Jews into pagans or annihilate them. He plundered the city by demolishing their homes and city walls, then burned them. He took women and children as slaves and forbid the Jews to practice religion or circumcise their children. He desecrated the temple by building shrines and altars to Zeus, then defiled the holy altar by sacrificing a pig on it. After all this, he issued orders requiring the Jews to follow customs that were against the Law of Moses.

When the Babylonians and Persians ruled, life wasn't bad, but it was a struggle for the Jews to remain faithful to God. When the Ptolemics and Seleucids fought among each other to rule Palestine, the constant turmoil caused their faith in Jehovah to increase; it was their faith that helped them survive the devastation. Now in their struggle with Antiochus IV, their faith was so strong that many chose to suffer horrible, torturous deaths rather than violate the old traditions of the Mosaic Law. They were determined not to forsake the God of their fathers.

There was an old priest from a small town named Mattathias who refused an order to sacrifice a pig on an altar. When the messenger demanded he do it, a Jew from the town agreed to do it for him. In his fervor to be obedient to God and the Law of Moses, Mattathias killed both the Jew and the messenger, then fled with his family into the mountains. Antiochus IV sent garrisons of soldiers throughout Judea to search for rebels like Mattathias, with orders to kill them.

Mattathias and his sons were joined by others who rebelled against Antiochus IV, and they soon became a small army. Mattathias was old and dying so he appointed his son Simon to be an advisor and his son Judas to command the army of rebels. Judas, who was also called Maccabeus, victoriously led the rebels against the Seleucid army in several battles. This enraged Antiochus IV so he ordered his commander to lead an army of four thousand seven hundred into Judah to destroy the people of Israel and give their property to foreigners. News of the eminent destruction of the Jews spread quickly and merchants from surrounding countries flocked to Judah hoping to purchase slaves.

Realizing the situation was critical, Judas and his army of three thousand decided to go to Mizpah to seek the help of Jehovah. They had heard the stories of the impossible battle the people of Israel were faced with after Samson died, and how Samuel interceded for them at Mizpah. If God could give them victory over the Philistines back then, He could do it again in their battle against the armies of Antiochus IV. They took the risk of being discovered by their enemy and traveled to Mizpah. When they arrived at Mizpah, they fasted and prayed, then put all their hope in Jehovah to deliver them.

A detachment of six thousand attacked the rebels but after Judas and his army killed three thousand of them, the remaining three thousand fled. The commander returned home with his army to report their losses, but returned a year later with an army of sixty-five thousand. By now Judas had learned that Jehovah was just as faithful as He was powerful, so he prayed and trusted God one more time, then went out to fight the battle. After killing five thousand of the Seleucid soldiers, the remaining army retreated out of fear and returned home.

With each victory their faith increased, and once again, a nation began to emerge.

FIGHTING FOR INDEPENDENCE
(1 Maccabees 4:36–16, 2 Maccabees 10–15, Reference Books)

When the Seleucid army retreated, Judas and all those with him went back to reclaim Jerusalem. They found the temple abandoned, the altar desecrated, the gates around the city burned, the courts overcome with weeds, and the priest chambers destroyed. They proceeded to remove the idols and stones that were in the temple, and dismantled the altar that was desecrated. After making the necessary repairs to the temple and purifying it, they built a new altar according to the law.

A new lamp stand, altar of incense, and table were made and placed in the temple, then they lit the candles and placed loaves of bread on the table just as Moses instructed. When it was all done, it was truly something to celebrate, and they did. For eight days they offered sacrifices on the new altar to honor Jehovah for delivering them from the Seleucids, then declared it a holiday to be celebrated for eight days every year. They called it the Festival of Lights, also known as Hanukkah.

When the celebration was over, they proceeded to repair the walls around Jerusalem and when they were done, assigned a garrison to protect the city. The Gentiles in the surrounding areas heard what they had done, and out of jealous anger became determined to completely destroy the Jews. Reports started coming in from all over that Jews were being killed, so Simon took an army of three thousand and headed for Galilee while Judas and his brother Jonathan took an army of eight thousand and headed for Gilead. They fought many battles in their efforts to save the Jews, and returned to Judah victoriously.

Antiochus IV was in Babylon dying during these battles with the Jews, and when he died his nine-year-old son Antiochus V became king (see Illustration 13). When the commander of the Seleucid army became frustrated with the army of the Jews, he convinced the young king to send an army of one hundred and twenty thousand men to destroy Judah. The battle had many fronts and went on for a long time, but in the end the Jews were hemmed in by the Seleucid army. The battle stopped and they proceeded to wait for the Jewish rebels to surrender. While they waited, the commander mysteriously had a change of heart and convinced the young king they should live in peace with the Jews, and allow them to practice their religious laws. Even though the Jews agreed to live in peace, Antiochus V ordered the wall around Jerusalem be torn down.

Antiochus V had a cousin named Demetrius who didn't agree with his decision to let the Jews live in peace. Demetrius took the throne by assassinating both the young king and his commander, then ordered the army to once again march into Judah and destroy the Jews. He learned quickly it wasn't easy to fight God's people and when his commander was killed on the battlefield, his army retreated.

Judas had heard that the Romans expanded their empire by absorbing smaller provinces through agreements to offer protection. Believing he could trust this new empire that was governed by a house of senators rather than a king, he sent men to Rome to negotiate an alliance of friendship with them. The alliance was too late for Judas because when Demetrius learned his army commander had been killed, he sent another commander. The new commander led his army into battle to defeat the rebels and killed Judas.

Demetrius ordered all remaining followers of Judas be hunted down, persecuted, and killed. When a man named Alexander claimed to be the son of Antiochus IV, the hunt stopped. Demetrius tried to make peace with the rebels because he thought it would give him an advantage over Alexander. Judas' brother Jonathan was leading the rebels now, and when Alexander offered an alliance to him, he accepted because Demetrius couldn't be trusted. Soon after, Demetrius was defeated by Alexander and he reclaimed his father's throne. Alexander also entered an alliance with Egypt by marrying the daughter of Ptolemy VI, and invited Jonathan to be his honored guest at the wedding.

About four years later Demetrius II tried to avenge his father, beginning with a declaration of war against the Jews. It was a long and fierce battle but Jonathan and his army were able to resist him. Alexander honored Jonathan like a king for his victory, because he knew it was just a matter of time before Demetrius II would march his army against him.

The victory didn't last long because Ptolemy VI came from Egypt to conspire with Demetrius II against Alexander. He broke his alliance with Alexander and defiantly took his daughter from Alexander and gave her to Demetrius II to be his wife instead. In the end, Ptolemy VI and Alexander were both killed and Demetrius II became king.

As king, he did his best to create an alliance with Jonathan, but Jonathan as well as the Seleucid army gave their loyalty to Alexander's son, Antiochus VI. In response, Demetrius II threatened war against the Jews, so Jonathan sent men to Rome to renew their alliance with them.

In all the turmoil, a man named Trypho surfaced, and in his determination to become king of Asia, killed both Jonathan and Antiochus VI. With Jonathan dead, the Jews implored his brother Simon to be their new leader and he accepted (see Illustration 14). Jonathan and Simon had both been recognized as governors, but now the people took a bold step and declared Simon king of Judah. They also kept with tradition and gave him the position of high priest.

Because of the devastation caused by Trypho, Simon appealed to Demetrius II to grant tax relief, and he accommodated Judah as much as he could. When Rome heard Jonathan had been killed, they renewed their friendship alliance with Simon and declared Judah an independent state. They also sent letters to all the surrounding provinces stating Judah was under the protection of Rome.

Demetrius II could not be defeated by Trypho, but he was eventually defeated by his own brother Antiochus VII. After stealing the throne, Antiochus VII bought the favor of the people by authorizing Judah to coin their own money, forgave all their debts, and acknowledged their independence. But it didn't last long and Antiochus VII changed his mind and declared war against Judah. Simon was getting too old and too tired to go to war, so his son John Hyrcanus took command of the Jewish army and defeated Antiochus VII.

It had been almost two hundred years since Alexander the Great defeated Persia, and it had been a long hard road for the people of Judah to win their freedom to live as an independent nation. Even after Simon and two of his sons were murdered by one of his son-in-laws in a plot to overthrow them, John Hyrcanus was able to preserve his position of leadership and their independence as a

Jewish state. They were finally a nation once again, a nation that chose to be faithful to the Law of Moses.

BEARING THE SCARS OF GREED
(Reference Books)

Like all the rulers before him, Antiochus VII kept trying to conquer Judah. John Hyrcanus hadn't been in leadership for even a year when Antiochus VII invaded Judah and took control of several cities. He took hostages and made them slaves, and eventually marched into Jerusalem. Antiochus VII destroyed the walls around Jerusalem and John Hyrcanus was forced to pay him tribute. However, less than ten years later he was killed in a battle with the Parthians, and John Hyrcanus seized the opportunity to take back the land that was taken from Judah.

During this period, politics and surviving as a nation dominated the efforts of the leaders and the high priest. They were unanimous in their belief that their survival was dependant on the study of the Torah. The Torah was the historical writings given to them by Moses, which included the books of Genesis, Exodus, Leviticus, Numbers, and Deuteronomy. Because the people were so committed to following the law of the Torah, there was often irresolvable controversy among them regarding the interpretation of the law. This controversy led to the formation of religious groups that taught opposing views.

The Pharisees were a devout religious group that studied the Torah, but they also believed that the writings of the prophets and the oral teachings that had been passed down were just as important. Their interpretations included the belief that angels and demons existed, and that life extended beyond the grave through the resurrection of the body. The Pharisees placed an enormous amount of importance on living in accordance to the law as an alternative to the traditions of offering sacrifices. They firmly believed there was either life after death or eternal damnation, an outcome that was determined by how each individual lived their life.

The Sadducees were another devout religious group that also studied the Torah, but they would not acknowledge that the writings of the prophets nor the oral teachings had any authority. They also did not believe in angels or demons or life after death. They lived life as well as they could for the moment, and held to the old traditions of offering sacrifices to atone for wrong doings. Because they claimed to be descendants of the priestly line of the Levites, this entitled the Sadducees to well-sought-after positions in the temple.

Wealth and power often came with these temple positions, and the Sadducees' interpretation of the Torah supported their lavish and materialistic lifestyles. They took advantage of the Jews through their Levitical business adventures, like selling animals in the temple for sacrifices. They took advantage of the Jews through their interpretations, like making the obligation to paying temple tax more important than the obligation to care for the elderly. Life was good for the Sadducees and they strongly opposed anyone who might threaten their esteemed positions in the community.

The court system in Judah was administered by the Sanhedrin, which was a council of people consisting of priests, members of privileged families, elders, family heads, scribes, Pharisees, and Sadducees. The outcome of their decisions could be influenced by the levels of membership among the interested groups.

These were hard times for the common Jews in trying to be faithful to Jehovah, and not because they didn't want to. It was just hard to live up to the expectations of their leaders, both morally and financially. Because of the importance the Pharisees placed on living by the law, their interpretations became just too demanding, and impossible to live by. When the people weren't able to live up to their high standards, the Pharisees would condemn them with their pompous, self-righteous attitudes.

Because the Sadducees placed so much importance on position and power, everything they did always seemed to be in their best financial interests. Because of this, the common people almost always suffered. Whether they followed after the teachings of the Pharisees or the Sadducees, ultimately both groups led the people to serve God through rules and actions, rather than from the heart.

Rome was growing and within two years of John Hyrcanus becoming the leader of the Jewish state, Carthage, Spain, North Africa, Macedonia, Corinth, Achaia, and Asia were just a few of the provinces that had become a part of the Republic of Rome. While Judah was an independent state under Rome and was allowed many freedoms, they were slowly becoming prisoners to greed and corruption, with an insatiable appetite for power. Before John Hyrcanus died, he designated his wife and oldest son Aristobulus to rule after him (see Illustration 14). However, Aristobulus didn't want to share the power he felt was rightfully his, so he put his mother and brothers in jail. He ruled for only one year and when he died, his wife Salome Alexandra married his brother Alexander Janneus who became the next king of Judah.

Alexander Janneus was king for twenty-seven years and after he died, his wife Salome Alexandra ruled as queen for nine years. When she died, their oldest son Hyrcanus II had the position of priest and everyone assumed he would be the next king. Instead, his younger brother Aristobulus II aggressively took the throne and had him removed from his position as priest. The dispute got the attention of Rome and they were forced to settle the conflict by awarding the throne to Hyrcanus II and moving Aristobulus II and his family to Rome.

Hyrcanus II may have been declared king of Judah but he ruled on the advice of Antipater, his astute minister. Antipater was a Gentile but was forced to convert to Judaism when Hyrcanus I was king. He took full advantage of his position as minister, and appointed his son Phasael governor of Jerusalem and a second son named Herod governor of Galilee. The Jews rebelled against their leadership because they were Gentiles, but Herod was always able to manage the rebellion throughout Galilee and that impressed Rome.

Antipater had been minister to the king for almost fifteen years when he advised Hyrcanus II to help Caesar in his fight against Pompey. When the battle was over, Caesar rewarded Hyrcanus II by reaffirming his position as king of the Jewish nation and returned land to Judah lost in previous conflicts. Caesar also rewarded Antipater by declaring him a citizen of Rome.

Caesar's victory was short lived because five years later he was assassinated and his generals Antony, Lepidus, and his adopted son Octavian temporarily became joint rulers of Rome. Within two years the west portion of the Republic of Rome was being ruled by Octavian, and the east was ruled by Antony.

Despite the splendor and excitement of Rome, the two sons of Aristobulus II that had been forced to move to Rome twenty years earlier, were drawn back to Judah in their desire to inherit the throne. Alexander failed in his attempt so he married his cousin Alexandra, the daughter of Hyrcanus II (see Illustration 14). Antigonus, like his father, was more aggressive in his attempt to defeat Hyrcanus II and joined the Parthians in an attack against Judah.

Antony was in Egypt with Cleopatra when the Parthians marched into Judah and attacked Jerusalem. Phasael and Hyrcanus II were both captured, but Phasael committed suicide and Hyrcanus II was tortured then taken prisoner to Parthia. Herod escaped and after going to Rome to seek their help, Antony and Octavian both convinced the senate to declare Herod king of Judah. Herod returned to Judah and with the help of Rome, defeated Antigonus after three years of fighting. Antigonus was brought to Rome once again, but this time he was beheaded on Antony's orders.

Herod claimed the throne and became king of Judah, and in time he would become a legend known as Herod the Great.

LOOKING FOR THE DELIVERER
(Reference Books)

Antony had failed in his attempts to defeat the Parthians, and with his funds depleted, returned to Cleopatra in Egypt who was willing to offer support. Herod had his own battles to conquer as king, primarily because the people didn't consider him a Jew. They had worked too hard for their independence and resented being ruled by a Gentile. They would have preferred Alexander be king, the one who returned from Rome and married Alexandra. They would have also been satisfied to have their seventeen-year-old son Aristobulus III as king of Judah. But Herod was determined to remain king and hoping to persuade the people, married Mariamne, the daughter of Alexander and Alexandra.

The people still resented Herod, so he began to eliminate anyone who opposed him. He ruthlessly executed forty-five wealthy Sadducees who had supported Antigonus. To help Rome look the other way, he gave all their possessions and wealth to Antony. There were also rumors that Herod had something to do with the attack by the Parthians when Hyrcanus II and his brother Phasael were captured, in order to be king himself. No one could quite understand how he miraculously escaped that attack.

His mother-in-law Alexandra had her son Aristobulus III appointed to the position of priest, but when the people favored him over Herod, he arranged to have him drowned when he was swimming in a pool (see Illustration 14). Antony could not overlook this one and ordered Herod to come to Egypt and explain the death of his brother-in-law. Before Herod left for Egypt he gave orders to Mariamne's uncle that if he should be found guilty by Antony, he was to kill both Mariamne and his mother-in-law. Herod was not found guilty, but he returned to discover the uncle had told Mariamne about Herod's orders to kill them. Herod repaid the uncle's disloyalty by having him executed.

Herod's biggest threat appeared to be coming from Egypt when Antony started giving portions of Judah to his lover Cleopatra, the queen of Egypt. First Herod lost portions to Cleopatra on the west side of Judah that cut off his access to the Mediterranean Sea, then she asked for portions on the east including Jericho. Herod, realizing he was in jeopardy of losing his entire kingdom to Cleopatra, established a military post in the east and one in the west.

As Herod was building fortresses in strategic locations throughout Judah, Octavian was in Rome undermining Antony. He convinced the senate that because of Antony's passion for Cleopatra, his allegiance had shifted to Egypt and planned to move the capital of Rome to Alexandria. Hardly ten years after Octavian and Antony divided Rome between themselves; they were at war with each other and the stakes were high. Even Herod realized how high the stakes were and quickly changed his allegiance from Antony to Octavian.

Within a year, Octavian emerged as the victor and Alexandria was incorporated into the Republic of Rome. As for Antony and Cleopatra, they chose to commit suicide and die together rather than be taken prisoners of Rome. Herod traveled to the battlefield to meet with Octavian after the victory, and because he had given his allegiance to Octavian, was reaffirmed as king of Judah and given back all the land Antony had given Cleopatra. Herod returned to Jerusalem ready to celebrate, but instead was met by Mariamne who refused to have any part of his celebration.

Mariamne had discovered he left orders again for her to be killed if he didn't return, and she angrily confronted him about it. Herod did love Mariamne, but the tension between them got to be too much so he had her placed in prison and eventually had her executed. Because Herod's grief for Mariamne was so intense, Mariamne's mother was sure he was close to death. She began to make plans for Herod and Mariamne's two sons to take the throne, but when Herod discovered her plans he had her executed and sent his two sons, Alexander and Aristobulus to Rome.

Within three years, in the year 27 B.C., the Republic of Rome became the Roman Empire and Octavian declared himself Caesar Augustus, the first emperor of Rome. Each province had two options under the new Roman Empire. If a province was peaceful, it was ruled by a proconsul who was appointed annually and reported to the senate. If a province was hostile or had problems, an army would be stationed within the province and it would be ruled by a prefect. This prefect was appointed by the emperor and reported directly to the emperor. Rome almost always took the advice of the proconsuls, and paid them well to manage the provinces.

Under the rule of Caesar Augustus, the provinces were allowed to have their own governments, mint their own coins, and were given the freedom to practice their own religions. The new Rome established Roman settlements within the provinces, and built roads, theaters, libraries, temples, bath houses and other public buildings. Even though Caesar Augustus encouraged the provinces to promote their traditional religions, he also built temples within the provinces to worship himself as a god.

Judah was flourishing economically so Herod followed the lead of Caesar Augustus by initiating several building projects around Judah. In Jerusalem he remodeled the temple and erected colonnades around the perimeter, built a huge luxurious palace for himself, rebuilt the theater, amphitheater, and stadium, and even rebuilt portions of the water system. He rebuilt the city of Samaria, which included new theaters, amphitheaters, and temples for pagan gods. He even built a temple in Samaria to honor Augustus, then renamed the city after the emperor. He built a port city named Caesarea with breakwater barriers, docks for shipping, theaters, and public buildings, then celebrated with athletic contests, performances in the theaters, and gladiator fights.

Despite all of Herod's good efforts to win the approval of the Jewish people, they always considered him an outsider. It had been about four years since Mariamne had been executed when Herod remarried. The Jews were furious when Herod's new wife convinced him to appoint her father Simon to the position of high priest.

They agonized over Simon's appointment for four years, but their anger gave place to hope when Herod brought his two sons, Alexander and Aristobulus, back from Rome. Even though they were Herod's sons, they could be traced back to the Maccabeus Jewish family through their mother. Herod had other sons by other wives but the Jews made it clear they wanted Alexander and Aristobulus to inherit Herod's throne. Herod had a son named Antipater who felt threatened by his two Jewish step brothers, and never missed an opportunity to turn his father against them. It was just a matter of time before Herod had them executed too.

The death of Alexander and Aristobulus meant the death of any hope to be led by a descendant of Israel. They had struggled so hard for their independence, even going back to when they first returned from Babylon. There wasn't a Jew in all of Judah that didn't share the dream of becoming the nation they once were when David was king. Now all they could do was stand by and watch as Herod ruthlessly robbed them of their dreams. Their only hope was the King that Jehovah had promised to send, the King who would be their Deliverer.

If they ever needed the promised Deliverer, it was certainly now.

Chapter 11

STILL WAITING

(Reference Books)

Caesar Augustus was emperor of the new Rome and because most of the civil wars among the provinces had ended, he retired a large part of the Roman army. Even though there appeared to be peace within the empire, the quality of life for most of the citizens had degraded to an unbearable level. Less than half the citizens were actually free because of the number of war victims that had been taken as slaves. When farmers and business people couldn't survive financially, entrepreneurs emerged to buy them out and nearly eliminated the middle class.

Unemployment was extremely high, forcing the poor and homeless to rely on government programs to survive. Politicians often took advantage of the poor by buying their votes with empty promises to help or feed them. The rich were living lavish pampered lives and taught their slaves to do everything for them. The law for a slave frequently meant whatever was good for their master, and because the slaves taught the children of their masters, a lack of integrity was instilled at a young age.

The theaters were filled with pornographic entertainment, and the amphitheaters filled with gladiators that satisfied the demands of bloodthirsty crowds. Because male children were preferred over females, baby girls were often killed by means of exposing them to the weather after birth. The Roman culture was reduced to one that had little respect for human life, and evolved around the pampered wealthy few. Society was filled with shameless people who were insolent, haughty, boastful, rebellious, and heartless.

Caesar Augustus initiated road construction and building projects throughout the provinces. In the city of Rome he built a water and septic system, and employed a huge force of police officers and fire fighters. He also ordered a census be taken in all the provinces. To register within Judah, the people were required to go to designated towns based on the tribe of their forefathers.

Most of the Jews were from the descendants of David, and they were required to register in Bethlehem. Jews from every corner of Judah came to Bethlehem, and it quickly became overwhelmed with travelers. There were so many people coming into the city that all the inns and boarding houses were filled. There wasn't a place in the city to rent, no matter how much money you were willing to pay. Some travelers even rented stables in barns just to have a roof over their head for the night.

There were however, three travelers from the east that caught Herod's attention. It was rumored they had been asking all over Jerusalem where they might find the baby that would some day become king of the Jews. The three were wealthy and wise men, who had traveled a long distance by following a star that had led them into Judah. Now that they were in Jerusalem, they weren't exactly sure where to go next to find the child. They had come with expensive gifts fit only for a king, and they were determined to find the baby.

Herod called a meeting with the Jewish leaders to find out what the prophets said about all this. The Jewish leaders told Herod that the prophet Isaiah promised a king would be born to a virgin, in the town of Bethlehem. Herod had the three travelers brought to him and told them they could find the baby in Bethlehem. He also ordered them to report back to him with the details of where the child was because he wanted to honor the Jewish king also. The three travelers went on their way but never reported back to Herod because of his untrustworthy violent reputation.

Herod was furious when he realized the three travelers had returned home without reporting back to him. Rumor or not, he would not allow anything or anyone to threaten his reign, not even a baby. Herod ordered his army to go to Bethlehem and kill every male child two years and younger. It was a horrible massacre, more horrific than can be imagined. Not long after this genocide, Herod became sick with a painful disease. While on his death bed, he ruthlessly killed again by ordering the execution of his son Antipater because he appeared to be overly anxious to take his throne. Then on April 1 of 4 B.C., Herod died.

Herod left a will and testimony that designated his son Herod Antipas be governor of Galilee and his son Philip governor of the districts north east of Galilee (see Illustration 15). His son Archelaus would be given the high honor of inheriting his throne, a throne that was stained with the blood of many innocent people. Caesar Augustus confirmed their appointments, but the Jews openly rebelled at the idea of being ruled by any of Herod's sons because none of them were Jews. After ten years of protesting, the Jews finally convinced Caesar Augustus to remove Archelaus from the throne. But rather than allow them to have a Jewish king, he declared Judah an imperial province of the Roman Empire and assigned a procurator to rule over it. Four procurators ruled Judah over the next twenty years followed by Pontius Pilate, who was assigned the position of governor.

Herod Antipas governed the area of Galilee and built his capital city on the shores of the Sea of Galilee. He frequently traveled to Rome, and while there stayed with his half brother Herod Philip I, his wife Herodias, and their daughter Salome. Eventually Herodias divorced her husband and married Herod Antipas, who took her and her daughter Salome back with him to live in Galilee. Even though Herod Antipas didn't care much that the Jews accused him of being an adulterer, Herodias despised anyone who dared condemn her for divorcing her husband and marrying his brother.

The majority of the Jewish population were poor just like those of other provinces, but the Mosaic law helped protect them from the extreme oppression experienced by most of the poor people in the Roman Empire. The average lower class Jew despised Herod Antipas and barely tolerated the Roman procurator assigned to

Jerusalem. The Romans lacked morals and ethics, and forced the Jews to live with temples that honored an emperor who thought he was a god. They were oppressed by the Sadducees who patronized the Romans in order to keep their lucrative positions in the temple. The Pharisees didn't make life any easier for them either. The Pharisees made the Jews live like prisoners to the Law, forcing them to wear a heavy yoke of strict rules. Even when the Jews appealed to the courts of the Sanhedrin, there was no guarantee they would get justice.

They needed the king promised by Jehovah through the prophets. Even though this king would come to bless the whole world, everyone had a different concept of who they hoped this king would be. Some of the Jews hoped He would be a king who would deliver them out from under the authority of the Romans, while others hoped He would be a king who would deliver them out from under the authority of Herod's descendants. The Sadducees looked for a king who would restore power and authority to them in the temple, while the Pharisees looked for a king who would lead strictly by the rules and regulations of the Law and the prophets. The Jews in the lower classes simply wanted a king who could deliver them from their lives of poverty and hunger.

Nobody had any concept of what time it was in God's plan. There was no way for them to know the promised Messiah would soon be walking among them, not as a king but as a servant. They couldn't know this, but one thing they did know . . .*they were still waiting.*

ILLUSTRATIONS

Illustration 1 - Generations from Adam to Noah

Name	Age When Son Was Born	Year Since Creation		Age When Died
		Born	Died	
Adam & Eve	130	0	930	930
SETH	105	130	1042	912
- Enosh	90	235	1140	905
- Kenan	70	325	1235	910
- Mahalalel	65	395	1290	895
- Jared	162	460	1422	962
- Enoch	65	622	987	365*
- Methuselah	187	687	1656	969
- Lamech	182	874	1651	777
- Noah		1056		
(God warns the people)		**(1536)**		

* Enoch never died - God took him

Illustration 2 - Calendar Events of the Flood

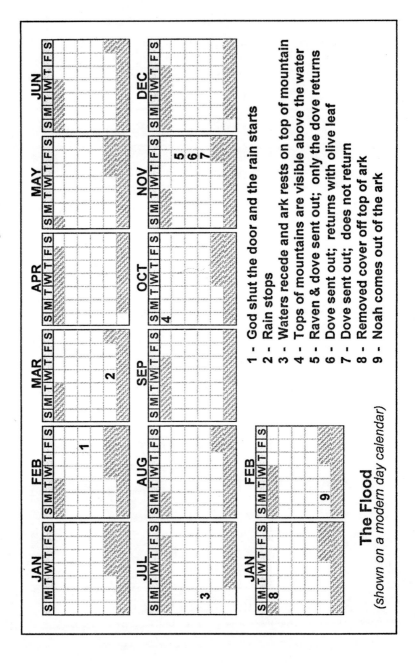

The Flood
(shown on a modern day calendar)

1 - God shut the door and the rain starts
2 - Rain stops
3 - Waters recede and ark rests on top of mountain
4 - Tops of mountains are visible above the water
5 - Raven & dove sent out; only the dove returns
6 - Dove sent out; returns with olive leaf
7 - Dove sent out; does not return
8 - Removed cover off top of ark
9 - Noah comes out of the ark

Illustration 3 - Generations from Noah to Abram (Abraham)

Name	Age When Son Was Born	Year Since Creation		Age When Died
		Born	Died	
Noah	500	1056	2006	950
SHEM	100	1556	2256	600
(the flood)		*(1656)*		
- Arphaxad	35	1658	2096	438
- Salah	30	1693	2126	433
- Eber	34	1723	2187	464
- Peleg	30	1757	1995	238
- Reu	32	1787	2026	239
- Serug	30	1819	2049	230
- Nahor	29	1849	1997	148
- Terah	70	1878	(2083)*	(205)*
Abram Nahor Haran (Lot)		1948 ⋮		
(Abraham leaves Haran)			*(2023)*	

* Terah died 60 years after Abram left Haran

Illustration 4 - Descendants of Abraham, Isaac and Jacob

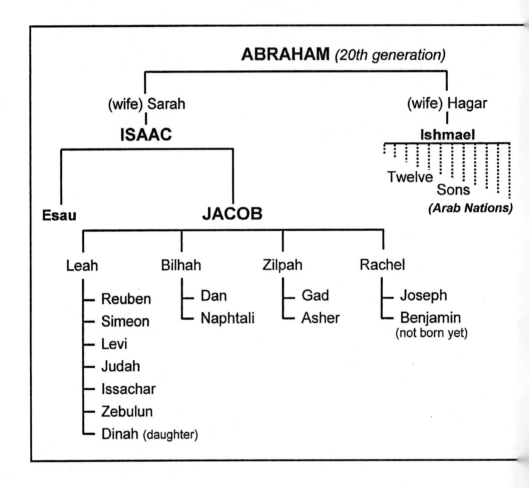

Illustration 5 - (Map) Entering the Promised Land

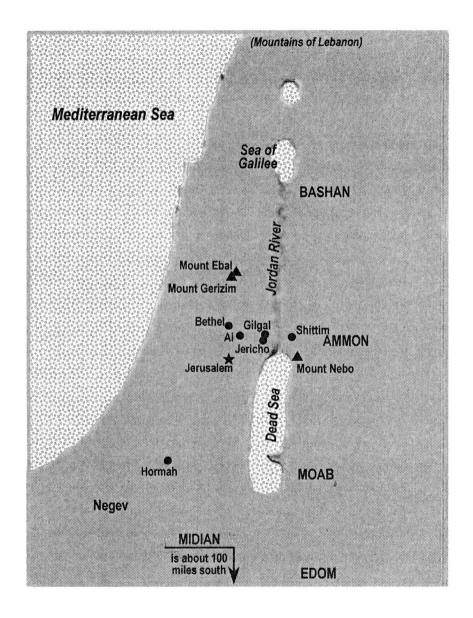

Illustration 6 - (Map) Conquering the Promised Land

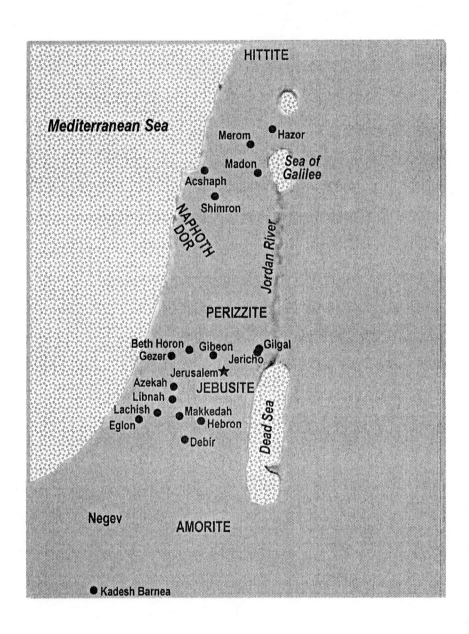

Illustration 7 - (Map) Dividing the Promised Land

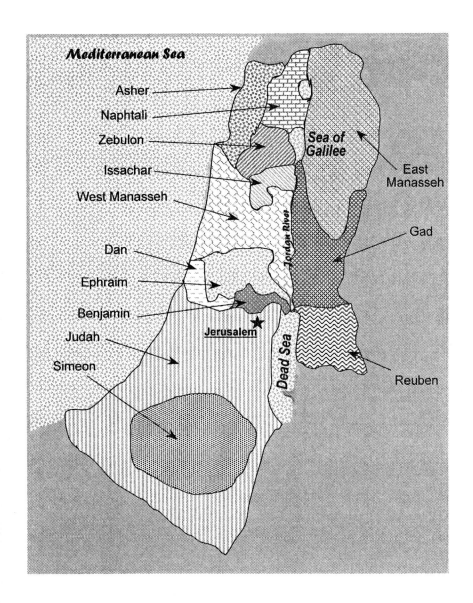

Illustration 8 - Generations from Judah to King David

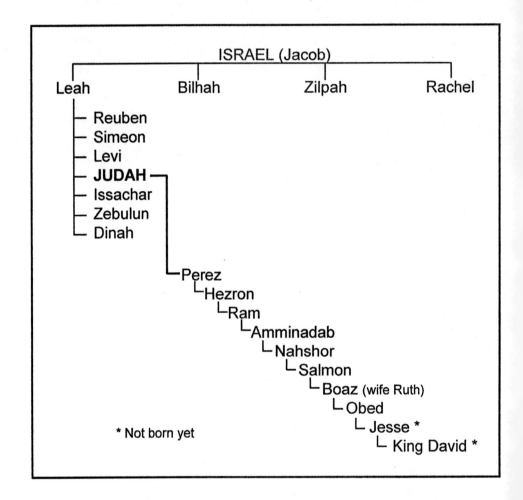

Illustration 9 - (Map) King Saul and King David's Day

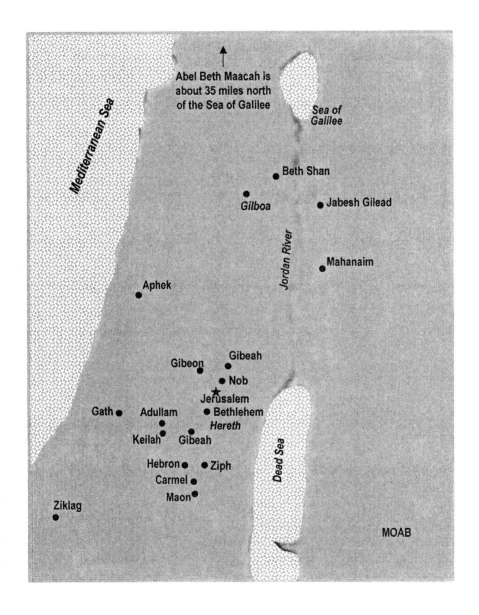

Illustration 10 - Kings of Israel and Judah

Nation of Israel	
King Saul	40 years
King David	40 years
King Solomon	40 years

(Nation of Israel Splits)

Judah		Israel	
(Southern Kingdom)		*(Northern Kingdom)*	
King Rehoboam	17 years	King Jeroboam	22 years
King Abijah	3 years		
King Asa	41 years	King Nadab	2 years
		King Baasha	24 years
		King Elah	2 years
		King Zimri	1 week
		King Omri	8 years
King Jehoshaphat	25 years	King Ahab	22 years (1)
		King Ahaziah	2 years
King Jehoram	8 years (2)	King Joram	13 years
King Ahaziah	1 years		
Queen Athaliah	7 years	King Jehu	28 years
King Joash	40 years		
		King Jehoahaz	17 years
King Amaziah	29 years	King Jehoash	16 years
		King Jeroboam II	41 years
King Uzziah	52 years		
		King Zechariah	6 months
		King Shallum	1 month
		King Menahem	10 years
		King Pekahiah	2 years
King Jotham	16 years	King Pekah	20 years
King Ahaz	16 years		
King Hezekiah	29 years	King Hoshea	9 years
King Manasseh	55 years	- *Israel Defeated*	
King Amon	2 years		
King Josiah	31 years		
King Jehoahaz	3 months		
King Jehoiakim	11 years		
King Jehoiachin	3 months	(1) *Married Jezebel*	
King Zedekiah	11 years	(2) *Married Ahab's daughter - Athaliah*	
- *Judah Defeated*			

Illustration 11 - Kings of Babylon

Nation of Babylon	
King Nebuchadnezzar	*604-561 BC*
King Merodach	*561-560 BC*
King Neriglissar	*559-556 BC*
King Labashi-Marduck	*556 BC*
King Nabonidus	*555-539 BC*
Belshazzar *(King Nabonidus left his son in-charge)*	
- Conquered by Persia -	

Illustration 12 - Kings of Persia

Nation of Persia		
Darius the Mede	539	BC
King Cyrus	538-529	BC
King Cambyses	529-522	BC
King Darius	521-485	BC
King Xerxes *(1)*	485-464	BC
King Artaxerxes *(2)*	464-424	BC
King Xerxes II	424-423	BC
King Darius II	423-404	BC
King Artaxerxes II	405-358	BC
King Artaxerxes III	358-338	BC
King Arses	338-335	BC
King Darius III	335-331	BC

- Conquered by Greece -

(1) Esther was his Queen
(2) Ezra and Nehemiah return to Judah

Illustration 13 - Kings of Greece

Nation of Greece	
Alexander the Great	*331-323 BC*
(Four Generals Ruled)	*323 . . . BC*

(Two General's Emerge as Rulers)

General Ptolemy *(The Ptolemics)*		General Seleucus *(The Seleucids)*	
Ptolemy I	*306-285 BC*	Seleucus I	*306-280 BC*
Ptolemy II	*285-247 BC*	Antiochus I	*280-261 BC*
		Antiochus II	*261-246 BC*
Ptolemy III	*247-222 BC*	Seleucus II	*246-226 BC*
		Seleucus III	*226-223 BC*
Ptolemy IV	*222-205 BC*	Antiochus III	*223-187 BC*
Ptolemy V	*205-182 BC*	Seleucus IV	*187-175 BC*
Ptolemy VI *(1, 2)*	*182-146 BC*	Antiochus IV	*175-164 BC*
		Antiochus V	*164-162 BC*
		Demetrius	*162-150 BC*
		Alexander *(1)*	*150-146 BC*
Ptolemy VII	*146-117 BC*	Demetrius II *(2)*	*146 . . .*
		Antiochus VI	*146-143 BC*
		Demetrius II	*. . . 139 BC*
		Antiochus VII	*139-130 BC*

(1) Ptolemy VI gave his daughter to Alexander in an alliance agreement
(2) Ptolemy VI took his daughter from Alexander and gave her to Demetrius II

Illustration 14 - Descendants of the Maccabeus

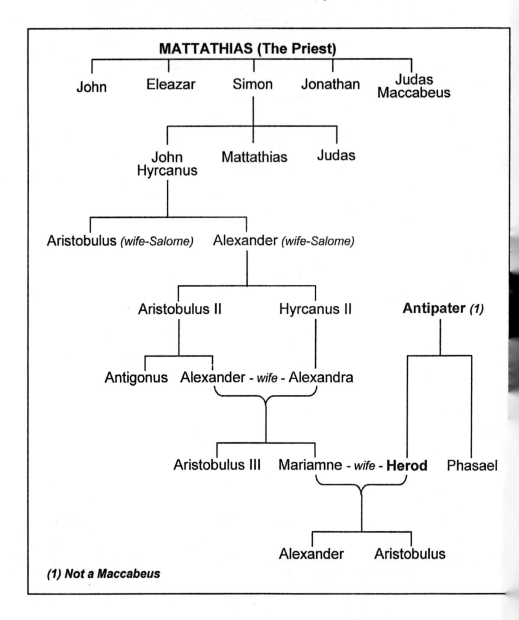

Illustration 15 - Descendants of Herod the Great

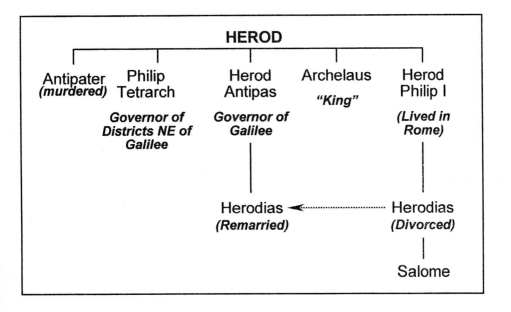

To order additional copies of

A STORY
FORGOTTEN...

Karen Geisler

Have your credit card ready and call:

1-877-421-READ (7323)

or please visit our web site at
www.pleasantword.com

Also available at: www.amazon.com

Printed in the United States
1308200004B/52-171

9 781579 217020